The Practitioner Inquiry

Marilyn Cochran-Smith and Susan L. Ly.

Starting Strong

A DIFFERENT LOOK AT CHILDREN, SCHOOLS, AND STANDARDS

Patricia F. Carini

FOREWORD BY JOSEPH FEATHERSTONE

TEACHERS COLLEGE PRESS

Teachers College, Columbia University
New York and London

Published by Teachers College Press, 1234 Amsterdam Avenue, New York, NY 10027

Library of Congress Cataloging-in-Publication Data

Carini, Patricia F.
    Starting strong : a different look at children, schools, and standards / Patricia F. Carini ; foreword by Joseph Featherstone.
      p. cm.
    Includes bibliographical references and index.
    ISBN 0-8077-4133-7 (hardcover : alk paper) — ISBN 0-8077-4132-9 (pbk. : alk. paper)
    1. Child development—Vermont—Bennington. 2. School children—Vermont—Bennington. 3. Schools—Standards—Vermont—Bennington. 4. Prospect School (North Bennington, Vt.) I. Title.

LB1117 .C28 2001
372.18'09743'8—dc21   2001033180

ISBN 0-8077-4132-9 (paper)
ISBN 0-8077-4133-7 (cloth)

Printed on acid-free paper
Manufactured in the United States of America

08 07 06 05 04 03 02 01   8 7 6 5 4 3 2 1

To all my families:

Prospect

The Swansons, Fitzsimmonses, Carinis

My parents, Hap and Ruth (Swanson) Fitzsimmons

My sisters, Faryl and Arlene

My son, Peter, his wife Johanna, and my dear little grandson, Eli

and most especially

Lou

without whom the sun doesn't rise

Contents

Foreword

Pat Carini is not as well known as some of the walruses who line the beach at educational conferences. To many of us she is an intellectual guide, an inspiration, and even a national treasure. This terrific collection of essays, along with the companion book focusing on teachers' efforts at descriptive review and child study, *From Another Angle* (also issued by Teachers College Press), may bring her work to a wider audience. Carini was cofounder of the Prospect School, which existed from the 1960s into the 1990s. This legendary place has over the years been an important force and symbol for the idea that good teaching practice and serious scholarly study of children ought to be intertwined enterprises. The elaborate Prospect Archive of children's work collected (in some cases) from the early years on into high school, exists in an archive edition—a gold mine with many untapped veins. Carini's daring claim that formal schooling should encourage children's thinking and creativity and that the core of good teaching practice is paying careful attention to kids and their work is, to say the least, still in contest in all our debates on education and school reform. Over the years, Prospect's example has spread around the county in many rippling forms, notably in teachers' groups, especially those dedicated to child study.

My own institution, Michigan State University, offers a case in point: The team that Sharon Feiman Nemser and I run within MSU's very ambitious teacher education program has been deeply influenced by Prospect theory, practice, and personnel. At one time our staff looked like the Prospect School's government in exile. Every entering undergraduate, for example, does a semester-long study of one child—a rare and invaluable introduction to the style of teaching we are aiming for. For us, Carini is, like John Dewey, an educational theorist whose work is fundamentally rooted in the experience of doing a real school with live children and bad plumbing.

She is a senior partner in a recent round of a long historical movement of democratic and romantic thought that seeks to lay rude hands on
what David Tyack calls the One Best System of teaching and research. From
the 1960s on, Carini and many others opened up a host of new and criti-
cal perspectives on education: promoting qualitative and alternative modes
of scholarship, attacking the cult of omniscient educational research, reminding an educational world too often managed by male big shots that
teachers and children are the real voices and characters in the educational
drama. The heart of this intellectual movement has been its insistence over
a very long haul on the root educational reality: that children and teachers are shapers of meaning and interpreters of experience. At bottom the
essays in this collection are an argument for democracy and the claim of
its great partisans, such as the poet John Keats. Keats argued that human-
kind may now appear to be low bushes with here and there a big tree—
but with a proper education, everyone would grow to the full height, and
we would see a grand democratic forest of oaks.

Prospect's method of oak production, if you will, and Carini's gospel,
is a passionate attentiveness to what makes a person—in her formulation—
"human." She might be described as a Henry James armed with a tape
recorder, portfolio-size file folders, and an incredibly longitudinal perspective. James called for the novelist to have "perception at the pitch of passion." Carini asks for this, but also for a close and detailed appreciation of
the vicissitudes of a child's growth as it spirals over time. All this flies in
the face of much current paper and pencil, and very, very instant, assessment. Certainly it goes against the grain of school environments profoundly
disrespectful of both kids and teachers. Against the mighty pendulum of
educational fashion distorting practice in so many schools, she reminds
us that the root of the word "evaluation" is the word "value." She calls for
paying close attention to Sean (a pseudonym) and his works over time.
Sean and the other children who appear throughout these essays (see
"Poets of Our Lives" and "To Help Us Start Strong" for particularly good
examples) turn out to have much to say to us about children's thought
and imagination, if we are prepared to listen, and if we are willing to work
at creating classrooms that are better places in which to be curious. Carini's
essays are in effect little handbooks for how to develop two great renewable classroom resources, listening and curiousity.

Carini proposes an alternative to the educational country we now
face—a radical alternative. These are radical essays, at least as sweeping
in their implications as any writings by Vivian Paley or Deborah Meier, to
take two parallel thinker-practitioners, calling for more democracy, respect,
and scrupulous attention to children's thoughts and meanings. Yet just as
many working classroom teachers view Paley and Meier as practical in-

spirations, many have also found a version of Prospect's Descriptive Review of the Child and Carini's talks and ideas to be immensely useful as tools for teaching and staff development. It may be, to paraphrase something Dewey once said about theory, that the visionary turns out to be practical day by day. As a poet impatient with the current educational scene and its Gradgrinds, I am grateful for Carini's far-sighted and humane vision. As a practitioner, I'm grateful for her help closeup.

Joseph Featherstone
Michigan State University

Acknowledgments

First and always, my heartfelt gratitude to Prospect colleagues present and past, the families and children of Prospect School (1965–1991), and most especially the three children whose works are the centerpiece for the lead essay in this collection. Without Prospect, the whole story for me would have been so utterly different that it is now, after 36 years, unimaginable. What I know about educating I learned at Prospect. The values and ideas foundational to this book are rooted there. I have said that Prospect remixed me educationally, philosophically, and politically. I can only affirm those words again.

To the Prospect Board of Trustees I owe enormous thanks for making it possible for me to set aside other work in the winter of 1997 to review and catalogue my writings and talks from 1965 onward; and subsequently, for giving a selection of these papers their undivided attention for an entire weekend retreat. Except that the Board started the ball rolling, this book would not have been written. Because the members of the Board are colleagues and friends who have contributed greatly, and in different ways, to my thinking and growth as an educator, I wish to extend my grateful thanks to each of you: Cecelia Traugh, President of the Prospect Board, and Beth Alberty, long-time board advocate for the Archives, who together conceived the plan for the review of my papers; Jane Andrias, Corinne Biggs, Paige Bray, Ann M. Caren, Kiran Chaudhuri, Ted Chittenden, Carol J. Christine, Cecilia Espinosa, Daryl Hartshorne, Mary Jane Hebron, Margaret Himley, Peg Howes, Brian Huot, Rhoda D. Kanevsky, Linette Moorman, Bonnie Navarro, Robert G. Navarro, Taeko Onishi, Ellen Schwartz, Alice Seletsky, Lynne Y. Strieb, Heidi Watts.

For the opportunity to develop papers presented in this collection, I thank the following persons and groups for inviting me to speak: at Michigan State University, Jay Featherstone, Sharon Feiman-Nemser, my former Prospect colleagues, David Carroll, Susan Donnelly, Dirck Roosevelt, and the family of Marianne Amarel, who together made possible "Poets of Our Lives"; at the University of Massachusetts, Peter Elbow who invited "In the Thick of the Tangle" as the 1997 Walker Gibson Lecture; Cecelia Traugh and Friends Select School who asked me to present the talk, "Another Slant on Knowledge," and Sheela Harden who so generously responded to and helped shape this talk as she did so many others; Carol Christine, Director of the Center for Establishing Dialogue (and valued friend) and the staffs of W. T. Machan and Sunnyslope Schools for the opportunity to develop the ideas in "Schools in the Making" as a frame for the 1994 summer institute.

And continuing: Prospect's Fall Conference under the leadership of Cecelia Traugh who invited two of the talks presented here: "What Would We Create?" and "We Love the Things We Love for What They Are," and for the latter, the members of the 1998 Prospect Summer Institute on Descriptive Inquiry for prompting my thinking, and very especially, Betsy Wice, who brought to my attention Frost's poem, "Hyla Brook"; at Sarah Lawrence College, Mary Jane Hebron and Sara Wilford who asked me to give the talk, "To Believe Ourselves"; the Philadelphia Teachers Learning Cooperative for their invitation to present "Valuing the Immeasurable"; the North Dakota Study Group on Evaluation for prompting the ideas explored in the Meditation: On Number; and Brian Huot and Kathleen Yancey for inviting the keynote address for a regional meeting of the National Council of Teachers of English that appears here under the title, "To Help Us Start Strong," and the members of the child inquiry group at the 1994 Prospect Summer Institute on Descriptive Inquiry who participated in the memorable study of Jenny on which this talk centers.

I want also to acknowledge with heartfelt thanks the many collegial groups, some in past times, some currently, many over decades, all of which have profoundly influenced the ideas on which this book is founded and, in times when energy flagged, have given me courage to continue. I take this opportunity to honor the membership and work of the following groups: The Art of Teaching program and Hudson Valley Teachers Collaborative at Sarah Lawrence, Bronxville, New York; the Center for Collaborative Education, New York City; the Center for Establishing Dialogue, Tempe, Arizona; the Center for Teaching and Learning, University of North Dakota, Grand Forks; the staff of Central Park East I, New York City; the Early Education Group at Educational Testing Service; the Elementary Teachers Network and the Institute for Literacy Studies, Lehman College, Bronx, New York; the Ithaca Child Study Group; the Mamaroneck (New York) Parent Teacher Collaborative, "Saturday Group," Seminars, and Summer Institutes; the staffs of W. T. Machan and Sunnyslope Schools, Phoenix, Arizona.

And continuing: the New York State Bureau of Child Development and Parent Education, and particularly the remarkable band of women who served as Field Consultants for the 5-year Indepth Study of the New York State Prekindergarten Program; the North Dakota Study Group on Evaluation; the Philadelphia Teachers Learning Cooperative (PTLC); the PTLC Archives Research Institute; the Prospect Institute affectionately known as "Summer II"; the Archives Scholars and Fellows Program; the Saturday Inquiry Group (members from Vermont, western Massachusetts, and New York Capitol region); the Workshop Center at City College, New York.

I wish to acknowledge here in friendship and with deepest admiration my friend and colleague, the late Professor Lillian Weber, originator of the Open Corridor in the New York City Public Schools and founder and director of the Workshop Center at City College, whose thought and work were inspiration for my own from the time we first met in the late 1960s until her death in 1994. There were many years when in winters I was privileged to join in the stimulating dialogues on education there, while in summers advisors from the Open Corridor came to Prospect Summer Institutes. I wish in particular to remember with love and high regard the first of these advisors to travel to Prospect, the late Catherine Molony and the late Norma Nurse.

In the same vein, I wish to extend grateful thanks to Vito Perrone, who from our first encounter at the charter meeting of the North Dakota Study Group on Evaluation has steadfastly promoted Prospect's efforts and supported my own work in countless ways. Limiting myself to only the contributions directly related to this book, it was Vito who sponsored the "Friends of the Prospect Archive" to promote wider interest in Prospect's Collections of Children's Works. It was through Vito's efforts that Prospect received a Bush Foundation grant to publish what became the *Reference Edition of the Prospect Archive*, from which selected works are presented in this volume. Except that Vito so consistently championed the Archive, Prospect could never have undertaken a project of this dimension. Naming just these specific contributions merely emblemizes all Vito has given to Prospect. Speaking for myself, I have benefited time and again over the span of a quarter of a century from his wisdom and his dedicated struggle to make positive change in education. As with Lillian Weber, it has been one of my great joys to make common cause with Vito. My thanks and my admiration for all he has contributed to education in this century are without limit.

I thank with equal gratitude Edith Klausner, who has been my dear friend and trusted advisor for nearly 30 years. I recognize with warmest regard the contributions of many others, not already included in these acknowledgments, to my growth as an educator, including Jessica Howard; the late Ann Gunning; the late Ruth Flurry; Carol Leckey; Nancy Miller; Marion Stroud; Clara Pederson; Sara Hanhan; Ernie Rouse; Marie Tervalon; Esther Kristol; Judy Buchanan; Margaret Casson; Elizabeth Heaton; Barbara Moffatt; K. Sue Updike Porter; Brenda Engel; Anne Martin; Eleanor Duckworth; George Hein; Posie Churchill; Joe Petner; Ed Yeomans; Ora Pipkin; Mary Burks; Ann Wiener; Norm Wilson; and in more recent years, Dr. Calvert Schlick, Jr. (administrator extraordinaire) together with my dear friends and colleagues Mary Jane Hebron, Darlene Adams, and Peggy Richards without whom the Mamaroneck (New York) project would not have happened.

I also take this opportunity to thank Cecelia Traugh who, as president of the Board of Trustees, played a crucial role in stabilizing Prospect during a difficult transition, and who has ably promoted Prospect ideas and processes for more than 20 years.

My thanks are owed as well to many persons for time and thought specifically devoted to making this book a reality. I start with Jay Featherstone to whom I express deep gratitude for writing the Foreword for this book, for the title of the lead essay, "Poets of Our Lives," for his deep appreciation of the children's artwork housed in the Prospect Archive, and most especially for his generous and optimistic spirit.

I give special thanks to Penny Colgan-Davis whose astute critique of an earlier version of this book led me to reconceptualize it in ways that were altogether strengthening. I thank Marilyn Cochran-Smith and Susan Lytle for inviting me to contribute this book to the Teacher Practitioner Inquiry Series, and I thank as well the members of their advisory board. I am grateful to Cathy McClure, development editor for this book, who gave wonderful encouragement and sound advice that has made it tighter and sharpened the focus. I also thank Carol Collins, acquisitions editor, for her continued support throughout the long process of turning talks into book.

There are not words to express my gratitude for the warmth, generosity, and unstinting support provided by my friends and sister Prospectors, Beth Alberty and Margaret Himley, who read the manuscript so many times over they must know it by heart. I also thank Beth, who played a central role in conceptualizing the Prospect Collections of Children's Works, and Margaret, with whom I worked with such pleasure on (among other things) the earlier Prospect book, *From Another Angle*, for countless hours of stimulating conversation that influenced in substance what I say here— but for which, of course, they bear no responsibility.

And then, there is my family who sustain me in all things, who put up with my often impossible schedule, who are with me in values, in spirit, in commitment to the idea that things can be better—in the schools and in the society. To my son Peter and my daughter-in-law, Johanna, my love and thanks for staunch support and for comfort when needed. To their son, Eli, just over one year old as I write this, I can only say that for me you are hope embodied, holding out possibility of all that is good that is yet to come. For Lou who has read every word of this book many times over and previously each talk in many drafts, who has ever had confidence in me, and who is always at my side no matter what, my love and my thanks for the great adventure it has been to work and think and make our lives together for the past 46 years.

I owe appreciation and love to my late parents, Hap and Ruth (Swanson) Fitzsimmons, and sister, Faryl, and to my surviving sister, Arlene, for their belief in me. I thank my extended family, especially the Jackson branch, who make appearances at times in these talks—I hope in ways that let them know how important they are to me. I was profoundly influenced by growing up in "Swansonville" among my cousins along the banks of the Des Moines River. Things I did later at Prospect in a school setting have roots in our play there. I especially wish to recognize here my one remaining aunt, Borghild, who from my earliest memories has been such a strong presence in my life.

I cannot close these acknowledgments without recognizing the teachers who had confidence in me during my growing up years and who may not know what lasting impression they made. Here I will particularly note among the many others, the late Marguerite Yager, mother of my best friend, Sue, who never once failed to appreciate some small accomplishment of mine and to encourage me to take the next step; Mildred Dymond who gave me piano lessons but whose independence of mind taught other lessons; my innovative third-grade teacher, Ruth Eide; my courageous seventh-grade teacher, Margaret Ames; my supportive ninth-grade teachers, Angela Pappas and Ruth Willey, who helped me across a tough year; my high school English teacher, Mary Lou (Huppler) Winzenburg who recognized and fostered my love of language by sharing with me her own. I had no desire in those days to be in education. When I found it was my greatest desire, I knew I was privileged indeed to have the memories of these strong and enlightened women to draw upon.

Introduction

In all the talks chosen for this collection, I take humanness, and the valuing of humanness, as starting place and center for education—and for society more generally. Taking this slant, I examine how views of humanness, and the status accorded to it, influence what we believe is possible educationally, socially, and politically. Mostly, I do this through an up-close examination of classrooms and the lives of those most intimately involved in the life of the schools on a daily basis: children, parents, teachers, and building administrators.

With these particularities and the public schools as frame, I turn my attention to a bigger social and political picture. Situating humanness in the specifics of actual lives and actual schools, I argue strenuously against the unrelenting and generalized critique of the public schools in the media and at policy-making levels. I trace that critique to a press for privatization and to an overvaluing of business concerns. I contest the devaluing of persons that results when the privatizing of schools and other institutions narrows the human horizon, and the measure of human worth is reduced to market value. Specifically, I resist the oversystematization and depersonalization of the school, which threaten to eclipse life on the human and daily scale. Among the thorny issues recurring across these talks, I choose for its particular perniciousness, the ever narrower definition of "normalcy" and the consequent classifying and pathologizing of children.

To resist a constricted educational vision and the devaluing of humanness, I offer humanness itself. I offer humanness as widely distributed capacity, as active making, as value, as resource, as scale, as process, and as responsibility. Drawing on my long history as an observer of children, I anchor this view of humanness in children, and ourselves, as makers: as drawers, story tellers, painters, sculptors, builders, engineers, teachers, writers, care givers, quilters, carpenters, gardeners; in short, as makers and remakers of a human world.

I represent us, humans everywhere, of all ages, across cultures and eons, as coequal in this respect, and through our works ever indebted one to the other. Although we may never meet face to face, your works invite and animate mine, and mine yours, while both of ours are unquestionably progenitors of works yet to come from persons unknown to either of us. Paired with this public character of works, I conceptualize the making of works and the making of lives as inextricably linked. That is, in works, and the making of works, my life acquires both circumference and definition, and equally, in my works, gestures, inclinations, and choices inescapably my own announce themselves.

From these conceptualizations, and others that expand or lend nuance, I weave together across these essays, a tapestry of values and ideas to envision a human and liberating education, the democratizing of the schools, and the reimagining of a society dedicated to fulfilling basic human needs and values. I do that weaving mostly with the help of stories. This is not accidental or incidental. In all these essays, I represent story as a democratizing force in educating us to our common humanity.

I rely on the animating power of story to connect your story with mine, and both of ours to larger public stories: stories of the era, stories of the race, stories of loss and sorrow, stories of hope and fulfillment, stories of human degradation and destructiveness, stories of human strength in the overcoming of stunning blows of fate; in sum, stories of how humanness happens in the making, unmaking, and remaking of it.

I equally rely on story to illuminate the thickness, selectivity, and complexity with which each person (and all persons) craft the stuff of a life into a personal poetic identifiably each person's own. Weighting story in two directions, I give it prominence of place for its pluralizing and publicizing function and equally for its twinned function of connecting both teller and hearer with personal memory and an innerness I see threatened on all sides by memory's (and history's) eclipse.

PROSPECT—IDEAS AND VALUES IN THE MAKING

This is one telling of what the reader can expect from this book: a selection of essays, joined by a view of humanness, each from a particular angle spelling out the consequences of those views for public education and schools. In this telling, I emphasize ideas and values long in the making and deeply rooted in the history of Prospect School and Center, of which, along with Marion Stroud, Joan Blake, and Louis Carini, I am a co-founder.

It was there in North Bennington, Vermont, that together with other Prospect staff I originated a discipline and method for observation and description with the aim of making visible the children's active engagement with the world, with other persons, with making things, and with learning. A further and related aim was to show that a comprehensive, continuing descriptive inquiry of this order and scale can be school based: that a school can examine its own practice and itself generate knowledge of children, of curriculum, of learning and teaching.

By the 1970s we had observed a generation of children, individually and collectively, making choices and making things, with the help of all the media and materials the school so plentifully provided: by writing stories, poems, songs, plays; by painting, drawing, sculpting; by constructing with blocks and cardboard and wood; by sewing and cooking and gardening; by doing science and math and geography and history; by dancing and doing sports; by singing and playing music.

At first casually and then with a clearer sense of purpose, we had collected enough works made by children to recognize their value as guides to a child's abiding interests, strong preferences, and propelling desires. The observations and collections of works, and following along with children over a 9-year period, gave us confidence that neither the works nor what we observed about a child was mere happenstance. We understood each child and every child to be animated by observable preferences, interests, desires, and curiosities that, as Dewey (1938/1963) says, "are sufficiently intense to carry a person over dead places in the future" (p. 38).

From observations carried out in the midst of the child's engagement with materials, we knew that gestures of the hand and body, the voice and manner of speaking, the motifs and ideas that attract a child, the child's preferences for particular media, and much, much more recur. By then we also understood that what recurs changes—and not merely additively, linearly, or in progressive stages, but in a more complicated fashion better described by the spiral with its double habit of touching back and arcing forward, and sometimes transformatively.

This may seem an ordinary insight that people, all of us and children, too, are continuous with ourselves and, at the same time, change. I think it is obvious. Or more precisely, it *is* obvious if you take the time to look with care at any person and that person's works over time, and it is the *person* you attend to. What is novel is that at Prospect we did strive to do that. We did to the best of our ability bend our attention to the children and their works, with care and caringly, and over the span of a child's school life.

We enacted that attentiveness with the help of reflective, descriptive processes originated at Prospect, the first of which, the Descriptive Review of the Child, set the pattern and tone for all the others. The initiating idea of the Descriptive Review of the Child was to bring the entire staff together on a weekly basis to give undivided attention to a child in the school. Using her or his own observations, and those of other staff, gathered across time, and including works made by the child, the teacher who knew the child best painted for the rest of the staff as full a picture of that child as possible. To do this, the teacher organized the portrayal under five headings, each designed to call out a facet of the child's presence. Beginning with physical presence and gesture, the successive headings for the portrayal are: disposition and temperament; connections with other people; strong interests and preferences; modes of thinking and learning. With the teacher's portrayal before us, everyone participating in the review added observations, and through questions and dialogue invited the presenting teacher to amplify the emerging portrait.

The primary aim of the Descriptive Review of the Child was to recognize and specify a particular child's strengths as a person, learner, and thinker, so that as a school we could respond to and build upon those capacities. As we came to the close of a review, our attention turned to suggestions for how that might happen, with all of us contributing ideas. In this way the first benefit of such a review was always to the child since the teacher(s) with major responsibility for him or her left the meeting with deepened insight and a widened repertoire of ideas for nurturing the child's growth and learning.

An equal benefit was to us as a staff committed to children. By immersing ourselves weekly in the school life of one child, we collectively and collaboratively honed our powers to observe and, foregoing the habit of critique and conclusive judgments hastily reached, to speak and think descriptively and reflectively.

From the practice of observing and describing enacted in the Descriptive Review of the Child, we learned to apply this way of looking across a whole family of reviews that evolved from it, among them, the Descriptive Reviews of Children's Works; of Issues; of Classroom Activities and Curriculum; and of Teacher Practice. In a layering fashion, alternating processes and perspectives, but always with the child as anchor, the habit of doing these kinds of collaborative observations and descriptions made us disciplined students of childhood, of learning, of curriculum, and of the classroom.

Writing about this experience on another occasion, I summed up what we were striving for at Prospect in these words:

> This was perhaps our great advantage at Prospect. Starting from the commitment to examine our own practice, we were oriented from the first towards noticing, with a responsibility to record, reflect on, and describe these

noticings. Starting from the idea of human capacity and possibility, widely distributed, we were oriented to look for and to particularize the capacities and strengths of each child. Starting from classroom settings rich in media and materials, we were in a position to see and make visible each child's strong interests and characteristic modes of engaging and learning. Committed to the long view and the child's growth over time, we were able to document these interests and modes of learning for as many as nine years of a child's school life. (in Himley, 2000)

None of this is usual in schools. In schools, children are mostly looked at through the assessment frame: as a good, bad, or indifferent reader; as at grade level or above or below it; as normal or disabled as a learner. Unhappily, this is all too often and increasingly true even for children of preschool age. This doesn't mean that individual teachers in schools everywhere don't give wholehearted attention to the children they are teaching. Nearly all do. I think it is rare to be immersed daily in the child world and not be deeply influenced by the humanness, vitality, and particularity of that world and of each child within it. As a result, most teachers and virtually all parents possess a deep and rich knowledge of children.

Yet mostly, and wastefully, this knowledge goes largely unacknowledged. For knowledge of children, schools rely almost exclusively on experts and specialists. The school seldom gives value or priority to teacher or parent knowledge of the child, or in any consistent way develops it. In any event, schools as institutions and systems are mostly taken up with other topics such as assessment and, alongside it, diagnosis, prescriptions, and services; teaching models, techniques, and curriculum packages; and scheduling. The priority is not the child but objectives reached and scores achieved. The assemblage of scores, rankings, IEPs (individualized education plans), and other official forms is mainly what is collected in what are called school "cumulative records" on a child.

The person and the person's continuousness with her- or himself is also not the conceptualization that frames most research. Longitudinal investigations, like those at Prospect, are rare if only because they are time consuming. Obviously, it takes years to do a study that spans years. Even when such studies do occur, the person and the person's learning are rarely the primary interest. More typically, the focus is language development or concept formation or problem solving or reading, with the child the necessary vehicle for gathering the data.

What happened at Prospect is that in some measure we unsettled these frames: the testing/assessment frame and the cross-sectional or longitudinal investigations in which a mental function or a predicted developmental progression is at the center. We did that unsettling in the ways I have used the Descriptive Review of the Child to emblemize, but they acquired dimension and further articulation in the other descriptive processes I have named, and in related inquiries.

For example, when we conducted inquiries into reading in the 1970s, we began with portrayals of children spanning 5 and more years of the child's school life. These portraits, besides spanning years, were also deliberately inclusive of a bigger picture than the child in connection with reading. Aiming for an embracing view of the child, we counted on the careful documentation of a child's interests, modes of expression as a speaker and maker of works, and ways of making sense of things more generally, to cast light on the specifics of the child's engagement with reading.

Some of what we learned from these studies, and especially through description of children's works, was applied subsequently in a 3-year study of individual children's entry into reading, in which Prospect, along with other schools, participated. Conducted by the Early Education Group at Educational Testing Service, this study was later published by them as *Inquiry Into Meaning: An Investigation of Learning to Read* (Bussis, Chittenden, Amarel, & Klausner, 1985).

During this same period, we also were compiling extensive documentation, published in house, of the Prospect classroom settings and the curriculum. At every step along the way, and especially through summer institutes held at Prospect starting in 1971, we sought opportunities to engage with teachers from other schools, mostly public, across a wide span of geographic locations, including Boston; Ithaca, New York; New York City; Paterson, New Jersey; and Philadelphia. Many teachers who came to these institutes were drawn equally by Prospect's anchoring of education in the child and by the envisioning of schools as the locus for generating knowledge.

At Prospect, we learned from the teachers who came, and by paying return visits to their classrooms, how observation and the descriptive processes might be adapted to the particularities of their settings. Through this give and take, Prospect's observation and description practices were altered and expanded, and continue to be, achieving in the process a nuance, complexity, and fullness that could not have happened except through these connections.

By the mid-1980s, I had written several monographs (Carini, 1975, 1979, 1982) positioning Prospect's methodology for observation and description. Naming it a descriptive, phenomenological inquiry, in each of these publications I called specific attention to its root in the particularities of the child's lived experience as that is viewable and describable across contexts, from multiple perspectives, and spanning time. The third of these monographs, *The School Lives of Seven Children* (1982), reports an application of Prospect's descriptive, phenomenological inquiry designed for the evaluation of the New York State Prekindergarten Program, which documents children's growth and learning from age 4 to age 9.

By 1985, a subset of 36 children's collected works, housed in the Prospect Archive of Children's Works, was available to other educators and researchers. Under the title *Reference Edition of the Prospect Archive* (1985; see Appendix), this publication in microfiche, typescript, and colored slides includes the children's numbered and catalogued works supported by compiled teacher observational records and narrative reports to parents. The cataloguing of these works was accomplished through an extensive study, spanning 2 years and conducted through the Archive Scholars and Fellows Program, which brought to Prospect professionals in education, literature, art, anthropology, and other fields. For this study, the Descriptive Review of Children's Works, the parallel process to the Descriptive Review of the Child, and guided by the same aims at fullness and attention to complexity, was used to trace the media, motifs, and themes represented in each child's collection.

I choose these several moments in time from the 1970s to the mid-1980s as glimpses of process, philosophy, and activities that happened at Prospect within that time frame to suggest a history and landscape that far exceed them. I also offer these glimpses to alert the reader to other paths to Prospect. For example, the Descriptive Review of the Child I have used emblematically and sketched only lightly above is the heart and substance of the companion volume to this book, *From Another Angle: Children's Strengths and School Standards* (Himley, 2000).

What remains to be said here is that the methodology for descriptive inquiry, the descriptive review processes that enact it, and description itself are subtext to all these essays—as is Prospect itself. None of the ideas and values on which these collected talks pivot is imaginable to me apart from Prospect.

LOCATING DESCRIPTIVE INQUIRY IN THE PUBLIC SCHOOLS

Another telling of this book relates it to a more recent history: a period of intense personal engagement in public schools, teacher centers, and parent/ teacher cooperatives spanning the years from 1989 to 1998. Mostly my part in these working partnerships with teachers and parents was to help start the kinds of observational, descriptive inquiries I had played a role in originating at Prospect. These inquiries, focused on children and based in public school classrooms, happened in a variety of locations, but most extensively and intensively in Ithaca, New York; Mamaroneck, New York; Philadelphia; and Phoenix, Arizona.

In practice, this meant that during these 9 years, I often was observing in classrooms, assisting parents and teachers to do observing, and helping parents, teachers, and children to collect and describe works. Children as makers of works, and the artworks, constructions, writings, and mathematical, scientific, and other projects that materialized from their making, were an intensive focus of all these inquiries. Grounded in this attentiveness to children and their works, the inquiries tended to expand to include description and documentation of classrooms, curriculum, the work and art of teaching, and occasionally whole schools.

Sometimes an essay in this collection refers to a specific descriptive inquiry and its location. Other times the connection to specific ongoing inquiries is oblique or goes unstated in the text of the talk. Whether the connection is stated or unstated, every one of these talks was powerfully influenced by what I was seeing and learning through my partnership with teachers, parents, and schools during these 9 years. For this reason, the reader will discover that many of the talks are urgent in tone, some are harsh. Situated in the very now of schools, these aren't talks that idealize. The ideas of humanness I advance as center and ground for educating and schools, I put to the hard test of the bleak, unrelenting realities confronting the schools and everyone engaged in them: high-stakes testing, the push for standardization of the schools, research- and technology-based reform, a proclaimed literacy crisis, ending so-called social promotion.

Across these essays, in response to these realities, I argue for change that is generative and regenerative, in which the school, itself understood as a work, is also understood to be makable and remakable. For example, in Chapter 4, "Schools in the Making," I locate the idea of the school as a work in the histories of two Arizona schools, W. T. Machan and Sunnyslope. With that idea as compass, I launch an inquiry for documenting both schools' histories with the aim of making visible each school's strengths and its generative potential.

By giving high priority to the making and remaking of the school, I call attention to the school as lively and animate, carrying within it the seeds of its own growth and renewal. I claim in these talks that uncovering the values and ideas, and the makers, that have inspired a school's liveliest educational accomplishments founds an energizing and empowering inquiry. My point throughout the book is that by accepting the task of making and remaking, working and reworking, the school and educating become squarely our (human) responsibility—to strive for their renewal, to keep them responsive to novelty, and to nurture their growth.

Arguing for (re)generative change, I am contesting educational aims, past and prevailing now, that project a utopian future, in which schools will be perfected, and ultimate solutions found for all problems. I make the argument on human and political grounds. I observe in several of these talks that reform policies that substitute one educational model or research-based technology for another, each successively promising final solutions to literacy or achievement or some other "problem," fail. And are fated in advance to fail. Aimed at generalized solutions, applicable across all schools, models and systems miss the human point: the point of human differences and human complexity. It is after all people—and most vigorously, children and youth—who learn, who make sense and meaning of the world, and they simply don't all do it the same way. Whatever the model, children tend to fall through these technological nets. The more refined and totalizing the model, the more fall through. Human complexity, the complexities of learning, the complexities of teaching resist systematization.

What I strive for in these talks by conceptualizing schools (and education) as works in the making is to expand what it is possible for schools (and education) to be. When I say "what is possible," in nearly all these talks I am projecting those possibilities in a double time frame: right now, as things stand today in the schools, in the face of grim realities, and in a foreseeable future in which I can envision education charted by other and roomier values than standardization.

Nearly all these talks spell out what you or I or anyone active in the schools can do on a daily basis and grass-roots level right now to insist on humanness and to resist the oversystematization and remoteness that threatens to totalize us all. While the suggestions are each time specific, the aim is always to keep the child—the child's humanness, the child's complexity, the child's learning, the child's well-being—at the top of the school's agenda.

The further and related aim is to value and make visible the knowledge of children and the daily work of those closest to the school scene: parents, teachers, and building administrators. Often, within these talks, I tell the story of how this vigilant attentiveness to the child's humanness is being enacted right now in actual schools by particular parents and teachers. The talk from which the title of this book is drawn, "To Help Us Start Strong," which tells the story of Jenny, is an example. The work every talk in this collection does is to call attention to basic human values and needs, to name the threats to those values, and to map ways to respond or to act or to have hope.

Envisioning the school as a work, a work with a history, a work permeable and open to influence, a work shaped and being shaped by human hands and mind, I also envision a future, not separate from the here and now, but already in the making. To translate what is right now germinating into focused, conscious mode, I urge vigilance to every opportunity to influence, to shape, to speak, and to enact. For example, in "We Love the

Things We Love for What They Are," I urge that each of us learn "to name and to say unhesitatingly . . . where [we] see capacity and possibility, to name what [we] know is working for children, for teachers, for schools, and to be alert to every opening to insert this other, and positive, language." Illustrating the point, I tell the stories of a principal and school director for both of whom the child and the child's humanness are center and standard for the school, and for themselves as spokespersons for children, childhood, and families.

The emphasis on what is possible, with twinned attentiveness to right now and up-close and to a future foreseeable and itself in the making, means that the talks I present in this volume are mostly two-tiered. Bridging the tiers, the workableness and reworkableness of human enterprises is the connecting link.

PAIRED BOOKS FORETELLING A SERIES

A third telling of this book is as companion volume to the book I cited earlier, *From Another Angle* (Himley, 2000), with both as pathbreakers for a projected series of books, each developing a facet of the institution. These first two volumes, with *From Another Angle* leading the way, were conceptualized as a pair. Besides their common root in Prospect, both are situated in public schools where in the hands of public school teachers and parents, the Prospect Descriptive Processes are at work. With Prospect, and Prospect's partnership with public schools, the common ground between them, the two books do different work, offering the reader two distinctive experiences.

From Another Angle, with its focus on the Descriptive Review of the Child, was composed from transcribed tapes of teachers from Philadelphia and New York City in the process of planning and doing this kind of review. Actively engaging the reader in the doing of descriptive reviews, it is a teaching book. Essays interspersed between the stories of the reviews flesh out the roles of the teacher presenting the child and the chairperson, and describe more generally what it means to take a descriptive approach in the classroom and school and how it is possible to sustain the discipline these kinds of ongoing descriptive inquiries require. Multivocal and multi-authored, it is, in every respect, an energetic book, meant to help teachers and parents get started with this kind of descriptive review process in their own locations.

Situated in the context of this earlier volume and in locations where Prospect's descriptive processes are happening, *Starting Strong* accomplishes other purposes. What these collected talks do, and what I often am asked to do when I am invited to give a talk of this kind, is to relate the irreducible particularity of teaching, classrooms, and children, and of doing descriptive inquiries, to a wider context of ideas and values. Viewed as companion pieces, *From Another Angle* provides the reader with a direct encounter that *Starting Strong* configures on a larger screen. Together the paired books engage the reader at interanimating levels: a face-to-face engagement with descriptive process and a no less up-close and immediate engagement with the ideas and values grounding and framing that process.

MIRROR IMAGES: TALKS AND BOOK

As it happened, I had many opportunities in the years this book spans to do writing in the form of talks. When I selected the nine that appear in this collection, I discovered to my surprise a corpus of about 50 such talks. Until I looked back over the accumulated texts, I had no idea of the volume. Reading through them, I was transported. I could see the faces and hear the voices of teachers, parents, and children in the places I was working. I could hear myself giving these talks, each forged in the realities of this ongoing work and intense conversation. I have tried in the versions of these talks as they appear here to retain as much as possible that closeness to the spoken, and as it seems important to do, particulars of the time and place that situate the talk.

In introductions to each of the four parts I have used to organize the texts, I signal connections I see among the pieces that dictated the order in which they appear. Yet, the reader should know in advance that while I have pruned for repetition and arranged and titled the parts, I have mostly left the talks themselves intact, each a whole unto itself. There is overlap among them. There is linkage of ideas and values. Story connects them all. In this the book mirrors the compositional structure of the individual essays.

Quite often I start a talk with a story or description of some close to home or school event. In "Valuing the Immeasurable," it is a story from my own life, as is also the case in "In the Thick of the Tangle." Sometimes I begin with a story further afield. For example, in "Another Slant on Knowledge," I start with a story from the learned world, juxtaposing in the telling the theories of color proposed by Newton and Goethe. Starting with theorizing on the grand scale, I turn about to connect that story with stories of children making sense of the world. In "Poets of Our Lives," I interleave the works made by three children with adult works and also political and social commentaries from a variety of sources.

Starting this way with a story, I expand the canvas and layer it by relating the intimate episode to contexts that enlarge it and give to what at a glance is highly particular a public face and meaning. Because the contexts are multiple, often interconnecting social, political, philosophical, literary, and aesthetic perspectives, these are not talks (nor is this a book) that narrow(s) to a point. Using this nonlinear, lateral construction, I am aiming for a kind of roominess in which one idea invites another and voices speak across discourses.

The image of these talks as each one offering a slant on humanness, is played out in this construction, which is intended to offer the reader a variety of entry points, all opening onto the same space but arriving there by different paths. For the reason that the talks are not strictly tied to educational discourse, I hope that readers from other disciplines and especially readers with interest in the larger social, political tapestry in which education is one of many figures may find the talks welcoming.

GROUPING THE TALKS

I have grouped the talks in four parts as follows: Part I, On a Human Scale: Works, Lives, Schools; Part II, The Politics of Educating/The Politics of Work; Part III, Standards in the Making; Part IV, Generation/Regeneration. The essays in Part I introduce the large ideas that recur across the talks and map the territory of the book as a whole. Among those ideas are the definition of the person as active maker of works, the dialogic interanimation of person and world, and the world itself as plural, ambiguous, and always larger than the systematized readings of it as "disciplines," or "fields," or "knowledge." Pluralistic in philosophical and political stance, these three essays connect the conceptualizing of the self with such democratic ideas as personal choice and freedom.

The talks included in Part II juxtapose to the wide ground carved out in Part I, the narrower vision and definitions of persons, of work, and of educating that prevail when as a society, we start (as we do) from an economic frame. The economic vision is, I assert, necessarily hierarchical, necessarily committed to a limited definition of work as "effort rewarded by pay," and to an equally limited definition of education that puts highest priority on marketability.

Part III selects standards as the locus of the struggle for human and humane schools. In these talks, I recurrently and across a variety of situations call attention to the root of standards (all standards) in values, and to the human capacity for conferring value and making standards. Returning standards to a human scale, I affirm that there aren't people who don't aspire. Specifically, I am attentive to children and the standards they hold—standards that are observable and describable in their actions and their works. Reclaiming standards as human work in the making of them, fired by desire and aspiration, I am insisting on a deeper and wider definition than worth measured by scores. I include in Part III two meditations, one on description, the other on number.

Part IV consists of a single talk that pivots on the responsibility of elders to children. I specify that responsibility in words adopted from Toni Morrison's 1993 Nobel Lecture in Literature, "to help [the children] start strong" (Morrison, 1994). Fragments from a spanning and comprehensive study of a child, following her life at home and school from ages 5 through 7, is the heart of this essay. As I say in the talk, this is a child who illuminates the educative power of story, and who by her values, her enacted standards, and her grasp of value priorities, teaches us, the elders, what it does indeed mean, "to start strong."

PART I

On a Human Scale:
Works, Lives, Schools

> The farthest horizons of our hopes and fears are cobbled
> by our poems, carved from the rock experiences of our
> daily lives.
> —Audre Lorde, "Poetry Is Not a Luxury"

Works (and ourselves as makers of works) connect the three talks that compose this section, which taken together step across the 9 years the book spans. Starting with "Poets of Our Lives," I begin with a talk that maps a big expanse of human territory, angling in on that territory from dual perspectives. One perspective is offered by three children, each represented by a selection of artworks and writings encompassing the child's school life up to age 12 or 13. With the help of these works, I visualize for the reader how, given careful and caring attention, the works offer insight into a child's persisting interests, choices, and preferences and a reliable guide to an education responsive to them. Then, juxtaposed to the children's works and lives, I offer as parallel perspective, the voices and works of a wide spectrum of adult makers, some celebrated, and others just as humanly consequential whose works and lives happened outside the spotlight of acclaim and fame.

The aim of this dual approach is to describe a human ground that is both spacious and inclusive. I insist on this wide embrace because without it, as parents, educators, and citizens, we find ourselves condemned to an ever narrower and undermining definition of normalcy—in the society and in the schools. If only a few children are normal and truly capable, it does not take great social or political acuity to guess which children and whose will be favored. In other words, I insist on this broad terrain of widely distributed capacity to propel a democratizing of the public schools, and the society.

The other essays in this section, "In the Thick of the Tangle What Clear Line Persists" and "Another Slant on Knowledge," translate and specify the idea of works and the making of works in two contexts: story (and the making of stories) and knowledge (and the making of knowledge). Both talks assert the act of making for its educational potency in life and in schools.

"In the Thick of the Tangle" gives full play to story, memory, and imagination working together in the child's self-configuring, in which the child discovers her- or himself a player in the wider human drama. The essay tells many stories, but the heart of the matter is a transcribed tape of my mother telling the story of the death of her sister, Faye, when Faye was 8 and my mother was 13.

The quotation from Eudora Welty's *One Writer's Beginnings* (1984), which I adopt as title, announces the valuing of the self's innerness, not for its privacy, but as a gathering place of many lives, with imagination as memory's animater and publicizer. In the essay, I pair the title quotation with Milan Kundera's (1988) prophecy of memory's loss, and with her departure, the thinning of the human fabric. I connect the threat to innerness and to our capacity to narrate ourselves to current school practice which, by a restrictive, habitually negative focus on behaviors, lacks, and problems, misses the child. I represent these practices as a forgetting of the child and, equally, a forgetting of humanness.

"Another Slant on Knowledge" affirms the human scale and its adequacy for living human lives and doing human works, by situating knowledge in its animated, bodily mode: the making of knowledge. In the talk, I root that activity in the strong desire of humans of all ages to make sense and order of the world and of their own experiences. Here, as in the two preceding talks, my aim is to democratize—not by claiming that all knowledge has equal weight but rather by claiming that as makers of knowledge, all of us, child and adult alike, enjoy a coequality of impulse and desire to engage in that activity. Locating knowledge in human effort and struggle, I represent it as necessarily plural, partial, and mutable, and as inseparable from the social and political surround in which it is made.

The lead essay, "Poets of Our Lives," was the 1995 Amarel Lecture, sponsored biannually by the School of Education at Michigan State University and the Amarel family to honor the memory of Marianne Amarel. The lecture prefaced an all-day conference held at Michigan State in November 1994 which engaged local teachers and university students and faculty in conducting and participating in Descriptive Reviews of the Child and Descriptive Reviews of Children's Works.

The second essay, "In the Thick of the Tangle What Clear Line Persists," was the 1997 Walker Gibson Lecture sponsored by the Writing Program at the University of Massachusetts at Amherst. Preceding the lecture, graduate students and faculty from the Writing Program and other programs within the English Department participated in workshops that applied Prospect's Descriptive Review of Children's Works to the writings of university students.

The third essay, "Another Slant on Knowledge," was presented at Friends Select School, April 1989, in Philadelphia at a celebration of "300 Years of Quaker Education in the New World," with the theme "Educating for Value in a Democracy." Later, some who heard the talk gathered to add their stories of knowledge making to the stories related in the talk, using a Prospect process called Recollections.

1

Poets of Our Lives

Some years ago now, educator and poet Jay Featherstone used the words "poets of our lives" in response to slides of children's collected works from the Prospect Archive, which I showed at a meeting of the North Dakota Study Group on Evaluation. I was enchanted by the beauty of the words and energized by the chords they sounded in me, resonating as they did with my long history as an observer and collector of children's works.

My first thought was that "poets of our lives" named a relationship between maker and works deeply familiar to me. I configure that relationship as a dialectic from which not only "things" result, but through which our very lives emerge as works, of which we are ourselves the authors. It is a dialectic that discovers in works and the making of works the self's medium and animating energy.

That dialectic carries other ideas which I understand to be intimately connected with it. One of these is what I name the *public* character of making. I mean by this the manner in which works observably build on works and, just as observably, lives build on lives. Here, I am signaling the generative potency of works and lives, a potency that joins a work or life in the making in an ever widening, deepening stream of works and lives, happening now or in the past—works and lives that are promise of ever more works and lives to come.

Next to the width and embracing sweep of this public dimension of works and lives, I place the philosopher Isaiah Berlin's (1969/1988) framing of conceptions of self as inseparable from conceptions of freedom. Or, as he says it, "Conceptions of freedom directly derive from views of what constitutes a self, a person" (p. 134). Drawing the consequences of that equation, he goes on to say, "Enough manipulation with [that] definition . . . and freedom can be made to mean whatever the manipulator wishes" (p. 134). In the waning years of the twentieth century with its legacy of hate and genocide, the issue is, as Berlin points out, "not merely academic" (p. 134).

The inseparableness of conceptions of self and freedom, twinned with the public character of making, gives to what I say here a specifically political cast, which is intensified by a third idea: the presence of human capacity, widely distributed, and everywhere witnessed to by our human works. As I was listening to Jay Featherstone's words, I could not help but hear their resonance with those of Walt Whitman (1860/1992), singer of work and workers, of the common man and woman. "Poets of our lives" are words he might have written, as a refrain perhaps within his "varied carols of America" (p. 177), that celebration of daily life and the ordinary capableness of our human hands and minds. And if we have eyes to see and ears to hear, its extraordinariness. I choose to enter this talk from that wing—the wing of human capacity.

HUMAN CAPACITY, WIDELY DISTRIBUTED

It is in just this sense that the works children make are both ordinary— and extraordinary: They reflect a widely distributed human capacity to be makers and doers, active agents in the world and their own lives; to be, as Jay Featherstone said, poets of their lives.

Children everywhere make things. Children make things from mud, sand, snow, stones, blocks of wood, or bits of cardboard or paper. They make things from their own bodies—from sounds, gestures, words. They use their hands and arms, their mouths, their eyes, their feet and legs. They make a mark on any receptive surface using a fingertip on a frosted window, a sharp stick in the dirt or sand, or a pencil, a crayon, or paint on paper, or lacking these, or just because it's handy, berry juice or some other natural dye. They connect things, sticking them together with nails or tape or glue or staples or string or yarn—or because it seems an interesting or challenging thing to do, with grasses woven together or a strip of bark.

Children do this enacting and constructing of the world everywhere— even, from the evidence available, in the terrible circumstances of desperate poverty, war, and concentration camps. It would appear that only the ultimate extremes of hunger, illness, and terror are able to interrupt that strong childhood urge to do and to make. Theirs is a sustained and powerful dialectic with the world, issuing in a seemingly infinite variation of activity and creations.

An ordinary capacity, widely distributed: to engage the world, to be a maker of things; a capacity observable in earliest childhood. Whitman (1855/1992) sings the song of that dialectic in the poem, "There Was a Child Went Forth," a child of whom he says, "the first object he looked upon . . . that object he became . . ." (p. 124). Although portraying his own child self, Whitman speaks for Everychild in those lines—and for each: a highly particular self revealed in the selections made by *that* child's eye and hand, a spectrum of noticings about the world and all its happenings specific to her or his perspective. He speaks for a self in the making, a making revealed in a trail of talk, activity, play, things drawn and built and written.

One of the useful things about having collections of children's works like those in the Prospect Archive is the lens they offer to highly particular selves—and to our humanness more generally. What I have just said about Everychild—and each child—is revealed there to any who care to look. There the viewer can see something otherwise associated almost exclusively with retrospectives of the works of famous artists: a continuousness of works with the maker. A continuousness that is made visible in a coherent, yet complicated variation of image, motif, and theme, growing and changing, but unquestionably that artist's signature from first to last; a continuousness descriptive of a highly individual and recognizable personal aesthetic.

Picasso is not Cezanne; Whitman is not Dickinson; Ives is not Ruggles; Stevens is not Bishop. We expect, anticipate, and relish the blazing individuality of these artists. We also discern, if we look, that they are participants in each other's works and lives, builders on each other's vision—sometimes sympathetically, sometimes oppositionally, sometimes in variation—and sometimes apparently unwittingly, as when an image common to us all, by crossing the boundaries from one work to another, assumes new dimensions and possibilities. This is true, for example, of railroad tracks which appear in Willa Cather's novel *O Pioneers* (1941) and also in Elizabeth Bishop's poem "Chemin de Fer" (1946/1994, p. 8)— but oh so differently—and then appear on the quite other horizon of Martha Graham's dance *Frontier* (1935).

And sometimes, one of us, the viewers and readers of others' works, draws an exquisite parallel, as Adrienne Rich (1993) does between Whitman and Dickinson, that "strange uncoupled couple" (p. 90), as she dubs them, or as she also names them, "a wild woman and a wild man, writing their wild carnal and ecstatic thoughts . . . as the empire of the United States pushed into the Far West, Mexico, and the Caribbean" (p. 95). Possibly hearing of each other, if at all, only tangentially, but each a pathbreaker, beginners, as Rich says, entering the same historical era from extreme and opposing angles, and mapping for us between them an American landscape. And by that mapping, naming for us the opposites we may combine—a combining that complicates and diversifies both the landscape and ourselves.

Yet these children for whom I claim similarly individual and mingled perspectives, a take on the world very much each child's own, are *not* acclaimed adult artists or thinkers. They aren't even children identified as prodigies or handpicked according to some other standard. They are children from all walks of life. Present among them are children who match the criteria used in some schools, although not Prospect, for designation as children with "special needs."

I propose, by this bringing together in one frame of the works of artists and children, *a continuum of makers* I believe worthy of our educational, social, and political attention. I do *not* with this proposal claim that all works possess the same value, or that a child's works are valuable in the same terms as those of an adult artist. My claim is for the *equivalency of the impulse,* the irresistible desire to make, and making, to make a mark on the world: to make a breakthrough that carries the child (as it does the adult artist) beyond the raw *fact* of existence to *own* that existence, that life that is her own. That is where I suggest we are well, and truly, met: artist and scientist, child and adult, worker and player, lives lived quietly and lives played out in the large, public arena.

Dipping into the collections of three children, whose works are published in the *Reference Edition of the Prospect Archive* (1985) (see Appendix), I propose to quilt together their three quite different perspectives—as persons, thinkers, and learners; or, as I think of it, following on Dewey (1916/ 1980), selves in the making.

Each collection spans at least 8 years of the child's life and contains about 1,000 items. The items are numbered chronologically within each year of a collection so that the first item for a child 5 years old bears the number 5.1, the second, 5.2, and so on; a "B" preceding the number indicates a work larger than 12" x 17"; "HC" indicates a collection item contributed from home; "nd" indicates no date. The names used for the children (Iris, Paul, and Sean) are not actual names but pseudonyms adopted to protect the privacy of child and family.

Although I am the spokesperson, what I have to say about each collection is selected from detailed, collaborative descriptions of these works carried out over an extended period, using processes originated at Prospect Center. Participants in these descriptions included Prospect staff, and in the period from 1982 through 1984, the members of the Archive Scholars and Fellows Program who numbered and catalogued the collections for publication.

In the discussion of the collections, I am attentive to representing important dimensions of each. Nevertheless, these are highly selective. What I am able to say in short compass, with the aid of a small number of supporting illustrations, can merely suggest the richness and complexity of these collections and, equally, the depth and detail of the full-scale descriptions from which these examples are drawn.

"Iris"

First, there is Iris, a prolific drawer and writer, her eye and ear attuned to what is at the heart of things. At age 6, she wrote this succinct fairy tale under the title "Snow White and the Seven Dwarves":

> Once upon a time
> There lived a pretty princess
> Had a pretty baby
> And she bit into a
> apple and a prince
> Came along.   The End   (6.91)

At ages 5 and 6, Iris also drew many pictures focused on people—usually duos of women—gesturally and dramatically lively, often sort of dancing along, but with a minimum of context (Figure 1.1, 5.82). Also worthy of note are the crowns, since these and other decorative treatments of heads such as bows and hats appear throughout the collection.

Or, the sort of scene depicted in Plate 3 (6.251) occurs: carved out, rather like a stage set in its lack of surrounding context, but filled with implied drama and mystery. Notice especially the slinky lady, on tiptoe behind the tree, lightly drawn but contributing greatly to the dramatic impact of the scene.

From age 7 onwards, individually depicted, strong female figures account for a dominant, recurring theme in the visual works. There are, for example, women at work, sturdy and self-sufficient, represented here by a country woman gardening, a basket of carrots beside her (Figure 1.2, 7.124).

Besides self-sufficiency, Iris's women tend to have the power of mystery. Often this is accomplished as it is in Plate 1 (B8.203) by seriousness of demeanor together with suggestion of inner depths. In this particular drawing, a female figure facing the viewer dominates the foreground, while the small scale of what appears to be a city skyline pictured behind her represents a distant horizon. Playing off this suggestion of distance, an echoing cityscape, perhaps a port, is drawn into the bodice of the woman's dress, as if to hold it in memory. Complementarily, what seems to be the prow of a ship decorates the skirt. The overall effect of time now and time remembered is intensified by the stillness of the female figure, her far-away gaze seemingly fixed on a yet further horizon existing beyond the space of the page.

Figure 1.1. Figures in motion. (5.82)

Figure 1.2. Woman gardening. (7.124)

At age 10, a striking trio of portraits repeats the theme of memory, employing similar visual devices. The first drawing in the series (Plate 2, 10.77) shows the upper torso of a female figure, foreground and frontal. Her costume with its bands of color on the sleeve and the heart-shaped pendant around the figure's neck connote a time not now, and perhaps in the distant past. As in Plate 1, the young woman's expression is serious and the gaze intense. On the bodice of her dress are painted three full-length female figures, positioned to form a triangle, with the middle figure at the apex. The inserted figures are depicted in what appears to be a moonlit landscape containing two bushes which, interestingly, are replicated on a proportionately larger scale behind the young woman. These elements also appear in each of the succeeding portraits in the series, each time with some variation in the positioning of the elements. That the three inserted figures foretell the two succeeding portraits in the trio seems inescapable. The total effect is haunting, redolent of memory. For the viewer, the fates, the three graces, all of the rich symbolism of female triangles is evoked by the figures on the bodice.

I would note in passing that the polish that characterizes the portrait shown (and also the two not illustrated) is somewhat unexpected in this collection. While Iris's works more usually display a kind of dash and drama, a certain offhandedness of execution, in these pictures the rough manila paper was obviously painted in advance to accomplish the smooth ivory of the figures' faces.

Attention to time and memory, however, *is* representative, as is evidenced in the following written piece, also composed at age 10. Composed in dialogue, the work combines largeness of idea with an elegant economy of style.

THE CONVERSATION BETWEEN PAST AND NOW

> "Hello now." Said Past
> "Hello then." Said Now
> "I wish that I had such great inventions like you." said Past.
> "Well my people have made something to destroy both of us so . . .
> I wish my people were like your people."
> "Well what is this somthing."
> "This something is a nuclear bomb."
> "How much Power does this bomb have."
> "Enough to Blow up half the world and kill what is left of it and
> also kill us."
> "How can we stop this."
> "I'm afraid we cant."
> "Are you Sure."
> "Yes. I am."
> "You mean the only way for this to stop is for the people to not
> want war."
> "Yes."
> "That's not fair."
> "I Know but there is nothing for us to do."
> "Good-bye."
> "Good-bye." (10.60)

The succinctness of the message, the grasp of human frailty, the effectiveness of the negative construction, "to not want war," and the confident poetic line are stunning in their power to evoke.

The predilection for packed imagery, the arrow to the heart of the matter, also is expressed in Iris's early adolescence. Poems like this one are continuous with "The Conversation Between Now and Past" and, although different in tone, with the poem titled "Snow White and the Seven Dwarves" written when Iris was 6:

QUIET EYE

A winter wind blowing
through a snowy field.
The doe is standing motionless, but to
quiet eye she is springing
in a field of joy. (11.160)

What I have called to attention through this selection of visual and written works is a strong theme of innerness and depth spanning the collection, and the inclusion of similar elements: mystery, memory, big ideas, women as a prevailing subject. Yet, in the full collection these threads are braided together with many others. Some are closely related, such as a fascination with outer space, UFOs, and the unknown more generally.

Another is a characteristically observational stance, typically illustrated in visual works by the presence of a watcher, pictured as a floating head above the action and looking down on it. The watcher also makes an appearance from above in the following piece of writing, composed when Iris was 6:

ONCE UPON A TIME

Once upin "a time there was a grandmother who died. And the girl was standing beside the grave and she was crying. The grandmother was watching down below from heaven and her grave was right beside tree and a balloon was watching down below too. It makes her happy because she thinks her grandmother is alive in heaven.

The End (6.165)

Another strong, but light thread woven through the collection is a delightful humor and whimsy that off-balance Iris's predilection for depths and mystery. For example, there is this play with words excerpted from a piece written at age 9—again featuring dialogue:

The moon said to the sun, "My you're looking bright today." The sun said back, "I'm glad I light up your life." Then the moon said, "Why are you so bright." I don't know, I studied a lot in school. . . ." (9.23)

A similar fancifulness is at play in the following journal entries made when
Iris was 8:

> Today Lydia found a worm. We are going to keep it for a day or
> two. It is so adorable I kissed [it] once so did Paisley and Lydia. a
> real sign of spring. She found [it] up in our fort which I will tell
> you about later. She found it under a board in the fort. He died
> yesterday the Worm died. Poor thing. Well today we are making a
> lot of progress on our fort. (8.139–140; Lydia and Paisley are
> pseudonyms)

To complete this tour of Iris's works, I return once more to the fascination with memory and interiors—this time by way of a recurring visual
form, an arch. Among the guises in which the arch makes its appearance
are the following: as a door marking the separation of indoors and out; as
a headdress; and as a tunnel designed to suggest infinite regression. Typically narrow and domed, the arch when doubled, as it is in Figure 1.3
(10.81), mirrors the interiority and distance accomplished by other means

Figure 1.3. Double arched passage with two figures. (10.81)

Plate 1 Woman in patterned dress
B8.203

Plate 2 Portrait
10.77

Plate 3 Scene with two figures
6.251

Plate 4 Design
B13.278

Plate 5 Night scene
B5.66

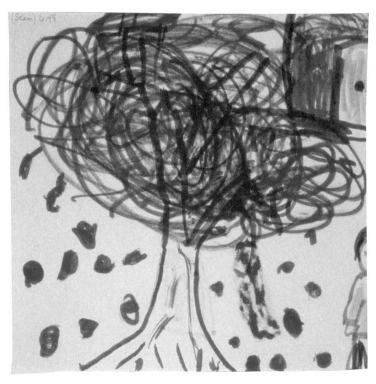

Plate 6 Autumn tree
6.48

in Plates 1 and 2. Here, that suggestion is accentuated by the long, opulent, red-carpeted curved passageway that separates the arches, with the diminutive scale of figures turned romantically toward each other to signal the distance traveled from here to there—in space or time or both. Represented here by a single drawing, arches span the collection, ever present from age 5 through age 12, and increasing in complexity and variation as they evolve over that span.

"Paul"

Next I introduce Paul. Here it is point and line and an inventiveness with the space of the page itself that span the collection from first to last. A very early piece contributed from home (Figure 1.4, HC3.3) illustrates attention to line as well as to point and geometric forms—all accomplished at the tender age of 3. A straight line marks the division of head and hat. The hands and feet, accomplished with similarly firm, clear straight lines, are drawn with remarkable precision for so young a hand.

The next two drawings, separated by a number of years from the one done at age 3, illustrate the persistence of line, point, and spatial dimension in Paul's works. The first of these drawings (Figure 1.5, B8.61) accentuates acute angles which appear in the bend of an elbow or knee. By depicting a tall figure about to stamp out a tiny village, the composition also represents a play with scale recurrent in many drawings in this collection.

Complementarily, Figure 1.6 (13.89) is a composition in points: the bird's beak, the humanoid alien's head with a point at the crown and sharply pointed teeth revealed in a halfmoon grin, and what appear to be icicles or stalactites descending from the top of the page. The addition of color in this drawing is notable in a collection in which the strongly preferred medium until relatively late in childhood is pencil.

As play with spatiality and line develops, there are numerous intricate designs. In many of these, geometrics are strong elements, and many defy expected figure/ground distinctions and boundaries. The design depicted in Plate 4 (B13.278) is especially complex in these respects—a complexity that is at least partly attributable to the interruption of the yellow border in the upper left quadrant.

As the drawing in Figure 1.5 suggests, humor is often hard edged and satirical. In some pieces, the veneer of civilization is rudely ripped away or, as in Figure 1.7 (13.153), which depicts a comically deadly attack on a man trapped in a bathtub by giant insects (especially bees) and spears, it is the frailty of humanness that is satirized.

Counterbalancing point, line, geometry, and edgy humor, there are drawings scattered across the collection just as meticulously rendered, but

Figure 1.4. Figure with pointed hat. (HC3.3)

Figure 1.5. Man with sharp angled limbs. (B8.61)

Figure 1.6. Composition with points. (13.89)

imbued with tenderness. Typically, these are of natural objects, revealing a sympathy with small creatures of all kinds, and a deep, urgent concern for the life of the planet. These surprisingly delicate, often lovely drawings complicate and soften the collection. Figure 1.8 (11.86) illustrates this quality of tenderness in the loving creation of a rabbit munching a leaf. Although done exclusively in pencil, the careful shading lends to the rabbit a palpable softness and vulnerability.

Poetry written in adolescence is similarly suffused with feeling and thought:

NOT HAPPY TO WIN

As I fall to the canvas
He yells, "Get up you overconfident
blockhead."

Staggering

Coach screaming to
get up

No time left

Retching
    Tired
        Sick

Standing
      Stumbling

Left
    uppercut

Right
      Knockout

Home now

Tired, sick, and bloody. Not happy to win. (13.24)

"Sean"

Sean completes this trio of children. In tandem with Iris, people, and especially faces, are a continuing preoccupation. But the single most recurrent motif is *eyes*, and eyes together with *looking* predominate across the collection. Three of the pictures he drew from age 4 through age 7 reflect this strong theme.

Figure 1.7. Man in bathtub. (13.153)

Figure 1.8. Rabbit munching leaf. (11.86)

Two of these drawings, at ages 4 and 5, besides featuring eyes, illustrate both experimentation and practice. In Figure 1.9 (4.6), the experimental dominates. Here the eyes on a huge, rectangular head diverge, with one a halfmoon or circle, the other a full circle divided down the middle, each half equipped with a pupil. In Figure 1.10 (5.13), what stands out to the viewer is Sean's mastery of the technique of using the line of an eyebrow to run on continuously to become a nose, while the eyes themselves are represented as large, horizontal ellipses.

In the third drawing (Figure 1.11, 7.148), the eyes are highly expressive, conveying here, as they do in so many of Sean's drawings, strong feeling. In this instance, they mime woe: downturned at the corner, the brows echoing their curve, the heavy black marker outlining irises that are checked (or crazed) by narrow green lines.

As these drawings suggest, Sean's attitude as an artist is one of playfulness, exploration, and inventiveness. For example, he exhibits a delight in the kind of unlikely possibility illustrated in Figure 1.8, in which a bird substitutes for the nose. In another drawing, not shown here, a teepee turns out on second glance to possess ears and a face. There is also a capacity to turn almost anything in the environment to his own purposes; for example, on at least one occasion, taking advantage of the presence of a fly swatter to make rubbings.

Yet another way Sean multiplies possibilities is by breaking through the confines of a single visual frame. For example, in Figure 1.12 (6.18), four visual planes are discernible: the rabbit in the extreme foreground, the lines of two rows of trees, and then the heavy black spot, perhaps the rabbit's hole, which suggests a space extending behind the page. Perhaps most striking in this respect are early experiments with duplicating an experience, as in Figure 1.13 (5.18) in which Sean draws a hand drawing and so inserts himself as artist within the frame of the picture.

As all these experiments with mixed images, multiple planes, insertions of himself within the frame of the picture, and spaces exceeding the page suggest, a wide variety of play with visual perspectives characterizes a substantial dimension of this collection. To offer just one further example, in Figure 1.14 (10.103), Sean presents the viewer with a back view of a boy, who is himself looking in a bathroom mirror as he brushes his teeth.

Across the collection are works, both written and visual, that explore themes of hiddenness or darkness. Represented here by a single early painting (Plate 5, B5.66), the images in these works are often haunting, while the style is characteristically experimental. In this night landscape, for example, it is the black trunk of a tree daringly and successfully portrayed against a black sky that announces Sean's experimentation with media, while the luminescence of the moon echoed in window and door

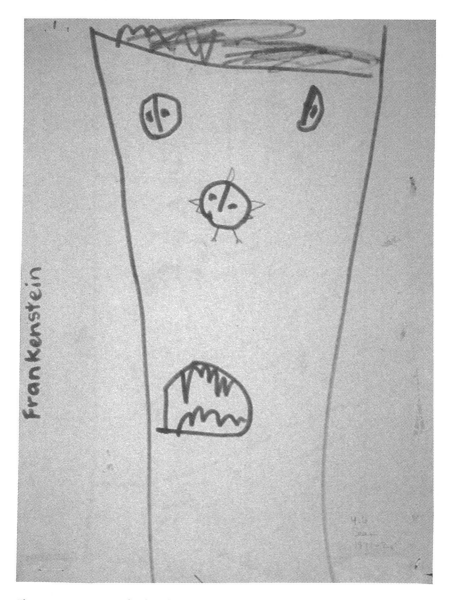

Figure 1.9. Rectangular head. (4.6)

Figure 1.10. Face with large, elliptical eyes. (5.13)

Figure 1.11. Face with heavily outlined eyes. (7.148)

of a house eerily punctuate the surrounding darkness. Later sketches from nature, not illustrated here, include a charcoal drawing of a covered bridge, the opening heavily shaded, echoing the mystery and darkness portrayed in Plate 5, and lending to a similarly pastoral scene, a suggestion of mystery and hiddenness.

The experimental quality of all these works makes the collection as a whole characterizable as a huge sketchbook—with Sean himself as a medium for the wide spectrum of images that flow through it, contributing to the whole a synoptic and metaphoric cast. Indeed, all Sean's work from beginning to end is self-referential.

Sometimes, as in a report on dolphins, this involves an imaginative relocating of himself to take the point of view from the inside out of what he is drawing or writing. Sean writes:

Figure 1.12. Scene with trees and rabbit. (6.18)

> The water is warm the way I like it and the moon is shining bright
> and the waves are very calm against my skin. When the water is
> like this it's very pretty. Its blue, deep, clear and warm and I can
> swim fast and easily. My snout is long and firm. My eyes are set
> back in my head. I'm grayish and my bottom side is lighter than
> my top. It's sort of off-white. I'm about seven and a half feet and
> weigh about 165 pounds. . . . (12.51)

The effect is a kind of dreaminess confirmed in accompanying watercolor
images, soft and with an overall blotchy quality, as well as in other writing. The following excerpt from a descriptive piece, also composed at age
12 and also watery, offers a further example of the blurring of the boundaries of inner and outer characteristic of much of the later work in this
collection:

> I look up to see what made the sky so dark. I see the clouds form-
> ing into black misty forms. A drop of rain hits the surface of my eye
> and rolls off to one side. I look down at my feet. I see another drop
> hit the cool crusty ground. It spread and soaked in. Now it's coming
> down hard. . . . (12.43)

Figure 1.13. Hand drawing a picture. (5.18)

Counterpoised to the blur and dreaminess of some of the later works, and running a parallel track with Iris's arches or Paul's geometrics, is line— a characteristic *quick, fluent, gestural line* that for Sean serves many turns, time and time again. It appears, for example, in recurrent pictures of burning houses or as shown here in flaming autumn trees (Plate 6, 6.48); and then again, in Figure 1.15 (nd12.1) to represent thought in the head of a person.

Figure 1.14. Backview of boy. (10.103)

Figure 1.15. Seated figure. (12.1)

THE WORKS OF THREE CHILDREN

These are glimpses of the works of three children; much is omitted. Paul, for example, built sculptures in wet sand that were astonishing for the dexterity required to achieve such fineness of detail and precise articulation in so difficult a medium.

Sean was accomplished at any kind of sewing but was especially in demand by peers to applique their jean jackets with motorcycles and race cars. His knack or feel for what a medium requires in order to "work" meant that his repertoire as a maker included almost every material the school made available.

Iris was an enthusiastic block builder and clay worker. In block building, her focus was on intricate interiors with hidden, secret places. She gave little attention to exterior finish and much of what she built looked, at a casual glance, like a somewhat untidy woodpile. Clay work was often sculptures of animals, also rough in execution, but with a flair for capturing some essential gesture.

Paul's dextrous hand and attention to geometrics, Sean's alert, discerning eye and feel for process, Iris's innerness and honing in on the essence—these are signatures of each child's dialectic with the world. Each is *true* and each is *partial*. Although partial, each discloses capacities to be trusted and relied upon by the child and by the adults responsible for the child's education. Trusted, unless that capacity, or some other abstracted from the whole, should come to fill the entire screen, and so obscure the person, living and growing: *a child, a person, possible in ways far exceeding single talents or particular inclinations, however strong.*

For example, there is the ability to geometrize the world as Paul does. It is an ability that allows him to see the line that isn't drawn in nature, and the shape that is not yet articulated, and the relationship between the two. It is a talent rich with possibilities. Yet it would be limiting for Paul or his teachers to see him only through such a narrow, if powerful, frame.

For Paul there is also the zest of the absurd, a keen, uncompromising eye for human frailty and elements of satire and irony. And beyond that, there are sweet and strong feelings of caring and expressions of great gentleness. Especially the latter could easily slip from view, hidden by the glitter of the humor and the analytic, mathematical power.

What to do with the satiric eye and the lampooning wit? What to do with sweet feelings? What to do with a great caring for the planet? What to do with an abstracting eye and a mathematical bent? What to do with a flair for words? These are not all easily compatible inclinations. Some conflict—or may in some situations do so. These are compelling, serious questions—questions on which hinge the education of the person: for Paul as his own teacher and for the adults responsible for his education.

I picked Paul for this example; but I might as easily have chosen Iris or Sean. These three children as makers shine through their works—each individual, each complex, each a vivid presence. One child does not call the tune for the others. Sean's proclivity for process does not detract from Paul's for analysis or Iris's for succinctness. *No one is made to stand in someone else's shadow.* Instead the works of each invite the works of the others, open onto them, not from sameness or even mere variation, but, as I think of it, conversationally.

Through the works there is figuratively a speaking back and forth, an interanimation arising from the distinctive voice in which each speaks. Sean's interest in perspectives runs on a continuum with Paul's geometry. Paul's skilled hand intersects Sean's versatility with media. Iris's capacity for the packed image resonates with Sean's metaphoric bent and Paul's pointed humor. And Sean's mixing and duplication of images echoes Iris's insertions within a figure of landscapes and occasions held in memory. Paul's sweetness of feeling for nature and small creatures is symmetrically reflected in the delicacy of Sean's later watercolors and both are counter-poised with the less gentle, haunting mystery of Iris's drawings.

Making works locates the maker as a witness and self-reflecter to her or his own making and life as it also locates the maker among other makers and their lives. Some of these makers are present together in a shared workplace—as can happen in a school among a group of children. Others with whom kinship is found are further distant in space or time. Works travel. Paul discovers Escher. Or perhaps Iris and Sean may find a poet such as Randell Jarrell good company. Or all three, from their different orientations, may relish myths across cultures and worldwide. Works are conduits for expressiveness, as conversation with oneself and in commerce with others.

In the making of works, there is grappling, challenge, frustration, exhilaration, anger, despair, and deep satisfaction. Works are channels for strong feeling. Works, and the making of works, join us together to stand on an equal footing not only on common ground, but on the very ground of that ordinary capacity, widely distributed: to be makers of works and lives.

This focus on the self places educational weight on that activeness of the person to which Dewey (1938/1963) calls attention. This is a self conceptualized not as a profoundly inner or psychological event, but an in-the-world, enacting self. As I have come to know it, this is a self, intermingled at the root with other lives; a self plural in its own orientations and interests and expressiveness; a self with a vital public, social permeability, both influencing and influenceable.

For these reasons, the self as I am envisioning it, is not ultimately "caused" as we understand the events of the physical world to be; nor is it, in important ways, predictable or finishable or perfectible. Instead, in its habit of breaking its own boundaries and ever leading on, this is a self that defies definition, but recognizes unequivocally the fierce desire that fires each life—and all.

Poets of our lives: A dialectic in which the human desire to make things authors works, and works, reciprocally, author lives. With these strokes I have drawn self and works into each other's arms. Doing that, I am suggesting that works and the making of works, ordinary works and high-culture works, bring us face-to-face with a person, another or ourselves, each of us intent on a bigger work and each coequal in that desire. Sean, reviewing his works years later as a young adult, put this mirroring of works to self into virtually these words. He said with wonder, tinged with awe, "It's my life!"

Given the bigness of this embrace, we might ask, what then of work itself and the doing of work? What light does the making of works cast on working? And, where may play, through works and the making of them, animate work? Taken altogether surely these are in important measure what we humans are about. What we know and name as identity, worth, recognition, and respect, and also independence, livelihood, and vocation, are held too in this wide embrace.

WORK

And so I turn to work, itself a hardworking word, covering almost four pages of dense, microscopic print in the Compact Edition of the Oxford English Dictionary. It counts among its meanings works as acts—"by their works ye shall know them"—and also daily chores and harsh, life-consuming, back-breaking labor. There is work that is a necessity of the body and work that is a necessity of the spirit. Sometimes work is understood to be a calling, a vocation, or it may be what puts bread on the table—or, should fortune smile, both at once. Work can be grueling; work can yield intense satisfaction and pleasure; work can destroy; work can save.

Whitman (1856/1992), in "Song of the Broad-Axe," sings the dialectic of person and world sturdily, honoring tools and workers. In this passage he composes a dance from workers joined in the common task and the common language of building houses:

> The blows of mallets and hammers, the attitudes of the men, their curv'd limbs,
> Bending, standing, astride the beams, driving in pins, holding on by posts
>   and braces,
> The hook'd arm over the plate, the other arm wielding the axe,
> The floor-men forcing the planks close to be nail'd,
> Their postures bringing their weapons downward on the bearers,
> The echoes resounding through the vacant building; . . .

From a kindred observational angle, Sebastiao Salgado (1993), the Brazilian photographer, more than a century later brings to life work and workers worldwide in the book *Workers,* which he subtitles *An Archaeology of the Industrial Age.* The photographs depict sugar cane workers from Cuba and Brazil; weavers from Bangladesh; coal miners from India; slaughter-house workers from the United States; perfume makers from an island off the coast of France; shellfish harvesters from Galicia; tuna fishermen from Sicily; sulphur carriers from Indonesia. And other occupations appear, on location in the world's workplaces—railroad yards, a foundry, a tobacco barn.

As in Whitman's poem, but now visually and in the very now of a photograph, we see bodies bent daily to the task, each shaped by its particular demands. Here are the faces of coal workers indelibly blackened except for eyes and mouth. Here is the broad swinging motion of the cane cutters. Here are the women clam harvesters, ankle deep in water, plying their hoes. And the sulphur carriers guarding their faces from the fumes, bent under their loads. In the faces we can read sometimes pride, sometimes striving, and too often bleakness, a deadening of the spirit.

I remember, as you may, a famous picture from the Great Depression. In it, the viewer sees a man sitting on a curb, but it is the hands that are hero: hands sculpted by years of repetition of the gesture of some skilled work, now reduced to unknotting string to occupy them. In recent years, when I think of that picture, an image of my father's hands as he aged is superimposed; rather long, slightly tapered fingers, the knuckles enlarged from 50 years of doing fine, close, exacting work on watches and clocks. A physician told him the same enlargement afflicts some surgeons. Exactness. Deftness. The work sets the terms of its standard. The work and its standards mold the worker.

There is a book by Michael Dorris titled *Working Men* (1993), in which the lead story, "The Benchmark," picks up the theme of making and standards. It features pond making—an occupation so unusual that I don't think even Whitman and Salgado refer to it. Frank, the pond maker, begins the story by telling us lessons learned in the trade.

He tells us, for example, that "[the] naked eye deceives" (p. 1), that sea level is irrelevant, and that seeking a constant is indispensable. Pairing process with standards held for the well-made pond, he tells the novice, "To start a job, . . . drive a nail into a peak of ledge, pound it deep, make it your benchmark, your one-hundred scale" (p. 1). Do that he says, and

> Weather patterns can alter, crops grow, houses get built and collapse, but you can return in fifty years and position a tripod, rotate the dials of the spirit until the air bubble precisely crosses the hairline, then aim an alidade at that solitary, centering nail and be in business. (pp. 1–2)

From a related, but distinguishable angle, work sometimes does what "deep play" (Geertz, 1973, pp. 432–433) accomplishes: creates its own world, governed by a rhythm that, breaking stride with the relentless march of measured time, transports the worker. Among the features of that kind of world-creating work (or play) is a communion of worker with the medium or a tool or some inner image or idea so complete that worker and it are one. I think of Sean and his fine-tip marker line, or Paul and geometry, or Iris and poetic form. I think of Casals and the cello. And I think of a 5-year-old I knew who reported to his teacher that he was trembling, not he assured her because he was sick, but because he "made the whole thing": a Native American village, complete with teepees and small figures—mainly from clay, carefully formed, but with additions of twigs, paper, and other materials as needed for campfires, bows, and various other props.

Such "deep play," such work, has life-saving power. A poet, Fay Chiang, says, "I write poems, songs, otherwise I would be crazy, rationalizing away the feelings and spirits which embody my identity" (quoted in Rich, 1993, p. 176). Puccini is said to have made a similar claim—that if he hadn't found music he would never have done anything in the world.

Should the maker lose the saving work, the cost may be high. I remember an uncle, magical with a pencil, gassed in the Great War, holding his right arm firmly below the wrist with his left to control its trembling as he painted flawless signs. At intervals, he drank himself into oblivion.

In his autobiography (1992), Jimmy Santiago Baca writes:

> When I was a kid growing up in the orphanage, I remember how I longed to learn to play the piano. Music and song always lifted me out of myself into rebellious reveries of enchantment. . . . When I sang, it seemed as if I were really talking to God and touching His ear. . . . But early on I noticed that my voice wasn't reaching Him. When it came time to choose those boys who would be taught to play [the piano], I pushed and shoved to the front of the line. . . . I knew I would be chosen. . . . Waiting for my name to be called, I saw myself flailing at the piano keys like a broncobuster holding the reins of a wild mustang, never letting go, mastering its power. . . . But they picked two other kids, Ricardo and Johnny, instead. I was told, with brutal indifference, that the piano was not for me. . . . Why them and not me? They were cleaner, neater, and better behaved. (pp. 84–85)

Another voice speaks, that of Sanyika Shakur, *aka* Monster Kody Scott. Joining the Eight Tray Set of the Los Angeles Crips when he was 11, Scott poured half his young life into gangbanging before he renounced that membership and committed himself to the New Afrikan Independence Movement. Describing the renunciation, he says that it was more than a change of mind that he experienced, more than outgrowing gang life. The roots were deeper than that, fed both by revulsion and by a great hunger. Shakur (1994) writes:

> It's not enough to say that I had transcended the mind-set of being a banger by this time. After having spent thirteen years of my young life inside what had initially seemed like an extended family but had turned into a war machine, I was tired and disgusted with its insatiable appetite for destruction. Destruction no longer fed my narcissism. It was not an expression of my thoughts. *I wanted to construct something*, which in banging is tantamount to treason. (p. 355, italics added)

To not destroy—to make something, to be constructive, to express thoughts: more a change of heart than of mind. Perhaps it does not go too far to suggest that it was the glimpse of creative possibility, of contributing to a work, that was the catalyst for that change.

Work leaves in its wake, made and gathered things—and lives. A person, living and working, trails behind a long train of acts and works. These gather around a life in ordinary and extraordinary ways. I notice these life patterns in obituaries in the local paper. The connection I make with them is fragile but evocative.

I read that the main interests of a woman, age 58, who worked for 20 years at the Eveready Battery Company, were "doll collecting, cookbook collecting, reading," and that, "she loved to travel." The word "avid," I notice, is the favored adjective locally to convey the passion of a pursuit. A man of 86 is described as "an avid gardener," honored for "winning many ribbons at local fairs." He is also noted to have had a great interest in baseball, following several teams but "especially the Red Sox." The obituary, though, begins with a pattern mingling his life and the seasons, a ritual started early and sustained for a lifetime: "He [has] made maple sugar every year since he was a child."

When I offered a tribute at my own mother's funeral, I picked a theme of mending and healing: Gluing together a doll's cracked skull; repairing a ripped jacket so you couldn't see the tear; coaxing ailing household appliances back into action. And with the same skilled hand, nursing back to health a dog given up as damaged beyond repair by distemper or, with mixed success, healing the injuries of birds, squirrels, and other small animals.

I might have chosen other threads such as a closely related knack for problem solving. Or, I might have selected quite different ones: A love of dancing, story telling, and singing; an unrelenting grip on reality; a shrewd eye for value and ways to stretch a dollar or a pound of hamburger.

Patterns in works and the pattern of a lived life, entwined, the one inseparable from the other. Works—words and gestures, made things and enactments: These compose the poem, emblemize the patterns of the life. The person, her preferences and aversions, strong interests, passionate pursuits, depths of feeling and thought made visible in works; the poet composing the life poem by becoming it.

Whitman in the preface to *Leaves of Grass*, composed in 1855, speaks of a poesy surging through humanity that exceeds the text and may attach to life itself, to the body. He commands us, each one, to nurture poetry and says if we do so, "your very flesh shall be a great poem and have the richest fluency, not only in its words, but in the silent lines of its lips and face and between the lashes of your eyes, and in every motion and joint of your body" (1986, p. 11).

One hundred forty years later, Adrienne Rich (1993) takes the title of her remarkable book *What Is Found There* from William Carlos Williams's poem "Asphodel, That Greeny Flower" and catches up Whitman's thread of poetry's nurturance with Williams's lines:

> It is difficult
> to get the news from poems
>   yet men die miserably every day
>   for lack
> of what is found there. (1944/1986–88)

Poets of our own lives: makers of works; workers making lives; lives creating works—our very bodies, poems; our very words, works.

FOR THE WORKER TO NOT HAVE WORK

We may rightly ask then: What does it mean to the worker to not have work? What is the measure of such loss? What measure is adequate to weigh not only loss of income but despair, sinking of status, failure of recognition, depletion of worth? What of the person who, misused, is shunted aside from her calling? What befalls the child left with only the opportunity for making things that he can devise from his own resources? What does that lack cost in the making of a life?

What happens to the piano player locked inside Baca—that wild broncobusting flailer of the keyboard—when there is no piano possibility? What happens when the creative, making impulse is starved or shut off? What happens to all of us, to society, to education when we blinder ourselves to the widely distributed human desire to be makers and contributors; to find some meaning in our lives; to be our own lives' poets?

What happens to democratic aspirations if we fail to recognize the wide distribution of that poetic desire and capacity—and instead reserve an education worthy of the name to some preferred group: "the best and the brightest," the inheritors of privilege? Or, we may ask what will happen if, with a rigidly even and stingy hand, the aims of education are reduced across the board to a narrow economic goal? What will be the human yield if we substitute technical training geared only to the demands of an emerging technocratic, information-age society for making and thinking, for poetry and wondering, for the liberation of minds? The question is not idle since the threat of that reduction is before us now in demands for absolute certainty of specific achievement assessed according to narrowly defined standards.

These are educational questions. They are also political questions. Contemplating these questions, we might for our edification turn back the pages of the twentieth century to 1903 and ask with W. E. B. Du Bois (1903/ 1989), mourning the loss of poor Josie, dead in her youth, ground under from labor, her aspirations for learning denied:

> How shall man measure Progress there where the dark-faced Josie lies? How many heartfuls of sorrow shall balance a bushel of wheat? How hard a thing is life to the lowly, and yet how human and real! And all this life and love and strife and failure,—is it the twilight of nightfall or the flush of some faint-dawning day? (p. 52)

These are also educational questions—and political ones.

Or, we might hearken to contemporary speakers. We might ask, for example, what *did* happen to the piano player locked inside Baca (1992) when there was no piano possibility? And we might listen to his desperate, haunting story, told in his autobiography, *Working in the Dark*, of years of imprisonment, of learning in prison from other Chicano prisoners, as he says, "my own language, the bilingual words and phrases explaining to me my place in the universe" (p. 5). And more. From these prisoners reading aloud, "the works of Neruda, Paz, Sabines, Nemerov, and Hemingway," Baca discovered, as he says, "the magic that could liberate me from myself, transform me into another person" (p. 4).

But years passed between that realization and the liberation, grinding years of prison life, of solitary confinement, of despair. And then in a textbook stolen from a prison attendant, Baca found the words, "p-o-n-d, ri-pple." Enunciating them to himself, in the dark, reading under a blanket with a pen flashlight, he writes: "It scared me that I had been reduced to this to find comfort. I always had thought reading a waste of time. . . . Even as I tried to convince myself that I was merely curious . . . the sounds created music in me and happiness. . . . Memories began to quiver in me" (p. 6).

He speaks of being for a time overcome by "deep sadness . . . as if I had chanced on a long-lost friend" (p. 6). As the heartache gave way, he writes that he was cured, "innocently believing in the beauty of life again" (p. 6). And continuing, he tells us that he fell asleep,

> Stumblingly repeat[ing] the author's name . . . saying it over and over in the dark: Words-worth, Words-worth. . . . Days later, with a stub pencil I whittled sharp with my teeth, I propped a Red Chief notebook on my knees and wrote my first words. From that moment a hunger for poetry possessed me. (p. 6)

The aspirant flailer of the keyboard is reborn in the music of words, in poetry.

To this renascence, Adrienne Rich (1993) replies, "Jimmy Santiago Baca writes of poetry as a birth into the self out of a disarticulated, violently unworded condition, the Chicano taught to despise his own speech" (p. 208). A birth into self through words, through the music heard in the words. A reborning of the piano in another medium, conferring wholeness, restoring desire. To adopt a phrase of Isaiah Berlin's (1969/1988), a self which is "unpredictably self transforming" (p. 171).

Or, we might understand Baca's story and yearning and rebirth in Cornel West's (1993) terms, as a conversionary experience that turns back "the nihilistic threat—loss of hope and absence of meaning" (p. 15). When I first read that, immediately I thought of another sentence that has haunted me now for several years: "These boys die like it's nothing." It is a line reported by Anna Quindlen (1992) in a *New York Times* editorial, under the title "The Lost Boys," a poetic line said in response to the shooting deaths of two young men at a New York City high school by the girlfriend of one of them. Quite recently, reading Luis J. Rodriguez's (1993) autobiography, *Always Running*, an account of his life in the Los Angeles gangs, I was caught by another line, a quotation from young Latinos at the scene of the 1992 Los Angeles uprising: "Go ahead and kill us, we're already dead" (p. 247).

West (1993) is not speaking in specifically religious terms when he calls for "a politics of conversion" (p. 18), which he explains as "a chance for people to believe that there is hope for the future and meaning to struggle" (p. 18). West goes on to say:

> This chance rests neither on an agreement about what justice consists of nor on an analysis of how racism, sexism, or class subordination operate. Such arguments are indispensable. . . . [But] nihilism is not overcome by arguments or analyses; it is tamed by love and care. (pp. 18–19)

Reading West's words, I felt the presence, the urgency of Jimmy Santiago Baca and of Josie and of Sanyika Shakur and of Luis J. Rodriguez and of the unnamed girlfriend of a boy dead in his teens and of the anonymous Latino spokesperson in the stand-off. In the circle formed by their lives, I asked myself these questions: When the strong desire to make, to create, has no channels, is everywhere thwarted, isn't it likely, more than likely that the barriers against despair and destruction will be breached? Isn't it altogether likely the maker may fall back from life, defeated, or become the destroyer, raining destruction on self or others or both?

On the heels of these questions, as if responsively, these followed: What, then, is the obligation of the school to the maker in every child? If work in school is empty or sheer drudgery, if there is no space or opportunity to be a maker, what happens to the child's intense desire? And denied the opportunity to see the desire written in the face of each child and young person, what happens to our visions of the self, of the possibilities of humanness?

Instead of selves and persons, fully human like ourselves, may we, the elders, their teachers tend to see not faces but "problems" or "violence" or "pathology" or "deficiency"? Instead of persons able to be educated, liberated in mind and spirit, may we not settle for training and justify the decision on the grounds that "these children" are not capable of anything more?

VIEWS OF SELF, OF FREEDOM, OF EDUCATION

I arrive now full circle to the words of Isaiah Berlin (1969/1988) I began with—specifically, his assertion that: "enough manipulation with [the] definition [of the person] . . . and freedom can be made to mean whatever the manipulator wishes" (p. 134). As even a cursory review of the historical record or a glance at the daily news teaches us, education and specifically the school are more than likely to be the manipulator's vehicle of choice.

About 20 years ago, at a history-making conference, The Roots of Open Education, convened by Professor Lillian Weber at the Workshop Center at City College, the African American scholar and educator Osborne Scott (1976) was among the speakers. Many years later, rereading the proceedings of the conference, I was struck with the light his analysis of the American enslavement of the African sheds on Berlin's point. Talking about "the advent of the African slave" on our shores, he says that what is challenged by the slave's presence is our allegiance to Judeo-Christian ethics, and specifically

> our attitude toward the person to be educated, which depended on our whole concept of what we think the person is, and his capacity to be educated. In order to resolve this dilemma, and the guilt that grew from it, *the African had to be considered as different from the ordinary person.* (p. 16, italics added)

The ordinary person: The person with ordinary capacities, equipped as humans commonly are to be a maker and doer. A person like Sean or Paul or Iris or Baca or Shakur or Rodriguez or Josie or the unnamed girlfriend or her murdered boyfriend or the young Latino speaker at the scene of the Los Angeles uprising. It is that ordinariness that Scott (1976) asserts has to be denied to justify depriving the African of his or her freedom:

> After all, if you were led to believe that the rights of man were inalienable, yours because you were alive, then what were you going to do with this person who came into your society to be used as property, and who was not going to be accorded the status of person? (p. 16)

He answers his own question by calling attention to the manipulative sleight of hand that denied the slave a self and justified the denial by asserting the incapacity of the slave to be educated. As Scott (1976) says it:

> So the African came to be considered by a measure to be uneducable, or, at the least, not quite capable of being educated as everyone else with the same type of training. Even Thomas Jefferson felt that while the African could be taught to do manual things, he was not quite ready for dealing with philosophical subjects. (p. 16)

Denied a self . . . uneducable . . . not a person . . . not an ordinary person with the rights of a self, to be an agent in the world and in his or her own life, to enact with his or her own mind, tongue, and hand the ideas, words, and works through which a life may be charted.

A liberating education for *all* children, an education that recognizes each as an ordinary person, a self-in-the-making, a maker of works. That sets a high standard. So do the principles of liberty, equality, and justice for all—the inalienable rights of the person on which this country was founded. Neither the principles of liberty, justice, equality nor an education that reciprocates those principles for all children is ever fully achievable in actuality. Yet, although unattainable, it is unthinkable that as citizens and educators we would not put those principles of freedom, and the rights of the individual as a fully endowed person, a maker and doer, as first priorities in our aims for education and in our struggles for the future of the nation.

So as an educator, parent, and citizen, I put my faith in an education centered on persons as ordinary—that is, *as fully endowed selves*. Doing that I place my confidence in children like Paul, Iris, Sean, the child Baca, the child Shakur, the child Rodriguez. For me, putting children as active agents at the center is not only a commitment to the best that education has so far offered. It is a political act.

Children (and ourselves) making things, engaged actively and dialectically with the world, have a broadly liberating influence—and sometimes, if unpredictably, a transforming effect. To affirm a view of our human possibility by calling attention to the widely distributed capacity of ourselves as makers and doers, in which works are understood as the self's medium, is an enactable educational, social, and political stance. For me that view of the self and the enactment of it offers a solid center and compelling aim for education: to be the poets of our own lives.

2

"In the Thick of the Tangle What Clear Line Persists"

Istart with story and with story's power to connect across distances of place or generation or experience. If I tell a story from my life, necessarily reflective of a particular era and location, a listener separated from me and the situatedness of my life, may nevertheless not only take its meaning but be reminded of a reciprocating story. Equally, although our circumstances are unlike, even disjunctive, a story told by another, even a stranger, may confirm mine or connect in such a way that our differences are bridged.

That bridging happened for me reading the poet Jimmy Santiago Baca (1992), writing from his Chicano roots, telling of his life in the barrio, describing his grandmother:

> My grandmother's face has a powerful dignity, like that of an old female eagle on a craggy peak, whose world is eternal. Her gestures are restrained, tentative and soft, as if the world around her, the innocent earth and flowers, were a child easily bruised. Her silence is sunlight sparkling in a freshwater snowmelt stream. (p. 31)

For me *barrio* is an exotic word I can't even pronounce gracefully, my tongue unused to curling around an "r" to soften it. But I recognize that beaked face, the far-seeing look. I recognize the quiet gestures. Restraint and silence were also my grandma's familiar greeting to the world. A Mexican grandmother. A Swedish grandmother. Grandmothers whose lives are synchronized in the shared look and fate "of women . . . bringing up large families on very low incomes . . . who are totally responsible for lives they have no power to save" (p. 107). These are the words the novelist Pat Barker (1991) uses in her novel *Regeneration* to epitomize the careworn lives of working-class women everywhere. Baca's grandmother. My grandmother. My embrace for grandmothers widens.

Other times, stories reflective of lives shaped differently than mine, marked by events that stretch my imagination to its limits, challenge my complacency, demand my unblinking attention. In a study group I conduct in Phoenix, that happened when one of the group, with permission, retold the experiences of a Bosnian woman she hired to do her housecleaning, with whom she soon became close friends.

The Bosnian woman's story was a story of rape and torture, not acts committed randomly, in the heat of the moment, but of systematized brutality, of horrors visited on her by people she knew. In a general way we, the listeners, knew of these kinds of atrocities from the news. But what we heard in the abstract, in generalized terms, muffled the horrors we understood so differently when brought to life through the experiences of a particular woman, and retold in the words spoken by her friend. We were doubly moved: by the story itself and by what the person retelling it had made of the story and its influences on her—as a woman, a mother, a teacher, a human being.

There was silence among us. We were reminded: Not all stories are warm and comforting. We were reminded: We humans commit against each other atrocities unlimited in their degradation of other humans. Stories like the Bosnian woman's offer instructive lessons, lessons likenable to those taught by the great myths and the founding stories of the great religions: lessons that reveal to us our mixed and star-crossed natures. Stories that call sharply to our attention the volatility of human nature and the shallow boundaries between love and possessiveness, or justice and reprisal, or creation and destruction.

Stories (and memory) pluralize us. Stories stretch our narrow, individual frames and minds, making us big and roomy. What was singular, multiplies. Through stories (and memory) we step across eras and even eons of time, glimpsing worlds we never knew but which also remain— through stories. Stories (and memory) are powerfully educative. Stories (and memory) hook us into humanness.

Family stories knit families together. Stories of the race sustain the people when they are beleaguered or scattered. Stories and songs and poems. That is the survivalist's strategy in bondage, in prisons, in extermination camps. Keep the stories alive, the songs, the poetry, pass them along, that is the unspoken message in the telling. If the people have stories, they exist. Through songs and poems and stories, the people bear witness—even to their own destruction. Through stories, art, poems, songs, the people defy extinction. Story telling, poetry, music, art in general are political acts. To deprive people of the stories, poetry, music, art that are theirs, of their making, molded in their idiom, is an act as death dealing to the spirit as murder is to the body. Language is lifeblood.

Toni Morrison (1992) writes, and truly, "[W]ithout one's own idiom there is no other language to speak" (p. xxix). "Under such circumstances," she says, "it is not just easy to speak the master's language, it is necessary" (p. xxviii). "One is obliged," she points out,

> to cooperate in the misuse of figurative language, in the reinforcement of cliché, the erasure of difference, the jargon of justice, the evasion of logic, the denial of history, the crowning of patriarchy, the inscription of hegemony; to be complicit in the vandalizing, sentimentalizing, and trivialization of the torture black people have suffered. (pp. xxviii–xxix)

Story and the making of stories don't merely preserve idiom. Story and story making spark the bigger, more moving, more active, more generative act. It is in story, in song, in poetry that idiom is renewed, animated by each maker, each teller bringing her own inflection, flavor, and texture to the language. It happens in families, among friends, within generations, this remaking of language, through the making and telling of stories. Happening, it bonds. As speakers or listeners, the zest of that language, *their* language—of the race or of the family or of the generation— is in the mouth, on the lips of each, each adding to the possibilities of more to say, more to feel, more to know, to understand, to imagine.

This is my interest in story: as an ordinary and daily affair and as such as an embracing human activity. Stories of human happenings that from the seemingly highly personal and deeply subjective persist—and persisting both remain and change. For me *persists*, with its implication of acting by staying, with its connotation of both permanence and mutability, is the apt, the salient verb. It is the rightness of that word that drew me to the passage from Eudora Welty (1984) that I have taken for my title: "in the thick of the tangle what clear line persists" (p. 90).

THREE STORIES

It is just such stories of the kind I have named "highly personal" and "deeply subjective" that are the heart of this talk. When I say those descriptors, "highly personal" and "deeply subjective," I mean that someone, to imagine the story, to make it, had first to experience an intensity of feeling: the fire or tears or longing or loss, the bulk or buoyancy or passion in her life. In brief, its value weight.

The slant of these three stories calls attention to the persisting lines that interweave them and, *in the same gesture*, loosen them from their moorings, launching them into a wider stream of stories that confer on the trio an expanded and more public dimension. Telling these stories, I intend, by animating memory, to invite your own. Plumbing these stories, I mean to cast light on the manner in which all stories invented from life, from memory, display acts of making and imagination. With this trio of stories as focus, I want to make vivid language and idiom and the making of stories as generative, consequential activities.

The first story in the trio is my mother's. I have chosen the version I have on a tape made by my mother in 1983, on a visit to my family and me in Vermont, when she was 82. The usual reasons prompted the taping. My mother was the last member of her generation on that side of the family. My surviving sister, my cousins, and I wanted to preserve some sampling of her large volume of stories. My mother was an enthusiastic participant in our plan. My role was that of the active listener, occasionally commenting, sometimes prompting or asking a question. When she had told some 30 stories, we stopped with some thought that we would sometime tape more.

That didn't happen. Neither did I listen again to the tapes or transcribe them as I had meant to. The usual exigencies of a busy family and professional life intervened. Then my mother's health began to fail. My sister and I became absorbed in her care, in trying to keep her independent. There was the grief of her death. I never touched the tapes. But they were there. Then, 2 years ago a family reunion was planned. I was asked to bring the tapes so everyone could hear "Ruth's stories." So much time had elapsed, I knew I had to listen to them in advance. I couldn't remember what was on them.

I tried to prepare myself for the emotional impact of hearing my mother's voice after all this time. I wasn't especially successful and I was even less prepared for what it is like to hear so many stories one after the other. The electrifying jolt, though, was experiencing the imprint of my mother in these works, these stories—her making, her imagining, just as I had first experienced these imprints of the maker in an extensive study of children's writings and visual works begun coincidentally at about the time my mother and I made the tapes. Making this connection, what had been securely (and lovingly) locked into a compartment called "family memories," assumed another meaning and dimension.

Transcribing the tapes was the first and best way I knew to immerse myself in a work. Listening and relistening, checking and double checking, I lived with this story for the more than 8 hours it took to transcribe it. My original plan was to transcribe all the tapes and to involve colleagues in describing them as we had done with the children's work. What I had not taken into account in my plan was that the story that was my mother's, drawn from her experience and memory, had a second residence long before the taping of it, in me—and there it had persisted, both influencing and influenced by life events far removed from it in time, in place.

I will tell this first story in my mother's words, including my own occasional comments and reminders. Then I will tell what that story catalyzed, sketching in broad strokes the trajectories of the story as it passed from my mother to me in my childhood.

The tape begins at the transition from one story to the next, with my mother looking for the list we made in advance of possible stories she might tell in this particular taping session.

TRANSCRIPTION OF FAYE'S STORY

Well, let's see . . .

(*Me: You were going to tell about Faye a little bit?*)

Oh, yes. She was just a very sweet, kind, patient little person. I don't know, I just thought she was an angel—like they say, unaware, as she was . . .

She must have been frail, don't you think? when I look back . . . but interested in school. The teachers loved her. She got along so well and they were so concerned when she was so . . . very sick.

And pneumonia. That was a *killer* in those days, they didn't have the antibiotics.

And she got over the crisis, they always had *that*. We had doctors. They came to the house but there wasn't a hospital in our town then.

But she reached that *period*. The fever had broken as they would say and now was the time for recuperation and they gave her a *tonic*. They used to . . . I don't know what it was when they talked a lot on *ton-ic* to become well . . . maybe a little alcohol in it, even, you know. They didn't have contents on anything, or I mean on your medications.

But it wasn't right. She wasn't well because her lungs were no doubt filled up because she should have had the lungs cleared. They do since then. They spread the ribs, that I know of, and they call it em-py-ema. And they drain that off and it's just like a . . . Well, that's a killer that is. . . . That's what caused her death.

And she just wasn't getting well. She was down in bed, down in bed.

(*Me: What time of year was it, Mother?*)

Well there wasn't snow. Because I kept running to town, running to town.

Well I went to . . . Well I went to what they called the Opera House on Main Street. Well there was going to be a performance. I think it was hypnotism, like that. And I went to it. . . . But you know I had a feeling of worry and I ran fast all the way home. Something seemed to tell me Faye wasn't good. My mother said, too, I burst in, "Is Faye all right?" "Oh, same," she says quietly, you know.

Then it was the next day she died.

I was sitting . . . you see we came home from school to eat, it was several blocks but we all came. And it was noon meal 'cause my Dad was working hard then so it must have been the kind of weather that . . . well, she was buried Good Friday, so it was spring.

And he came to eat that day and my mother was putting dinner on the table for all and I was to feed Faye. And it was broth, I can remember that. We propped her a little. And I was alone with her. And I put some in her mouth and all at once she . . . I could see . . . I'd never witnessed a convulsion before . . . but that's what it was. . . .

I ran out quick to the folks and they came and I remember seeing my Dad pull her tongue. He got hold of it with his finger and pulled her tongue out because sometimes in their . . . to keep it clear, and then he tried to . . . between my mother and he, they worked on her.

Well, then I was the runner again. So I ran for the doctor and Mrs. Marsh first, our neighbor, our closest neighbor, and I heard her say, "Oh my God, she's gone."

I ran like the dickens to the doctor. Dr. Benson. And I don't know if he drove a car but he came.

But she was gone. My Dad . . . he just fell face down on that cot. . . . Wept and wept you know.

Well, then it was an undertaker to find and all that. I remember they . . . we had no funeral homes. They placed her in a little casket in a small room upstairs. Closed it off. Nobody used that. We just managed.

The funeral had to be quite soon. The way they embalmed in those days was very different. My Dad watched and he [the undertaker] just poured formaldehyde into her mouth. And that would I suppose be in her stomach.

(*Me: Oh, Mother, it must have been horrible for Grandpa*)

Yuh, it wasn't the right . . . the right way. So they had to have the service quite soon. I can remember the day. It was Good Friday that fell on.

And it was awfully hard to understand, you know, for me. And one of the neighbors—'course they all come and help and bring things—and when something happens so fast like that. . . . I suppose I was terribly upset. She told me that if I would feel her . . . brrrrr if *that* didn't give me chills! just like a chunk of ice y'know . . . the sensation, the same sensation as if you put your fingers on a chunk of ice. But she thought I should know that . . . that life . . . the life force was gone, y'know. I was 13.

(*Me: That's not a very good time* [*meaning her age*])

Oh, terrible. So those were hard times.

I remember we didn't have music, an organ at that time. A little later a neighbor gave us . . . we had an organ in the house. But the Presbyterians or Methodists? I don't remember which it was . . . we kids usually went to the Methodists 'cause that was the closest to our home. But it seems to me they brought a little organ in, portable.

And, I'll never forget the hymn, "A Jewel in Her Crown"? Is that *it*? And other songs or hymns, there were a couple, and then that one. That stuck with me. And there was another song that must have been suitable for a young child.

And then it was all over and we went to the cemetery and all back to the house. 'Course people stayed and there was coffee, cookies . . .

All at once there was a fire, about five, four, five o'clock, still light, the fire whistles blew, y'know. My Dad was such a faithful fireman but he was dressed in the best they had, that was his clothes. But he said, "We'll go for a walk." There was a flour mill [on fire]. So he took us by the hand, one on each side of him. We walked up so we could watch it, but very quietly, sedately you know. No running and excitement, y'know.

(*Me: You told me once the flowers were lilies . . .*)

Yes. I admire them *out, but to this day* I don't want them in my home. Just the odor reminds me. Other flowers . . . One whole family—I should remember names better—they sent carnations . . . just beautiful the way they were arranged.

But there weren't a lot of flowers. People didn't seem . . . I don't think there was in our town . . . It was larger towns around us who had greenhouses. The Easter lilies were what were there that time of year.

(*Me: You mentioned she did well in school . . .*)

Yes. Very bright child and serious. Some of her work, her spelling, pages and pages, 100, *all right*. She wrote very carefully, neatly. I can't remember her being rambunctious like Melvin and I. We'd fight. But not Faye.

Melvin and I, we'd lie down and I should be ashamed old as I was, how much older than Melvin was I? We'd have kicking battles and like that. So, I think I was more or less a tomboy.

Faye wasn't like that. So sweet, and followed the law. She never got into anything.

Faye Swanson died at Easter in 1914 when she was 8 and my mother was 13. As I construct it, Melvin, the youngest, would have been about 6 or 7. John, about 3 years older than my mother in age, was himself seriously ill from pneumonia. Anne, the eldest, by then 25 or 26, was married and homesteading with her husband, Jay, in Dakota; Art must have been about 23, but I am not sure where he was at that time. Until Faye's death, these were the six surviving children of (Selma) Carolina and Gust Swanson, Swedish immigrants, settlers in Jackson, Minnesota, in the 1880s; three other children died in infancy.

A STORY MANY TIMES TOLD

I have heard this story of Faye since I was a very small child, so young that I don't remember when I didn't know it. For me it is a story that reaches to the back of beyond. I begged my mother to tell and retell it; it gripped my imagination. Images of the spoon with the broth and of the formaldehyde being poured; images of grandpa, but a young man throwing himself across the bed, and of grandpa with mother on one side and Melvin on the other walking hand in hand up a hill I knew and often climbed; images of my mother, a young girl, supporting Faye's shoulders to feed her, and of my mother, a young girl, reaching out to touch the icy body; images of bright flames shooting up and bright white lilies.

The lilies. In this version of the story, I prompted that detail, yet I remember them as a striking feature of the story as my mother usually told it. I don't remember hearing ever before about the carnations or the family who sent them. The Easter lilies in my version of the story were brought by women from the Royal Neighbors, which I understood to be a lodge. The pots of lilies I see in my mind's eye are tied with purple ribbons. There is a banner, in white, with Faye's full name, Lillian Faith, in gold; the banner has an insignia or motto of the lodge embroidered in purple. The neighbor, Mrs. Marsh, whom I remember as a very old woman, and who figures quite often in my mother's stories from childhood, says in my version of the story, "Such an angel of a child with a name so pure can only die young."

Lilies. Purple and gold. Lavender and yellow. Decades later, my mother's oldest sister died at a time close to Easter. My mother specified no purple or yellow flowers or ribbons in her order to the florist. When that was what faced her standing in a place of honor near the casket, she told me it required an act of will not to march up and throw them out. My father told me it made her physically ill.

The deep familiarity of a story many times told, many times imagined. The deep familiarity of my mother's voice, her way of saying, the rhythms of Scandinavia caught in her inflections. Her language was alive in me—when I was a child hearing this story and others. Her words were the story's words. This is how it had to be told. It wasn't that there couldn't be deviation; deviation wasn't possible. Variations of detail were enfolded in the larger drama of voice, idiom, gesture, inflection—braided together in the telling—the telling and the story itself inseparably joined.

Transcribing the tape, listening so closely, I loosen the words, release them onto a larger landscape. Running, for example, which itself runs, a refrain, through the story of Faye: "She was down in bed, down in bed. . . . I kept running to town, running to town. . . . I ran fast all the way home. . . . I ran out quick to the folks. . . . Well, then I was the runner again. . . . I ran like the dickens to the doctor. . . . But she was gone."

Mother favored the verb *run*. It was a daily word, alternated with *hike*. She (and we) ran over town; hiked across the yard to my grandmother's or an aunt's house to borrow, to return; or ran up to the west end of town for her cousin Hazel's help with some complicated sewing. Fast, forward motion, taking action, without delay. A problem solver. A modern woman, future oriented. A relisher of new information and words, like the carefully enunciated em-py-ema on the tape. A good home mechanic, interested in tools and technology. I hear the note of contempt for old wives tales and home remedies in the intonation of "ton-ic."

The runner, the errand doer, the rambunctious child, the tomboy, the fighter: the frail child, the good student, the patient, serious child, the law abider. Like Rose Red and Snow White, in my mother's stories, she and Faye are forever counterpoised, my mother dark, olive skinned, Faye blonde and fair: each the other's balance, each the other's foil, perhaps neither quite imaginable to herself without the other to stretch and complicate the picture. Rose Red and Snow White—interrupted midsentence; Faye's side of the story left voiceless.

I never heard anyone else in the family tell the story of Faye's death. Certainly not my grandmother. I don't recall asking anyone. It was my mother's story—and then, mine.

"In the thick of the tangle what clear line persists . . ."

THE STORY CATALYZES

Perhaps all big stories, all life stories as they travel from the teller to the receiver, are catalytic agents—mixing the boundaries of possession and memory, firing imagination, energizing more making, more stories, magnetizing others. And so it happened with this story. Released from "calendar time," Faye was in me a free agent, unconstrained, and she was in me soon linked with another story—which as a child I thought of as "the same story." If I imagined one, the other followed close behind. For this story my grandmother was the teller, and like the story of Faye's death, I knew it from a very young age. The story grandma told was from long ago, when she was herself a child or young girl in Sweden, of the death of a boy, possibly a brother—or so I thought of it, listening. It was, like most of my grandmother's stories, barebones, rendered more in singsong, it sounds now in my ear a litany. It has occurred to me that the bareness, which had its uses for me as did the bareness of certain fairy tales, was probably a function of her limited English. Then, it was just grandma's way of telling stories.

As I recall it: The boy was sick. He seemed to get better and then fell sick again. He had brain fever. He was "out of his head." His head swelled up. His eye "ached out of his head." I would wait suspended for that fateful line. I saw the boy sewed into his winter clothing (a fragment picked up in another story), lying on straw (I don't know where that detail comes from), his head growing, growing, and the eye, open and blue, looking out and sliding down his cheek. . . . Death following that image was anticlimactic.

The same story as Faye's—early death, early sorrow, early loss. The weight of the stories, the vividness of the images, interlaced them, symmetrical tragedies, the same tragedy: my mother's, my grandmother's. That is how the stories persisted in me, twinned—until I listened to my mother's telling of Faye's story in 1983. I was speechless, stunned when my mother said that Faye died of pneumonia. I wanted to argue the point. In the story I carried paired with the other story, Faye had long since become a second victim of that mysterious malady, "brain fever," that forced that long ago boy's eye from its socket and squeezed his brain until he died. Under the spell of these early, terrible deaths, called to myself "the same story,"

I had reshaped Faye's story, to achieve a symmetry of events to match the tragic weight that braided them together inseparably in my life.

The third story—the one that completes the triad—is my own, although I know it only as another story I was told. Unlike the other stories, I remember the first time I heard it. My mother was the unwilling teller. At about 10 months I was stricken with a more than usually severe case of whooping cough. I didn't fully recover. Apparently a secondary infection followed the whooping cough.

Here is the story of that infection as my mother told it to me: The fever was very high. My head swelled to "twice its size." The pain or the fever was so intense, I pulled the hair out of my head with both hands. Prior to the illnesses, I am told, I had just started to talk and walk. The doctor cautioned my parents that if I lived, I might never do either. I lived. I talked and walked. My parents moved away from that town, but as I understood it from my mother the doctor kept in touch until I started school.

I didn't hear this story of my own illness until I was about 6 or 7. This is almost certainly after I had heard the stories of Faye and the boy in my grandmother's story. An aunt let the cat out of the bag. As I recall the scene it went this way: I made a characteristically snappy, sassy remark, backtalking my mother—what it was I don't remember, but I had a quick, sharp tongue. One of my aunts was there, visiting and drinking coffee with my mother. She laughed and said when a kid's brains got fried, they either turned into idiots—or, tossing her head in my direction, came out like that. It's the head toss that I see when I recall this episode. At the time it was "fried brains" that stopped me.

A child's sure instinct told me not to ask any questions right then. Later, I pressed my mother for an explanation. She was tight-lipped, displeased with my aunt. Reluctantly she told me the story I have repeated. Illness frightened my mother, made her angry: "We'll have to call the doctor if you are that sick." When I was hospitalized with acute appendicitis at age 16, she was ready to help me get dressed and leave the hospital because momentarily I felt a little better. My father intervened.

THE STORIES SLIP THEIR MOORINGS

A child says, "Tell me a story. Tell me a story of when you were a little girl. . . . Tell me a story about your sister Faye. . . . Tell me about Sweden, about when the boy died. . . . Tell me the story of when I was a baby. . . ." Hungry for life, children are story starved. With sharp little nails and piercing eyes they dig for places to hook in. Not picky or squeamish, children swallow stories whole, in big gulps, raw, terrorized only by what they cannot name. With stories for bait, they fish out more stories, more language. Even while their lines are out for more, they forage in the ones they have, relentlessly prizing out nuggets, chewing over tough gristle: Trying to understand.

At the same time, in my own home there was an undercurrent of anxiety. My own oldest sister, 12 years my elder, was mysteriously, if subliminally, ill, sleeping for long stretches of time, seeming better at times, falling ill again. I adored her. Sometimes, when she slept so long, if I begged hard enough, my mother would let me try, very gently, to wake her. I would take off my shoes and run up the stairs, but softly. Fitting my feet between the rungs at the foot, I would rock the bed a little, chanting, "Faryl, Faryl, Faryl, wake up, wake up"—as if she were the sleeping princess in the fairy stories I loved. Later, much later after the terrible damage was done, she, and we, learned that her strange affliction was rheumatic fever.

My cousin Jim, two houses away, became seriously ill with the dreaded pneumonia. In the late 1930s antibiotics were still in the experimental stage. For a breathless period fear hung in the air. More whispering. It was *his* ribs, I think, that got spread to drain the lung. This is probably the context in which my mother learned the word *em-py-ema* she enunciates with such care on the tape. He didn't die. For what seemed a very long time he "recovered": thinner than his normal thin, his carrot-red hair brighter in contrast to his white invalid face, but he lived.

On the other side of my family, during this same packed period, my father's mother, my other dearly loved grandmother, died, and within months of her death, my father's older brother—dead of heart disease at 43. I recognize it now, looking back, as one of those intensely emotional periods common to all families, when in a packed period of time, a lot of living and dying happens; for us, from 1936 to 1940. Strong feeling. Few breathing spaces. Loss. Sorrow. Regeneration.

Casting the story line wider, wading further into the stream, there were books. People read to me. I learned to read. Well padded with home stories, I was astonished to find those stories in books. Never a whole story, but pieces and chunks.

Although in our house, books were almost never bought, the Christmas I was 7, my mother gave me a copy of her favorite book from childhood, a Victorian tearjerker, *The Birds' Christmas Carol.* It is a story of a frail little rich girl who dies at Christmas—but only after doing great good for a hearty, rambunctious, poor family of Irish immigrant children, who idolize her. There was tissue over the color plates. When I lifted the tissue, the blonde, blue-eyed Carol pictured there was, inescapably, Faye. The rough, healthy Irish children blurred in with my mother's self-described tomboyish wildness. Some had red hair like Jim.

There was *Little Women*, read to me that same year; read by me over and over for years after. Beth, of course, I already knew. She was Faye's twin—but in this version, dead at 13, the age my own mother was when Faye died. My energetic middle sister, a runner and doer like my mother, slid with ease into the figure of Jo. My oldest sister was surely Meg. Through the poor, German immigrant children from whom she contracted scarlet fever, Beth's death blended in with Carol Bird's. Both were a bridge to my mother and her immigrant family, with Faye singled out to be the angel, the fair one, the good one, the dead one.

My mother's personal heroine, apart from Eleanor Roosevelt, was Helen Keller. Before I ever read Keller's book, *The Story of My Life*, I knew that story. I knew how everyone said Helen, blind, deaf, and mute, was damaged beyond repair by that strange illness that struck her down as an infant. Meningitis. I knew how Anne Sullivan proved them wrong. I tried out blindfolding my eyes. Not talking was beyond my imagination. Could I have been her? With her temper fits and stubbornness, she felt much closer to home than Faye.

Then I read the story of "The Little Matchgirl," dead of poverty and neglect, freezing to death for the want of a fire. I was appalled. I slammed the book shut. I informed my mother I was going to read only "real" stories in the future. I avoided the fairy tale shelf I had previously haunted at the library. I held stubbornly to that resolve for a very long time.

The whole summer following I played at being poor. The joke is, we were poor. It was the depression. Everyone was poor. All the time leading up to that summer, I was busily *not* thinking about the Matchgirl. I meant never to think of her again. Night was the hardest. My habit when I was small was to put myself to sleep by continuing the loved stories in my head, revolving images, visualizing myself in the appealing roles. I blocked the Matchgirl out by giving myself feature parts in "real" stories—contemporary stories of the era like *The Saturdays*. I discovered *Heidi*.

But the Matchgirl didn't let go of me so easily. My mother helped me play poverty. She sewed me two plain, dark blue cotton dresses so I could pretend I had nothing else to wear but this one dress. She gave me bread and milk or porridge (a word I savored) for supper. I often went barefoot anyway but that summer I deliberately walked on stony gravel and hot cement. Looking back, it seems a useful experiment, alternating the dresses, looking for berries to eat, burning my feet. I think doing that I partly warmed the image of turning to ice. Like the Matchgirl. Like Faye. Years later, when I closed my parents' house, I came across my mother's button box, merged years before with her mother's button box. Inside were small,

red, ball-shaped buttons from those two dresses. Immediately, that long ago summer flashed into my head, still fresh. And the Matchgirl. And Faye.
    "In the thick of the tangle what clear line persists . . ."

EYES

Images. Images of body bursting sickness: Eyes ache out of heads; heads swell; hair is pulled out of the head by the roots; brains fry; children turn to ice. Influences. Not benign. Wild. There is nothing tame or predigested about childhood. Through hard play, visceral, bodily play, I made a world, a play world, but a world for those images. In that world, I was not merely who I was, but other things and other people. Looking in a mirror, I tugged at my hair, hard, and saw myself screaming and redfaced tearing it out by the roots. I was I both now and then. I was the I I couldn't remember. I was the I who existed someplace, just beyond reach. This was the I in other stories of "when I was little" or "when I was a baby." I was my mother, rambunctious and brown, and in the same moment the hearty, rough children across the Birds' alley. I was my grandmother in a mean, dank hut in Sweden watching, powerless to save a young boy trapped in fever, and in the same moment, my mother placing that spoon of nourishing broth in a mouth she could no longer nourish. I was the eye watching the eye ache out—and the eye itself.

When I think of this hard play, opening lines from a famous poem by Emily Dickinson (1862/1951) arrive hard on the heels of those memories: "I felt my life with both my hands/To see if it was there . . ." (poem 351).

I grew up. The play faded. The stories languished. The images slipped back into the wonder world. I was into life. Doing things. Miraculously, 18. Miraculously, at the university. Sophisticated—a reader of literature. A reader of important books by famous authors. I was in the library, at the very beginning of Joyce's *Portrait of the Artist* (1948), when reading Stephen's half-remembered, shadowy childhood impressions pushed open the doors of my own story world, abruptly, shockingly:

> [Stephen] hid under the table. His mother said:
>   —O, Stephen will apologise.
> Dante [his aunt] said:
>   —O, if not, the eagles will come and pull out his eyes.—
>
>> Pull out his eyes,
>> apologise,
>> apologise,
>> Pull out his eyes.

> Apologise,
> Pull out his eyes,
> Pull out his eyes,
> Apologise. (p. 2)

Leaping across 45 years of reading—and books like Toni Morrison's *The Bluest Eye* (1970) that forced my own eyes to open—the eye image has in the past year found me again—so raw that I could hardly look at the words on the page.

I was reading the trilogy of the Great War by Pat Barker. The setting in the first volume, *Regeneration* (1991), is Craiglockhart, the facility for British officers suffering from shellshock and memory loss. The Great War poets—Sassoon, Wilfred Owen—were treated there. They figure in the story, but the protagonist is that exception, a British officer from the working classes—Billy Prior, ambitious, smart, shrewd. He is at Craiglockhart because he has lost his voice for no known physical reason. Slowly, his voice returns—but not the memory of what happened before it vanished. It is under hypnosis that the lost thread is finally retrieved.

What happened on the fateful day he was left with no voice began ordinarily. Prior was on duty for trench watch. He stopped briefly to talk with two soldiers, Sawdon and Towers, who were cooking bacon. He walked on, thinking to himself that it had been a quiet day, a quiet watch. Then almost simultaneously with that thought, there is a shell screaming down, landing behind him. Prior hurries back, retracing his steps. There is nothing or almost nothing where the two soldiers had been. As Barker (1991) describes it, "Of the kettle, the frying pan, the carefully tended fire, there was no sign, and not much of Sawdon and Towers either, or not much that was recognizable"(p. 102). Prior and another soldier, Logan, set about to shovel the dirt, the flesh, the charred bone into an empty sand bag; Prior retching, Logan swearing.

> They'd almost finished when Prior shifted his position on the duckboards, glanced down, and found himself staring into an eye. Delicately, like somebody selecting a particularly choice morsel from a plate, he put his thumb and forefinger down through the duckboards. His fingers touched the smooth surface and slid before they managed to get a hold. He got it out, transferred it to the palm of his hand, and held it out towards Logan. He could see his hand was shaking, but the shaking didn't seem to have anything to do with him. "What am I supposed to do with this gob-stopper?" He saw Logan blink and knew he was afraid. At last Logan reached out, grasped his shaking wrist, and tipped the eye into the bag. . . . [Prior] wanted to say something casual, something that would prove he was all right, but a numbness had spread all over the lower half of his face. (p. 103)

From Rosemary Dinnage's (1996) review of the trilogy, I learn that "a gob-stopper is a cheap, round children's candy" (p. 20). Even as I was reading that explanation, for the American reader, of the reference to "gob-stopper," I was hearing my grandma's quiet, resigned, fateful voice: "His eye ached out of his head."

A blue eye,
deep, dark blue like grandma's,
like mother's,
slipping out from the corner of the socket
sliding sideways
down a boy's cheek
still looking.

THE RACE TOWARD LIGHTNESS OF BEING; THE NEUTERING OF LANGUAGE

Even as I was transcribing my mother's story and experiencing the flood of answering stories, feeling their cumulative weight, I also was registering other words—jarring words, clashing words. As surely as Eudora Welty (1984) affirms memory and her thick tangle, from which she also asserts no strands are ever entirely lost, Milan Kundera, whose words are clamoring in my ears, mourns memory's passing. It is not just strands or threads he glimpses at the exit. It is memory herself. Or more precisely, that memory for which, in the West, Proust is prophet. In this response to interview questions about his novel, *The Incredible Lightness of Being*, Kundera (1988) puts it this way:

> With Proust, an enormous beauty began to move slowly out of our reach. . . . [T]he weight of a self, of a self's interior life . . . becomes lighter and lighter. And in that race toward lightness, we have crossed a fateful boundary. (pp. 27–28)

I might have chosen the final phrase, "in that race toward lightness, we have crossed a fateful boundary" as a companion title for this chapter.

I work in the schools, mostly the public schools. I am committed to children by profession. More important, I am committed to children—to their health, safety, and education—as a member of this society, responsible, as all of us are, for doing what I can to make it better. It is in this context that Kundera's words ring true to me—as I wish they did not. I recognize that those words resonate with what I see happening to children and to education—as I wish they did not. I recognize, too, that in that race toward lightness, not only density goes. Along with weight loss, there is an accompanying neutering and flattening of who we are humanly—to ourselves, toward others, and of others toward us. Transparent, we lose our faces. The children lose theirs. We erase them. The power to animate leaks away. I find it deadly.

When I say *deadly*, when I say *neutered*, I am thinking of the "policing language," as Toni Morrison (1994, p. 13) names it, that dominates and degrades discourse about children, parents, teachers—and the schools themselves. There is, for example, the dead language of education plans for children—called ironically enough, "individualized" education plans. These are designed for children who aren't making it in school. These are the children who do not fit the school's agenda for learning—and so are referred for evaluation and retooling.

The language of choice for "adjusting" the nonconforming child is impersonal, imperative, and goal driven: "The child *will* learn . . . the child *will* do . . . the child *will* achieve. . . ." The child, nameless, dwindles. Percentiles are substituted for passions and desire; grade levels for aspiration; IQ scores for thinking and imagining. The parent sitting at the table, witness to this remote, dissecting talk, is forced to participate in the language of reduction and diminishment in order that the child, the "needy" child, the "misfitting" child can receive "services"—services for which the cost may prove immeasurable. The teacher sitting at the table who knows the child in other contexts—how he loves to draw or shines on field trips outside the school—finds those stories marginalized, pushed to the sidelines by the sheer weight of the expert, specialized testimony that preempts any description of the child in the ordinary talk of ordinary daily life in the classroom.

The "prescription" that follows the diagnosis of disabled learner or victim of attention deficit disorder or language disorder is typically for training in unrelieved and humiliatingly tiny skills: to recite names of colors, to write the numerals from 1 to 10, to spell correctly five new words a week, and so on. The passport the "classified child" carries is mostly marked "not valid" for education. It is a passport to low-track or contained special classes, and trivialized learning—learning devoid of big ideas, learning devoid of stories, learning devoid of inspiration.

I find it deadly to witness the medicalizing of the schools. I find it deadening to ordinary human feeling to witness a pathologizing of children that denies the humanness of error and the humanness of strong desire, that reduces passions to the lusterless language of "behaviors" (the euphemism for breaking rules and other wrongdoing). Using language leaked in from mental health agencies, checklists of criteria to make the case for an array of disorders, proliferate. An example: Children or adolescents with [Conduct Disorder], the reader is told, "often initiate aggressive behavior and react aggressively to others. . . . Criterion A1: [the child or adolescent] may display bullying, threatening, or intimidating behavior; Criterion A2: [the child or adolescent] may initiate physical fights" (pp. 85–86)—and so on, to compose a list of 14 criteria, followed by this warning: "The prevalence of Conduct Disorder appears to have increased over the last decades and may be higher in urban than in rural settings. . . . Conduct Disorder is one of the most frequently diagnosed conditions in outpatient and inpatient mental health facilities for children" (American Psychiatric Association, 1994, p. 88).

The political and racist implications of that warning, and its message, hardly require explication. The message of oppression and conformity and the school as the agent for achieving those goals is clear. Writing off the children. Erasing their faces, rendering them mute before they begin because we have taken their tongues, denied their stories, squelched their aspirations. I have a tongue. I have words. I am old. I cannot consent to a neutered language, to an educational landscape barren of ideas, of stories. I ask: Whose interests are served by this objectivizing of children, by this rendering of them educationally, socially, and politically as the enemy, as "the utterly other" (Fussell, 1977)? What is at stake for education? What is at stake for them? For you? For me? For all of us?

In this reading of children and of our humanity, you are merely circumstantial to my existence; I to yours. If I am represented to you as tongueless, passionless, a cipher, a statistic, a demographic phenomenon, a "problem," at best a commodity, an "object of use" (Schachtel, 1959, p. 167) somewhere in your scheme of things, then it is as true that you may enjoy equity with me in this. As we float weightless and melt featureless into each other's faces, a certain blandness relieved by intervals of commerce in the titillating and horrific overtakes us.

This is my interest in memory, this is my interest in telling the stories I have told—to lend weight and flesh to the self, to make the tangle thick. It is these interests that define a larger work I set for myself: to animate memory so that memory animated enlivens and deepens the vision of humanness. For this essay, my mother's story and the stories, personal and public, that it carries in its train have served as the animating agent. It might have been your story or your works. It might have been a child's story and works. What matters is that by stories and by works I am forced to recognize that your life and the child's life, like my mother's or my grandmother's, is full and complex, rich with desire, longing, caring; troubled by turbulence and loss; flawed by the extremes of our own natures.

I undertake that task of animating memory, mindful of all that works against it. I undertake it because of that lightening of our being, that deadening and neutralizing of our perceptions of children, and of ourselves, who, if hollow, can neither protect nor educate them. I undertake my task in a spirit of defiance of neutralism and in the conviction of human possibleness, unpredictableness, and complexity. I undertake my task in the spirit of the need for continuous vigilance in the struggle to keep present before us the blur and blend of human experience, the rich and generative mingling of selves and lives.

3

Another Slant on Knowledge

In a 1988 paper, I explored a way of looking at humanity which calls attention to the *activeness of persons*: in making sense and order of the world and their own place within it; in seeking connection and relationship with each other; and in pursuing worth and conferring value. This essay continues that exploration in the context of knowledge, and from the slant of our own human engagement in the making of knowledge.

It is my conviction that persons, collectively and individually, are caught up in that knowledge-making activity. As co-authors of this enormous and continuing "work," we happen upon, or struggle mightily for, connections that through their yield of new meanings and visions, remake, in large or small ways, the face of the world—and along with it, the face of humanity. The making of knowledge, as I understand it, is a *spanning* activity.

Its inclusive span and the potency that making knowledge releases in the individual suggest that it would occupy a ranking place in discussions of education—and especially so in a society that harbors and aspires to democratic principles. Yet neither the activity and strength of persons as makers of knowledge, nor knowledge itself, is much in evidence in the vocabulary that mainly dominates the discussion of schools and school reform. This discourse has tended instead to favor the language of curriculum, information, instruction, skills, and tasks. In large degree, learners, and to no less degree, teachers, have tended to be portrayed in the negative language of weakness, deficiency, disability, and failure.

I am not unmindful of the difficulties arising from the introduction of knowledge into a discussion of education. It is to my ears, and I suspect to others, one of those big, solid words whose smooth surfaces make it hard to grasp, or even to say (without placing it in inverted commas). Its connotations range far and wide. It easily travels the distance from the familiar to the esoteric; the conventional to the boundary breaking; the dry and

72

boring to the fresh and invigorating; the self-evident to the proven; the carnal and sexual to the spiritual and mental.

Positively, knowledge is often twinned with truth and portrayed as a beacon—a light penetrating the darkness of ignorance. Other images and metaphors with which it is interwoven include trees, fruit, harvests, books, mines, and portals such as doors and windows. Through the Greeks, knowledge is linked with wonder and quest, with novelty and adventure. It tends to confer power and freedom on those who possess it—and also, obligation and responsibility.

Negatively, knowledge is associated with loss of innocence, with secrecy, pride, possessiveness, and exclusion from power. Knowledge can be used to betray and deceive as readily as to enlighten. A little of it can be dangerous and so can a lot.

In myth and story, the price of knowledge has tended to be high. Through knowledge Adam and Eve lost paradise, and Faustus, his soul. In real life, Giordano Bruno went to the stake for it. In equally real life, through knowledge we unleashed upon ourselves the means for the ultimate destruction of the world. The gains also have been high in the yield of power, security, material goods, and intellectual and spiritual growth. In the era perhaps now passing, knowledge has enjoyed a lofty position. Some would argue that it successfully usurped the authority formerly claimed by a Supreme Being.

It is also the bigness and richness of meaning encompassed by knowledge that attract me to it. For that reason I have chosen for the purposes of this essay not to refine its definition or to distinguish with any precision between familiar (or cultural) knowledge and systematic knowledge, or between the making of knowledge and its near neighbors, learning and thinking. When the search is for an embracing idea, one which may call previously drawn boundaries into question, it seems to me some latitude, and even vagueness or ambiguity in this respect, may prove useful.

I have for much the same reason chosen to start with the activity of making knowledge rather than knowledge itself. It is an obvious thing to say but if we humans did not engage in that activity, and regularly, neither accrued bodies of knowledge, nor subject matter disciplines, nor cultural heritages, nor academic canons, nor any of the artifacts of knowledge which we recognize in the form of "works," would exist. I choose, then, to emphasize activity because I perceive it to be prior to and determining of knowledge. I also make that choice because I believe approaching knowledge from the side of creating it, casts a fresh and useful light on us as makers and on knowledge itself.

To illustrate: Taking the approach of us as makers calls attention to the root of knowledge in the hands, bodies, and hearts of people as well as in their minds. Planting knowledge in bodies lends it an other than purely mentalistic or cognitive dimension. Embedding knowledge and the making of it in bodily activity calls attention to the contaminations, confusions, impurities, error, and the general messiness that are the inevitable accompaniments of that activity. Embedding knowledge in ordinary activity roughens its smooth surfaces.

My exploration of the making of knowledge will be through stories— one drawn from the European learned world, and the others from the worlds of childhood and adolescence. I hope by this concentration on the particular to illuminate and also ground an abstract and overarching idea in the ways I just alluded to. My other purpose in telling these stories is my belief that it is through lives and stories of lives that we educate each other with respect to our common humanity.

THE NEWTON/GOETHE STORY

In the early years of the seventeenth century, when Newton set out to investigate color, he held a prism to the light. Goethe, almost 100 years later, bent on the same task, held the prism not to the light but to his eye. Those divergent gestures spelled out the world of color in altogether different terms.

Holding the prism so a ray of white light passed through it and directing it toward a white surface, Newton found displayed before him the full spectrum of colors. He was led by this experiment to conclude that pure colors are the units which, when combined, produce white.

By all accounts, Goethe misunderstood Newton's experimental procedure (Magnus, 1906/1961; Matthaie, 1971; Mintz, 1959). Setting out to repeat it, instead of holding the prism to the light, Goethe looked through it at a white surface and saw not colors but a uniformly white surface. Being more observationally inclined than the brilliant theorist, he repeated his own experimental procedure with many variations under natural and contrived conditions.

What Goethe discovered through his observations was that a display of color will be perceivable on a surface only if its uniformity is interrupted; for example, in nature by a cloud, or in everyday experience by a demarcation such as a window frame, or under experimental conditions by introducing a spot. Looked at from Goethe's angle, color appears when light approaches darkness. Countering Newton's finding that colors produce white light, Goethe drew the conclusion that color arises from the dynamic interplay of light and dark—and that combining colors produces a gray hue, not white (Magnus, 1961).

If I select this juncture to leave off the account of these opposing conclusions on color, there is much to recommend Goethe's theory. What he describes is observable in nature, confirmed through carefully conducted experiments that as much as possible replicate natural conditions, and understandable as an extension of our ordinary daily experience with color and the natural world. By comparison, Newton's experimentation begins, as Magnus (1961) points out, from a "circumscribed individual case" (p. 136). While sharply focused, the experimentation was rather scanty and the echoes it evokes of our actual experience with nature are, at best, faint.

But the story doesn't end there. Newton was a physicist and mathematician. Understanding color as it occurs in nature or in human experience was not the focus of his inquiry. These ordinary occurrences are from the physical standpoint unruly and blemished by impurities. It was Newton's purpose to abstract color from nature and to subsume it under a rubric of mathematical laws, and it was to that end that he fractured light into bands of color. His thinking in this respect was on the cutting edge of a world view just emerging in the West in which objectivity would shortly be acclaimed as the only reliable method for making knowledge, and measurement as the only the reliable standard for its evaluation.

Cast more broadly, his purposes and preferences fell in with a burgeoning belief that through the separation of phenomena into their component parts science would fall heir to nature's secrets and through physical laws rise to be her ruler. It was in the context of this fast-changing intellectual climate, his own disciplinary habits of mind, and his own intuitions that Newton, on slender evidence, made a sure-footed leap of faith that carried him far beyond it. He conceived the brilliant colors refracted by the prism as *frequencies*—that is, as measurable wave lengths.

A RETELLING OF THE NEWTON/GOETHE STORY

I am going to tell this story again and in slightly other terms. Newton positioned the prism away from himself—figuratively, at arm's length and in line with a ray of light. With that gesture, he assumed some degree of distance and detachment. In a manner of speaking, he stopped blocking the light with his own presence. That gesture of humility, of paying homage to objective truth, when twinned with a newfound freedom of inquiry composes, I think, the important subtext of values invigorating the spirit of a new intellectual age.

Goethe's countering gesture—bringing the prism close to his own eye—pointed in another direction and discovered its orientation and vigor by way of other values. Through this gesture, the prism was positioned as if it were a window between the person and the world of light and color. The gesture and the investigations that followed emphasize the creative powers of human consciousness and call attention to the malleability of the world. As the German literary scholar and interpreter of Goethe, Erich Heller (1975), observes, "It is indeed amazing how malleable the world is and how easily it models and remodels itself according to the inner vision of man, how readily it responds to his 'theorizing'!" (p. 26). Starting from the same "world stuff," but according to their own perspectives and methods, Newton and Goethe divined, fashioned, and placed before us different world interpretations: Newton's pure, abstract, and measurable; Goethe's profusely varied and subject to influence and change.

Embedded in Goethe's reactive gesture and belief is a contradiction of Newton's vision of immutable and objective laws of nature existing in perpetuity and in detachment from human consciousness. Because Goethe believed from the depths of his being that how we *look* at the world has no less than determining effects on the reality in which we find ourselves, he was appalled at Newton's indifference to the human factor in the physical equation.

At the time, and for many years to come, the intellectual tides in the West ran strongly in the direction of Newton's perspective and values. As another man of letters, Owen Barfield (1963), points out, Galileo's isolation of the physical world from the perceiving subject led ultimately not only to the exclusion of such qualities as color, sound, smell, beauty, and ugliness, but also extension, figure (shape), solidity, and motion.

Once relegated to the perceiving subject, these qualities and features of the observable world were accordingly ranked as secondary properties. In the final analysis, this restriction left only number to enjoy an independent and objective existence. In general, what we now call subjective qualities—those dependent on a human perceiver—were considered henceforth to be largely without importance for knowledge of the physical world. In the emerging Western scientific world view, attention was unqualifiedly fastened on the *physical* world and focused on *number* and *measurement.*

Goethe's attention to color as a qualitative dimension of nature was not compatible with that physical definition or the perspectives and values in which that definition was rooted. It is a sign of the rising tide of enthusiasm for the *physical world view* that Goethe's painstaking observations and careful investigations were judged exclusively from that perspective and by the measurement standard. That judgment prevailed and mostly has continued to prevail, even though as psychologist Norbert Mintz points out in his 1959 re-evaluation of the color theory, the knowledge yielded by Goethe's studies has contributed to the fields of human physiology and perception and been applied in the visual arts and in such color crafts as printing and dyeing. Not withstanding these influences and applications, the potency of the physical world view remains such that even so recent a commentator as James Gleik (1987) observes in the science best seller *Chaos* that Goethe's color theory has "faded into merciful obscurity" (p. 164).

As the physical-mathematical star rose on the Western horizon, objectivity and measurement became the only values and standards by which knowledge was evaluated and accorded a ranking status. Accordingly, diversity was diminished. In the West, the arts, the humanities, and education would all be powerfully influenced by that overriding perspective. Once the Western world was divided along the subjective–objective axis, the continuum along which perceiver and perceived, or person and world, might be understood as interanimating *and* as distinguishable no longer enjoyed any effective reality.

In spite of Goethe's efforts, and those of others, the power of that thought was weakened and the values from which it sprang were overshadowed. Lacking a value context in which person and reality are understood to form an inseparable whole, subjectivity and all that has to do with human value sank into a merely negative conceptualization. To be subjective was to be *not* logical (that is, fanciful); *not* analytic (that is, vague); *not* physical (that is, intangible or immaterial); and *not* real (that is, unreal, magical, or spiritual; not based in the physical world).

By the standards of the physical-mathematical, Goethe's descriptions of color could only be judged to be subjective and so, fanciful, vague, and of little consequence. That is the judgment he received. It is important to my retelling to stop for a moment to say this: It could have gone the other way. A different intellectual climate, a different rising star, and Goethe's fate could have been Newton's. And that being so, our predicament would have been the same: A contradicting idea for the sake of clarity and certainty and simplicity would have been submerged. With that important aside, I return to the Newton/Goethe story as it happened and for what it has to tell us.

When Mintz (1959) sought the second hearing on Goethe's scientific contribution that I just referred to, he prefaced his essay, "Concerning Goethe's Approach to the Theory of Color," with the Biblical story of Joseph's coat of many colors. Employing the metaphor for my own purposes, I wish to draw some lessons from the story I have told—to treat it as a sort of parable of knowledge making. For the sake of brevity, I will treat these lessons schematically.

As the story just told suggests, knowledge may itself be thought of as a coat woven from many colors and the makers of that knowledge as weavers whose color choices reflect different visions and values. Some of the colors will be happily complementary or at least compatible; others, as in this story, will clash. As the story I have told also suggests, the *way* of knowing something is irreducibly perspectival and value-imbued. This is so when the way of knowing is based in theory (as was Newton's) just as it is so when the way of knowing is based in observation (as was Goethe's). Different ways of looking and diversity of method color the world in hues, pure and blended, not achievable by a single eye or a solitary mind or by a single cultural slant or a single world view.

Saying this, I am saying that the knowledge made of something cannot be synonymous with it. The world is much bigger and immensely more complex than our visions of it. Color, for example, is vaguer and more ambiguous than either Goethe's or Newton's conceptualizations of it. What knowledge gains by definition and clarity is necessarily at the expense of width and variety. As I understand it, any knowledge refers to large and uncharted territories beyond the borders it has drawn—territories that await the eye and hand and perspectives and consciousness of other thinkers or artists or scientists to map them. That is, knowledge for the reason that it is a made thing—not different in this respect from any "work" (a picture, a novel)—is always partial and never complete. In this respect, it also bears a striking resemblance to cultures and social orders.

From these "lessons," I understand that there isn't any piece of knowledge or way of knowing that is altogether separable from a context of assumptions, purposes, and values. Even if unannounced or overlooked, these intuitions of worth and importance spread an aura around even those hard bits of reality to which a particular discipline or social order accords the *status of fact,* and the rules and methods of investigation and theorizing that it acclaims.

Taking the next step, by treating knowledge as a made thing, I place responsibility for knowledge squarely in human hands. The status accorded to knowledge, who is given access to it, whose knowledge counts, whose ways of knowing are privileged, maps a history of power. Women's knowledge, the knowledge of persons ruled out of the academy, the denial of access to knowledge to the many peoples relegated by race or culture to a low rung on the social and political ladder arrow to that history—and to now. That it requires vigilance to keep before us the question of who benefits from a particular construction of knowledge, and who is ruled out by that construction, testifies to the authority of knowledge I spoke of earlier. To practice that vigilance unsettles the received wisdom that knowledge is context free and equatable with truth.

It seems to me that major shifts in knowledge and ways of knowing, those that dislocate authoritative knowledge or eclipse previous world views and sponsor new ones, do not occur primarily through changes in technique or specific methods. These occur from revolutions in perspective. Sometimes occurring gradually. Sometimes abruptly. Always there is struggle. Always there is tension. Always these novel perspectives change in small degree or large the face of the world as we know it—and the face of humanity along with it. When geometry as a single and absolute law, with God the geometrizer, was toppled at the turn of the nineteenth century with the invention of multiple geometries, the last stronghold of a some one and only way, some one and ultimate truth, was breached.

Saying this, I am drawing the lesson that knowledge is plural, inexact, mutable, and potent. I am saying that knowledge is subject not only to additive change describable as a sort of linear progress from the relatively more concrete or naive or inadequate to the relatively more abstract or sophisticated or adequate, but equally as reversal, inversion, controversion, and transformation.

Finally, the story just told illustrates rather vividly that standards transferred from one world view or discourse or social order to a world view or discourse or social order rooted in other values, lead inevitably to inadequate, misplaced, or misleading judgments. These failed translations have the further effect of obscuring diversity and divesting us of the vast richness of human feeling and thought—and of knowledge itself.

As I see it, the story I have told, and the lessons I have drawn from it, have far-reaching consequences for education. How we as adults, as teachers, as citizens stand in relation to knowlege and the making of it deeply influences how we present knowledge, how we treat contradictory interpretations, how we engage children and adolescents with ambiguity, and how we make available and recognizable to them the power of their own perspectives as thinkers.

CHILDREN AND ADOLESCENTS AS MAKERS OF KNOWLEDGE

I am going to encircle this parable of knowledge making, drawn from the annals of scientific and intellectual history, with stories of children's and adolescents' ways of knowing the world and themselves as knowers and thinkers. These are stories much lighter in weight and tone and on the smaller scale of ordinary, daily life. Unlike the bigger story, these stories cast no long shadows on the intellectual horizon nor do they alter in noticeable ways the course of knowledge or the character of the culture.

Their value lies, I believe, in that very commonplaceness. These are stories that easily strike chords of responsive recognition in any parent or teacher—or for that matter, anyone who recalls their own childhood and youth. In my ear, they also echo the intellectual adventures of Goethe and Newton. These, too, are stories of discovery, of intense feeling, of highly individual and insistent points of view, of the making of new and, if weighed on their own scale, powerful connections. These stories verge on the same territory of values and, with respect to standards, raise similar questions.

Because these stories are about young people, those only just embarking on life and on knowing, they also carry us closer to the world of schools and, I hope, to ways of grappling more directly with the place of knowledge within the schools. I am telling them mostly because they reveal a level of sense making that I believe defies abstraction and the categorization of children and their learning according to such rubrics as "higher-order thinking skills," "visual learning," or "multiple intelligences"—as if we were each somehow a sum of fixed traits or progressed as thinkers along a linear path from lower to higher levels. Sense making, as I am using it, is more ordinary, more to be counted upon, and more complex. I sometimes call it making connections.

A PERSONAL ENCOUNTER WITH THE MAYFLOWER

About 50 years ago, as a second grader in the elementary school of the small Minnesota town where I grew up, I made a riveting connection between my own life and the larger world. It was possibly in the autumn of that year since the teacher was telling us the story of the pilgrims. When she reached the part about their voyage on the Mayflower, I understood in a flash what this story was about. It was a very exciting story, one I quite regularly requested my grandma to tell, about how she came from the old country (in this instance, Sweden) to America. I knew the story in several versions and by heart. My understanding that this was the same story was unshadowed by any question or doubt. What surprised me was that the teacher knew it and was telling it in school.

I raised my hand, and called upon, announced the fact of my grandmother's journey to America on the Mayflower. I suppose the teacher must have been amused, but if she was she hid that—or I didn't notice. What I remember is that she tried to persuade me that my grandmother could not have come over on the Mayflower. I insisted. Although it would be impossible for me to reconstruct a word of what she actually said, I remember that her tone became firmer and her explanations lengthier. Overborne by words and authority, I held my peace. Inwardly, I clung to my conviction. After school, I indignantly told my mother what had happened. To my astonishment, she sided with the teacher. Again, I retreated.

It would have been a short trip to run next door and ask Grandma, but I didn't do that. In part that may have been because I didn't usually ask her questions or seek information from her—just stories. In part it may have been that by then I suspected my error—although I pretended to myself to be unshaken. The feeling of "rightness" remained strong—which reflects in part I suspect just plain obstinacy. Yet I also think that sense of "rightness" I felt was because the connection with the historic event was so satisfying. It made so much sense to me. In a pleasing way, it elaborated and expanded the original story. I am quite sure I never again voiced the idea aloud. In the way that children not infrequently seal off a belief in Santa Claus from contradictory evidence, I think I encapsulated and protected this conviction from further challenges.

It was to me a thrilling discovery. Aboard that tiny, storm-tossed ship, the Mayflower, I was there with the pilgrims—and my grandmother. I was there in the same way I was present with my grandmother, her twin and co-conspirator, in *all* the stories she told of her childhood and girlhood in Sweden. I felt with her the meanness and drunkenness of the pastor schoolmaster, suffered with her the swollen joints and fever that plagued her youth, and, on better days, skied with her to school.

The effect of this new connection was to fire me with an even more intense passion for family stories and, with the passage of time, anything to do with exploration, settlers, and pioneers. The connection I made, although mistaken, opened up whole new regions of possibilities. To this day, I can feel the glow of wonder when as an older child of 9 or 10 I felt in my feet, knew in my bones as I walked along the river in my town that where I walked the Sioux had walked—on this very ground. And in my ears I heard the clatter made by covered wagons as they later rolled over the tall, tough prairie grass on their journey further west into Dakota territory. When at age 12 or 13 I discovered that same image in the opening pages of Rolvaag's *Giants in the Earth*, the connection I felt with the author brought that same feeling of awe.

I recall, too, the painful moment when as a fourth grader, reading some other version of the pilgrim story, I unearthed that "forgotten" earlier mistake from memory. Stripped of its protective cover and beheld in the light of my own knowledge and reason, the foolishness of it and my own stubbornness caused the blood to rush to my face. I was briefly, but deeply, embarrassed. No one knew and I hoped they never would. But by that time the mistake had done its work—I had become a participant in history, was its willing captive.

The story I have told is at several levels about the making of connections. I think it is reasonable to say that at age 7 I was predisposed to seize upon the pilgrim story or any other piece of history. In general I had a big appetite for stories. In particular I hungered for those that told what was before I was or what I denominated globally as "olden times." The specific link I made through the image of a tiny boat on an immense, stormy ocean to my grandmother's voyage was forged from *likeness* at the level not of fact or information, but of *feeling*. If I may put it this way, the two voyages separated by over 200 years, and historically disparate in scale of importance and every specific detail, were *expressively equivalent*—held for me, the same *value-weight*.

In making that connection, my "mistake" was to confuse the world of image and feeling with the world of fact. Using accuracy as a standard, I was dead wrong. Employing meaning and literature as a standard, and allowing for age, perhaps I wasn't so far off. Both were stories of leave taking and loss, of danger and adventure. Each bordered on the same existential issues and the same values. Of course I don't mean to say that I made these connections or had any such conscious thoughts. I do think, though, that the two stories, taken together, opened up the possibility for exploring such ideas, such ways of being—which I did in the ways of childhood through books, play, drawing, and especially more stories. In other words, I remade them and did so by turning them into works of my own.

Another way to talk about the connection I made is to see the new story—the pilgrim story—as falling on ground already fertile with story-knowledge. I already knew what story was, I already had a supply of "olden times" knowledge and, however vague, some sense of "pastness." Looked at from this angle, the new story can be seen as understandable or assimilable in the terms of the story already familiar to me to which it bore the closest structural similarity. Emphasizing such a structural or logical similarity is credible but fails to encompass the expressive participation through body and feeling that made the stories told by my grandmother and mother such an active force in my own memory, perspective, and ways of knowing.

The enjoyment, satisfactions, and excitement I found in my grandmother's and mother's stories of their lives came, as I have suggested, from reliving, retelling, re-experiencing those stories in my own thought and play. There the stories were also transformed. Listening to those stories and enacting them, my imagination filled them with details of my own making. When my grandmother told of skiing to school, she described that journey as sometimes beginning and ending in the darkness of a Scandinavian winter. In *my* mind's eye, a snow-covered expanse, dotted with pines and firs, dimly lighted by a rising or descending moon, was the landscape through which the skis cut our paths. When in my daily life I walked to school over the snow-covered, frozen river on dark Minnesota mornings, I was within myself, her, and the scenes of our lives merged.

The boundaries of my life with my grandmother's and mother's lives blurred in this play and retelling. In imagination I became both of them and also neither of them, but somehow a fourth person expressive of all three of us. From the fragments and materials at hand I did what all children do in play: I made a world in which I became not merely who I was, but many things and many people. In inestimable ways, their lives and stories widened and complicated my own—making room for thinking, imagining, and increased meaning.

That the connection I made was "wrong" seems to me at one level not important and at another altogether consequential. The inward grasp of the pilgrim story as the "same" as the grandmother story fueled the fires of curiosity and desire: to hear more and to know more. It seems reasonable enough and indeed, predictable, that the teacher would seek to disabuse me of my fancies. It was also predictable that in time I was bound to discover this particular kind of error. I suspect that the strength with which I defended my mistake was not so much for itself as for some vaguer promise that connection held for me of more good things to come—to paraphrase the words of that remarkable interpreter of childhood, Edith Cobb (1977, p. 28). And I was not, in that respect, disappointed or mistaken.

THE GOETHE/NEWTON STORY; THE MAYFLOWER STORY

However I measure it, the distance between my personal recollection and the Goethe/Newton story is vast. Positioning them next to each other nonetheless illuminates some broad and common human ground. Allowing for differences of scale and weight, the making of knowledge in both stories is inseparable from a vague but potent substrata of preferences, perspectives, and cultural and personal values. They both involve *valuations* of the world which, except at a high cost to understanding, are not separable from these shaping circumstances. Again allowing for differences in scale, both stories call attention to mistakes, error, partialness, and incompleteness as characteristic of all human activity—including the making of knowledge. While these may have a limiting effect on knowledge they may also, as these stories illustrate, be incidental to larger purposes and may exercise an expansive and energizing influence on the *making* of knowledge.

For all these reasons, I am led to conclude that evaluation of knowledge reached in isolation from the way of knowing, and the perspectives and values shaping the knowledge made, is likely to lead at best to weak or inadequate judgments. Sometimes—and this was true for Goethe—the judgments made are seriously skewed and end by limiting the possibilities for all of us.

TWO MORE STORIES: "RAIN" AND "REAL THINKING"

Bearing these commonalities in mind, positioning my own recollection next to observations and recollections more comparable to it in weight and scale calls attention to features of making knowledge that expand its meanings and implications in other directions. Since counterparts to my own recollection abound in the worlds of childhood and adolescence, I have with difficulty selected just two: a short observation of a very young child and a recollection of an adolescent experience.

Those familiar with my work will recognize the first brief observation as a favorite of mine. Many years ago now, while in a laundromat, I noticed a small girl, certainly no more than 3 years old, who was watching her mother take the laundry out of the dryer. When the mother straightened up, she tossed her head back. Her hair, long and glossy black with red lights, shimmered in the sun as it fell back from her face. The small child standing behind her caught her breath and whispered, "oh, rain," while at the same time shimmering her hands held outstretched before her, palms down, in a rhythm responsive to the wave-like fall of the hair down her mother's back. The child's face was filled with wonder.

I don't know what followed from this discovery of a likeness that linked hair and rain. In a way, I don't need to. I know that she was transfixed—onto something, something exciting and wondrous. What I don't doubt is that it led somewhere, made possible other connections—as it would for any child.

The next story I am going to tell makes the leap from childhood to adolescence. It is the account of what a teacher friend of mine, Anne S. Fogg, describes in a personal communication as the moment "I became conscious of actually thinking." She writes: "It was in an eleventh grade English class. *What* I thought is long forgotten, but the excitement (so *this* is what thinking feels like) and the astonishment that I had apparently not really thought anything before that moment remains a strong memory."

Qualifying that statement, she notes that she had probably "done plenty of thinking before age 16, at least in other people's terms." Questioning herself she wondered "what the quality of that moment was that defined it so sharply for me, as in some dreams that have such apparent reality that one is disoriented on waking."

Pursuing her description of this "first thought," she describes it as "almost like a physical sensation." After speculating that it might have been a physical experience ("a final connection of neurons"), she compares the "first thought" to the thinking she previously had done in school that got her passed from grade to grade and not without distinction. She says of that school thinking:

> It was usually done in response to a question, or group of them. It was performed orally or in writing. It needed to be quiet and orderly. It was finished if the answer was right, or recognized to be appropriate in certain ways. If it wasn't right, sometimes the teacher exhorted us, "Come on, Think!" It was definitely an act of will.

This was not like the "first thought" which was "quite a surprise, arriving unbidden by anything in particular." She continues by noting again the excitement she felt "by the recognition of a process which indicated that whatever I had been doing in school before was not thinking, not REAL thinking anyways." She concludes the recollection with these thoughts:

> I suspect that this memory is strong because I had found some personal meaning in a bit of school work, had seen a connection between myself and an idea, for the first time. . . . *It must have been the first moment that I heard my own voice clearly.* It was startling to be the observer and the facilitator of this moment. I felt the excitement of having powers, and being free. (italics added)

CONNECTING THE STORIES; LEARNING FROM THEM

Without specifically linking these stories to school—that is, to teaching and learning in that more formal way—I am going to call attention to some of what they tell us about children and people. I pause to do this for the reason that what I understand these stories to tell us are all things I think need to be, really must be, present in our ways of looking at children and adolescents as we set about to teach, to plan the curriculum, to administer the school, to make educational policy.

All of these stories bear witness to the power of the human mind to free events from their moorings, to freely mingle inwardly what is outwardly set apart, and to freely make and remake the world and our own experience in ever varied and novel ways. For us humans, hair doesn't stay on the head, rain doesn't stay in the sky, grandmothers and pilgrims may escape their respective centuries and pursuits to engage in an unexpected dialogue, and thinking does not remain bound by the conventions of school.

The connections that are made in these stories are of the global and far-reaching variety. To make the connections between hair and rain or a grandmother's journey and that of the pilgrims, the children leapt lightly across wide distances. In Anne Fogg's recollection the growth of thinking did not inch along in baby steps but by a giant step; thinking itself and Anne along with it were catapulted into an altogether new and other dimension.

Although highly personal and individual, the connections discovered in these stories are altogether understandable. Even when the connections are not our own, they are foretold in our own possibilities and enjoy for that reason a self-evidence and public character that belie their particularity and individualness. The children's perceptions arouse our own, cull from memory related but divergent experiences, awaken us again to the richness and variety of the world, and engage us, in however small a degree, in the remaking of it.

These stories also illustrate that the making of close connections coincides with *bursts* of meaning, an expansion of interest, intensification of feeling, and a freeing of the will. There is, as Anne Fogg says explicitly, the experience of freedom and power. These experiences are immediate, sensuous, physical, full of feeling—and not merely mental and abstract. As Whitehead (1938/1958) observes, and Anne's recollection so vividly illustrates, "A thought is a tremendous mode of excitement" (p. 50).

Viewed most widely these stories are about the transforming effects that even small-scale making and remaking of knowledge have on the world and the maker. Anne Fogg's connection with "real thinking" endowed her with altogether new capacities and an altogether new perspective on the world. My mother's and grandmother's stories and memories were nothing less than a magnetic force in my life. Into their orbit they attracted all sorts of stray experiences and pieces of the world: scraps gleaned from the radio, items from overheard conversations, images from movies and books, knowledge from school.

The direction of that kind of force is best described as time-spanning; certainly it is not linear. I choose that phrase because I believe this kind of connection is open-ended with respect to regions of possibility and to the rediscovery of the past. With each connection made, the ground of understanding and the boundaries of the self are altered. The dislocation may be slight, as perhaps it was for the 3-year-old—an age when almost every new experience may evoke such imagery and intuitions. Or the earth may shake as it surely did for Anne.

By calling attention to knowledge making as an *expressive* activity, these stories are reminders that all of us, even the very young, are passionately entangled with it—are captured by it. Positioned alongside the Goethe/

Newton story, these stories are a reminder that from the outset the making of knowledge displays its bigness. It is an adventure for which we are configured and to which we are fated.

If we were not as these stories portray us to be—in the first place and without exception, makers of knowledge, and for that reason *educators of self*—it seems to me that no horizons would exist for education beyond the limited boundaries of training in skills. The purposes of education with equal necessity would be fastened tightly to short-term results and shaped by narrow and minimal expectations.

PART **II**

The Politics of Educating/
The Politics of Work

> [If] you start from the activities of production and trading
> . . . increasingly these are seen as the essential purposes of
> society, in terms of which other activities must submit to
> be judged. All forms of human organization, from the family
> and the community to the educational system, must be
> reshaped in the light of this dominant economic activity.
> —Raymond Williams, *The Long Revolution*

As the lines from Raymond Williams affirm, the views a society starts from and lives by are profoundly consequential. Right now in this society, economics is undeniably the starting point and the determining, largely unchallenged arbiter for all other societal activities. The negative consequences of that framing for the family, for the community, for the arts, and for education is a recurring theme across the three talks that compose this part of the book. In response to those consequences, ideas of work, works, and human memory introduced in Part I are applied and further explored.

Chapter 4, "Schools in the Making," conceptualizes the school as itself a work—a work I claim, as the title announces, to be in the making, and indeed (and desirably), ever in the making. Picturing the school as animate and in motion, contingent on and particularized by shaping influences and a history peculiarly its own, I envision it as likenable to a living organism, holding within itself the seeds of its own renewal.

One aim of this reconceptualizing of the school in active mode is to unsettle the definition of the school as a fixed entity—a cog in the system's wheel interchangeable with any other school, incapable of change except through manipulation and reform instigated by agencies external to it. The related aim is to advance the idea that a school can lay claim to its own history, examine its own practice, and discover by this discipline, its value roots and so, too, its positive growth points and leading edges. In the discussion surrounding these definitions and aims, I contrast substitutional, incremental change via reform agendas on a massive and uniform scale with change that is regenerative and transformative of the school conceived as a collective, and particularized, human work.

The second essay, "What Would We Create?," deepens and expands ideas about work first introduced in "Poets of Our Lives." Specifically, meanings of work and its human value are juxtaposed to traditional economic definitions capsulized in the phrases, "effort rewarded by money" or "what we are paid to do." Among the larger meanings of work the essay explores are the following: Work that is done for the love of the work itself; work done to benefit others; work that fulfills desire through the disciplined pursuit of a medium; and that vast domain of work often discounted as "women's work," which safeguards and nurtures a quality of life essential to all our social arrangements. Within that domain, I call particular attention to teaching, caring for the family, and ministering to the ill and infirm.

This essay also continues the discussion of history and regenerative change introduced in "Schools in the Making." In particular, I spell out the consequences for all dimensions of civil life, and education in particular, of substituting for history and remembering what Milan Kundera (1988) describes as "a present that is so expansive . . . that it shoves the past off our horizon and reduces time to the present moment only" (p. 18).

However, it is in the third essay in this part, "To Believe Ourselves," that I most carefully distinguish the ahistorical construction of the school as a corporate entity from the school envisioned as in the making. Evoking the liveliness and particularity characteristic of the classroom and the many histories embodied and unfolding in that space, I use the language of "two worlds" and "worlds apart" to describe the conflict that divides this densely textured, close-to-the-bone human world from the upper and business level of the school hierarchy. At the end of the essay, history is also the perspective I choose to talk about classrooms as I perceive them to be now, some 30 or more years after the social, educational, and political changes that occurred in the 1960s and 1970s.

The talk, "Schools in the Making," framed a summer institute held in Phoenix in 1994 for the purpose of doing a Descriptive Review of two schools: W. T. Machan and Sunnyslope. At the time the institute happened, the staffs, parents, and principals from both schools had been doing inquiry and documentation rooted in the Prospect descriptive processes for about 5 years. For the occasion of this institute, working together across schools, we developed and gave a trial run to a new process which we called the Descriptive Review of the School.

The 1995 session of Prospect Center's annual Fall Conference was the venue for "What Would We Create?" Held in the New York City area, the conference included teachers, school administrators, and teacher educators from a variety of geographic locations, some with long-standing membership in the Prospect network and others new to Prospect. The talk followed a day in which participants joined in a variety of reflections, recollections, and descriptive reviews.

"To Believe Ourselves" opened a conference held in 1997 at Sarah Lawrence College (Bronxville, New York) to honor the tenth anniversary of the Art of Teaching program, and attended both by graduates and students at that time enrolled in the program. This Master of Science program, directed by Sara Wilford and Mary Hebron, involves students in extensive observation and description and introduces them to the processes for descriptive inquiry evolved at Prospect Center.

4

Schools in the Making

Today, principals and members of the staffs of two schools, W. T. Machan and Sunnyslope, begin a 5-day summer institute, sponsored by the Center for Establishing Dialogue. The aim is to do a descriptive review of each school, initiating a process rooted in the Prospect descriptive processes now in use in both schools, but devised among us specifically for this occasion.

The timing and the pairing of schools for this joint review are not coincidental. Although not even in the same district, these are sister schools in history and philosophy. Starting with history, about 5 years ago now each school experienced a sea change. At each, a newly appointed principal—Lynn Davey at Machan and Pam Clark at Sunnyslope—seized the opportunity of public institutions fallen on hard times to bring together staff and parents to rededicate and to remake these schools. At both schools, independently of each other, this rededication affirmed children and families as starting place and center for the school's philosophy.

Of course, there is so much more. Charting a new course for a school is strenuous, asking everything of everyone: principal, staff, parents, children. There are challenges to be met on all sides. There is the daily work to accomplish and the larger vision to sustain. Yet both schools have come through these 5 years committed to the course chosen and to a philosophy that counts children and families as their greatest resource.

THE SCHOOL AS A WORK

I take the starting point for these framing remarks from this shared history of rebuilding, by conceptualizing the school as a work, and more specifically, a work that is ever in the making. I do that with these questions as guideposts: How is it possible in a public school to start from the idea of the school as a work? That it is makable and remakable? That it is for this reason ever in process? That it is not only unfinished but unfinishable? That unfinishable it defies perfection?

I state these questions boldly because the idea of the school as a work and a work in the making (and remaking) breaks it free from more familiar definitions; for example, the school defined as a system, the school defined as a service, and in recent years, the school defined as a corporation (with a CEO to head it). That is, the idea of schools in the making is a different starting place, with different aims than schools conceptualized as businesses or systems or based on technological, economic ends.

Starting places, like cornerstones, matter. Beginning with schools in the making, I start from views of the person and of humanity with the aim of keeping the school workable and lively with possibility for each child and for all. Starting here, I start with different aims than the goal of developing specific skills and expertise or discovering and skimming off the cream of the crop.

Conceptualized as a "work in the making," the school isn't static or fixed, but in motion. Being in motion, moving along open to its surround, it is subject to influence and change. As a work that is ever in the making, the school is in the hands of many makers, and is responsive to their visions of what it is possible for the school to be. It is for the reason that the school is in motion, in process, that I say that it is (and necessarily must be) in a state of unfinish. What is unfinished or unfinishable, what is animate, is difficult to box in, to routinize or to confine to a schedule. Definition is eluded.

Understood this way, the school seems to me more likenable to a living being than an object or corporate structure or site. A school understood in these terms is more like our own lives or selves: permeable, ambiguous with respect to its boundaries, mingled, and in action. In its likeness to a life or person, the school is not a bounded, definable entity. It is a locus of activity, an energetic field.

It seems to me that much of our frustration with schools is linked to a conceptualizing of the school as an object-like structure, a kind of box composed of parts that are interchangeable or can be reassembled. The implication is strong in that definition that all the parts needed are present and to hand and all that is needed for the school to run smoothly, efficiently, well, or successfully is to tinker with the parts until we hit the right combination. Once that combination is found, there is the unspoken presumption that the school will continue in a state of perfection—and of changelessness—governed by routine, custom, schedule. The goal of perfection achieved, the task of keeping school would be reduced to maintaining the structure or machine in good running order—a matter of adjustment of routines, accommodation of schedules, fixing worn parts, or replacing them.

The evidence that makes me think this is the prevailing image of the school is all around us. Reform that goes further than substituting one "model" with another is regarded with suspicion. The most radical mainstream suggestion about schools is to restructure them; that is, to rearrange the parts. Assessment of schools is stubbornly and resistively one-dimensional and tied to standards external to the school. The dominating climate tends to be one of conformism and docility—even as children and schools confront us daily with the desperate need for bold action. The intellectual discussion is mostly fragmented and compartmentalized by specialized expertise and jargon, and by contradictory beliefs and standards. In New York State, for example, there is a simultaneous commitment to "learner-centered education" and to state-mandated Regents exams and benchmarks. This contradiction appears to occasion not the slightest internal disequilibrium or intellectual indigestion.

There are other evidences closer to home. In schools, when work teachers and others thought was accomplished has to be redone, there is angry, frustrated talk about not reinventing the wheel. I or you or others may think that if we could just have a newer, smaller school free of the bureaucratic surveillance of the public sector, everything would be fine. There is disillusionment and shock when, should the wish be granted, we find that the new, small school with a certain predictability finds itself engulfed in crises—not all of them attributable to outside sources. In all these disappointments I feel us haunted by standards of excellence, a utopian dream of the perfect school, and by a framing of the school as a "something"—a something fixed and so inanimate.

As educators we are not accustomed to the idea of "schools in the making." We are not accustomed to the idea of schools as "works." Last October I sent along to my friend and colleague, Professor Emeritus Lillian Weber, the preliminary plans for the annual Prospect Fall Conference for her comments and suggestions. Those of us doing the planning had shaped the conference around the work and art of teaching. Weber wasn't altogether approving. On the phone she admonished me, "Teachers and teaching, yes! But the center has to be the child and the context that will support the child. The issue is the schools aren't *doing* it. Restructuring misses that point. Deschooling the schools—*that's* the point!"

That became the phrase around which the conference was shaped: Deschooling the schools. Deinstitutionalizing them. Starting over again, this time by visualizing the educative surround that will support the child. From this perspective, *support, caring, and the benefit of the child name the positive primary moral obligations of the teacher.* The paired negative or restraining obligation is that imposed on all the humane professions: first do no harm—or, as I like to translate it, as little harm as possible.

DESIRE AND THE EDUCATIVE SURROUND

Speaking in these terms, I am speaking in human terms. The making of schools is human work for human benefit: the protection, nurturance, and education of human young—of the rising generation. In this institute and more generally we might usefully ask, what sort of educative surround will sustain the children's possibility, their wonder, their enchantment with the world? How will they make connections with the ideas, knowledge, and lives of the time and place in which they are living and with ideas and knowledge ascribable to other times, places, and persons? From making those connections, how will they be enabled as persons, as selves, to contribute new possibilities and knowledge, novel ideas, and works?

Adrienne Rich (1993) says of poetry that it "can break open locked chambers of possibility, restore numbed zones to feeling, recharge desire" (p. xiv). Paraphrasing her words, it seems to me precisely the function and aspiration of education to *prevent* locking, numbing, and loss by keeping alive and nurturing possibility, feeling, and desire. *Desire is the operative word.* It is both a wonderful and a terrible word: to be filled with desire, to be fired by longing and passion, to seek with full intensity and power of feeling, to imagine, and to visualize the unimaginable.

Desire isn't antiseptic. It is full-bodied, not merely mental. Desire doesn't easily lend itself to specific goal setting or narrow objectives. It does, though, neighbor on aspiration and lend itself to seeking and searching. Desire fires us, puts us in motion. From desire, we reach out. Something beyond compels us. Childhood is redolent with such desires: to touch, to hold, to possess. Think of it for yourself, things you wanted, desired terribly when you were very young. For myself before the age of 5 I can remember being filled with desire for (among other things) a field of dandelions; a stack of folded, thin, dry, papery-smelling Christmas gift wrap, bright with many patterns; patent leather tap shoes (for the shine, the bow, and the steel tap); and a child-sized bright red car I could sit in and drive. By no means were all of these fulfilled but that does not dim either the fervor or the vividness of the images they inspired.

Not so starchy or forbidding as will, desire, with its animating power, may be will's wellspring, the progenitor of discipline and perseverance in the face of obstacles. Think of its power in your own life. I went back to earliest childhood. What drew you, deeply interested you as a school-age child? What in adolescence inspired you? What at any time in your life has drawn you to go beyond yourself? The fire and strength of desire points us toward the gutsier side of a child-centered education, beyond the pale, neutered language of manipulatives, learning centers, and motivation.

What kind of surround can respond to such strength and expressiveness of being, such vividness of spirit? What does the school have to be (and not be) to lend itself to the uses of full-bodied children—children with heart, will, desire, a positive and vigorous thrust toward the world and learning? In other words, children fully endowed. Children each on an equal footing with the other, each able to think, to choose, to act.

Just the phrases *to think, to choose, to act* place enormous obligation on education, on teachers. How as teachers do we make an educative surround that enables the child to be a speaker, acter, agent in her or his own life—to make informed choices on her or his own behalf? How do we make an educative context that enables each child to be on an equal footing with others, and do that in a society that proclaims but has yet to enact this kind of democratic principle?

THE SCHOOL AS A COLLECTIVE WORK

The school as a human work is also, of course, a *collective work,* involving many makers, both adults and children. A school centered around its humanness, around the teaching–learning relationship, with the person, the self, as context, begins on the human scale. And so, if I or you are clear-eyed about it, it begins in the knowledge that like all human enterprises it will be flawed, and will quite probably fall short of its most inspired hopes and dreams.

For example, if the dedication to a *collective work* (with its democratic implications) is sincere, time will have to be allowed for missteps, for changes in course or emphasis, for discussion and disagreement. Time has to be taken to circle back to respond to the persons, both children and adults, who join in after the first flush of new beginnings, who may not share the originating enthusiasms, who challenge the school's boundaries. *That can be a stretching experience.* The demands of the situation may well pull in opposing directions.

At the same time that room has to be made for newcomers, for dissidents, for challengers, care, great care, has to be taken not to lose sight of that broad vision which inspires the school, which centers it on children and the provision of an educative surround worthy of their strong human spirits. There has to be a weighing up of the rights of individuals and the hopes and the obligations and responsibilities that are understood to be primary by those deeply committed to the school's vision and aims. As I know from experience, the temptation to remove those who don't "fit" can be very strong. Casting the school's vision broadly without losing essence and substance requires intense thought and deep reflection.

And then, surrounding a school in the making there is the larger societal context, and especially the school *system* which tends to allow change or novelty only to a point: the point at which its own boundaries are threatened. So a school in the making may be a feather in the cap of an ambitious and serious-minded chancellor or superintendent, but not if there is controversy or if the school breaks too far away from the received image of "school." Quite often it is assessment and standards that trigger the alarm.

In other words, in a *collective work*, in the making of a school, always at least two things and usually many, many more than two have to happen at once: for example, both to enact and sustain a broad vision and also to make room for novelty and for newcomers. And always there are at least two arenas in which action and thought have to occur: within the school and without. Both tend to involve values that compete for attention and allegiance.

Here, I add to the questions I have already named, another layer—all as guideposts for this institute. In these complex circumstances, how do each of us and all of us together keep striking the balance between the requirements exacted by the surrounding school system and the human obligations and responsibilities of a school centered around children and families? How do we make "children at the center" an actual and enacted value and not merely agreeable rhetoric? How, in the climate of an ever expanding testing technology, do each of us and all of us together keep alive ways of inquiring and talking about children that safeguard us and them from definition in the terms of narrowly conceived assessment strategies?

TO KEEP THE SCHOOL IN THE MAKING

Holding fast to these questions and holding fast to the idea of a school as a collective work ever in the making, accepting the responsibility of continuously rethinking and reimagining, I think the most I or you or any of us can do is the best we can in the light of the prevailing circumstances. Sometimes that will mean just a few teachers working along together to create pockets of possibility for children. Sometimes, more propitiously, as is true at Machan and Sunnyslope right now, there are larger opportunities, the door is open wider than just a crack. The possibilities for children and families and teachers expand.

But whatever the circumstances, I or you or anyone can always do *something*, even when the something is limited by the narrowness of prevailing trends. And what I or you or all of us together can do, we must do. In a late paper titled "Reflections," Lillian Weber (1986/1994) sets that standard for us when she says, "We have a depression in our visualization of possibility right now and I'm saying that it's both the task and the challenge to keep alive the visions that do exist . . ." (n.p.).

With these thoughts, we turn now to the descriptive reviews of Machan and Sunnyslope—to visualize each school's possibilities, to keep alive the vision that each embodies. As everyone participating in this institute is aware, these summer reviews are understood to be trial runs to be reenacted this fall, in part or in whole, and involving the full staff at each school.

5

"What Would We Create?"

I start with us, with persons. I start with the conviction that how we see each other, the view we carry of the person, profoundly influences what we see as possible for us to make of our lives and of society. It is an influence felt both individually and collectively; it finds expression in all our political and social arrangements. It matters greatly, therefore, to whom we accord the *status* of person. I mean by that, whom do we see and *act toward* as capable? Whom do we see and *act toward* as contributing? Whom do we know to have, *as we know ourselves to have*, hopes and fears, joys and struggles? Whom do we know to have, *as we know ourselves to have*, the strong desire to have their lives mean something, the deep desire to add some measure of worth to the world?

It matters greatly whom we recognize to have, *as we know ourselves to have*, moments of pain and falling back and doubt and moments of experiencing the fulfilling satisfaction from work well done—work of benefit to ourselves and to others. It matters greatly whom we know to have, *as we know ourselves to have*, the strong desire to be part of the world; the strong desire to be *in relation to* others—to experience acceptance and love, to be valued. It matters greatly whom we recognize to have, *as we know ourselves to have*, the urgent hope that we can feed and shelter and protect and make opportunity for those we love. It matters greatly whom we know to be, *as we know ourselves to be*, vulnerable to loss and grief, vulnerable to shame and humiliation and pride, vulnerable to the extremes of our own passions, vulnerable to self-satisfaction and greed.

This is, as I understand it, what it is to be human, a person. To enjoy and suffer that status is to be complex and mingled, pervasively and continuously influenced by other lives and events, near and at a distance, in the immediacy of vivid, present feeling and in the ebbs and flows of time and memory. To enjoy and suffer what it is to be a person is neither to be reducible to the status of mere product nor to be explained, as are events in the physical world, as caused; that is, as merely the sum of the external forces impinging on our lives.

To enjoy and suffer what it is to be a person is to be active, impelled by desire, fired by the impulse to make and to do. It is to be capable of imagination, to entertain what *might* be and not only what is. It is to be transformative of experience, of ourselves, of the world. It is to be, as I phrased it on another occasion, "poets of our lives" (see Chapter 1).

The large point of what I said on that occasion, and what I am saying now, is this: That to deny the *status* of self or person to anyone, to categorize them as not having, or not being capable of having, selves, of being persons, *differs* them so fundamentally as to separate them at the root from humanness. That done, and it *has been done*, there is nothing that cannot be done *to* them—and justified by some others of us on the grounds that they are less than human. Individuals or entire populations denied the status of being persons can be, and have been, systematically enslaved, raped, murdered: denied all possibility.

What I want to say about this is that it takes vigilance, hard, recursive work, and educating ourselves in the largest sense of that word to keep alive this awareness of human complexity. It takes an active attunement to the fullness of passion in each person, to the driving desire of every person to make and to do, and to the strong, basic *need* of each person and all, to know, as Doris Lessing (1994) phrases it, "that [we] are valuable and valued" (p. 103). What I want to say is that this isn't weak stuff to be human, to be a person. It isn't in any simple sense good or bad, positive or negative stuff. It is strong stuff. In the face of such complex impulses, passions, and needs, the tendency is to look away; for me to occupy myself with my own affairs (and you with yours), to blinder our eyes to what isn't immediate to our own interests.

But it isn't affordable to do that. To fail to keep the fullness of person, of humanness, consciously and actively in view has consequences. What isn't looked at ceases to be seen. What isn't seen is easily dismissed. What is dismissed from discourse and public reference can be altogether overlooked and silenced: It doesn't matter anyhow. What has no importance, what sinks from view, can be trampled and discarded.

Any inroads on humanness must be major concerns, and especially for educators. What I am addressing is this kind of incursion—happening for a long time, moving now at an accelerated pace: a redefining of the person, the self, in narrower terms; a disallowing of dimensions of possibility; a reduction of human agency—and especially the human desire to make, to be a maker.

During this conference, we have addressed that incursion into human-ness by looking at and describing work: works made and work done. We have described drawings, constructions, and writings by children and ado-lescents. We have joined together with colleagues, to explore and describe their teaching lives. And locating ourselves in this way, we were brought face-to-face with the presence of the maker in each work. In this looking, describing and reflecting together, we made a space for the work to be, and for the maker to be.

By doing this, we raised questions to ourselves about schools and educating—questions such as these: What does the school, the educating place, have to be like for making and doing, for effortful work to happen for all children? For there to be room for the strong desires of each child to be fulfilled? For there to be opportunities for all children to contribute and to be valued? For there to be opportunity for each and every child to encounter and find in themselves and in the world, a loved medium—a medium that joins and releases, that satisfies and leads on?

I am going to place around these questions the words of two poets, each speaking to the power of the medium to release the maker in each of us. The first is the Chicano poet, Jimmy Santiago Baca (1992), speaking to the life-saving power, indeed the transforming power, of the love and discipline of a medium. He speaks of how that happened for him in words such as these:

> Writing bridged my divided life of prisoner and free man. I wrote of the emotional butchery of prisons, and of my acute gratitude for poetry. . . . I wrote to sublimate my rage. . . . I wrote to avenge the betrayals of a lifetime, to purge the bitterness of injustice. I wrote . . . to affirm breath and laughter and the abiding innocence of things. I wrote the way I wept, and danced, and made love. (p. 11)

Writing: the creator of wholeness, the wellspring, the avenger of betrayal, the sublimater of destruction and rage, the purger of bitterness, the dis-coverer of compassion, the affirmer of hope and innocence, the liberator of creative human energy.

Another poet, Adrienne Rich (1993), also testifying to the power of the medium to release the maker in us, to bring deep satisfaction, says it this way:

> What is represented as intolerable—as crushing—becomes the figure of its own transformation, through the beauty of the medium and through the artist's uncompromised love for that medium, a love as deep as the love of freedom. These loves are not in opposition. (p. 249)

THE DESIRE TO MAKE; THE LOVE OF A MEDIUM

Poets speaking. But what they speak to is neither exalted nor specialized. The desire to make, the love of a medium, the capacity to see and to say the world—these are widely human. As an educator, I attach great importance to the pervasiveness of these broad and basic needs and desires.

For this reason, I am going to expand the idea somewhat further, drawing examples from other phases of life and other circumstances. There is, for example, the contagious delight of the baby—each baby and all—who, with effort, succeeds in making a mark on a page, and is inspired by that success to make more, and still more, wherever a receptive surface is to be found.

Looking at ourselves, humans everywhere, as makers, and not merely inheritors of language, there is the invention of phrases and words and gesture that crops up as regularly as flowers in spring, generation following generation, in the slang of adolescents. In this manner, each succeeding generation remakes and claims for itself both language and world and, doing so, changes the language climate and possibilities for us all. It was by appropriating this lively, novel language, the slang of the nineteenth century, that Walt Whitman created a distinctively American poetry.

Or staying with ourselves as speakers, we can observe that same creative struggle in language that worked its way in from the margins, given birth to collectively by persons the dominant society forced into slavery. These are people who by dint of great effort broke the prevailing language mold in order to make a language that is theirs. These are persons possessed by such strong desire to make what is, what might be, and so to own that future, that, as bell hooks (1994) says, "enslaved black people took broken bits of English and made of them a counter-language" (p. 170). And so successful were they as language makers, that, as hooks also says, "they put together their words in such a way that the colonizer had to rethink the meaning of English language" (p. 170).

This strong need and desire to do the work of making is evidenced in the imprints of the human hand, voice, and mind across the globe and spanning millennia. Wherever in the world we look there is testimony to human inventiveness and imagination in the making from and making over of the natural world. Yet somehow, even though the vitality of making and its potency are everywhere and ordinarily visible, the work of making things doesn't tend to be featured in schools. In schools, the definitions of work tend to be narrower. In schools, what is recognized as success or as having value is mostly judged in other terms. That this is what tends to be the case in schools has given direction to my thinking and reading for some time now.

Recently, in a more focused way, I have been thinking over what the specific influences are that disallow attention in schools to the active agency of the person as I have been describing it—and which itself describes a common human history. In particular, I have been examining dominating contexts of value that command our attention and effectively eclipse from view that agency: the capacity to make, to do, to be transformative of experience, world, and self.

ECONOMICS AND THE DEFINITION OF WORK

The heart of this talk is the examination of one such context of value: economics and its overriding influence on our definitions of work, reality, and the person. I do this examination as one woman's attempt to understand what I see and feel to be happening and to relate that to the thinking of others; among them, authors whose works are current and which I have only recently read, and, alongside these, authors encountered many years ago but whose writings continue to speak to me. I do this describing to strengthen my own resolve, so that I don't falter or turn away from work that I know needs doing and that I know I can help to do—as all of us as educators and parents can. Doing this description of my own process, I invite your thinking and analysis—and *action*.

Guided by what I see and hear around me—what is being proposed in Congress, what is promoted in educational marketing, what I read in the newspapers and see on the television—I discover myself living my life in a society in which attitudes and policy tend to be framed in almost exclusively economic terms. In the terms, that is, of the marketplace and in the terms, therefore, of the production and exchange of goods.

The making of works as I understand and value it doesn't easily fit in that frame. In the context of the serious business of profit taking, the questions and ideas I posed as I began this talk seem trivial or frivolous. That is, if I hold very firmly to "work" and "worker" and "works" as valuable only as economic activities and as commodities, then Rich's context and Baca's in which love of the medium dominates, appear beside the point. In the economic frame, these ideas are easily dismissable as romantic ramblings that have nothing to do with the hard stuff of the marketplace, of earning a living, of being a competitive earner, of succeeding.

For example, right now in this society, making is hard to see or to value, except as the made "thing" can be ranked as high or low culture, vulgar or refined, vernacular or formal, skilled or crude, craft or art, mass produced or custom designed, and assigned a monetary value. Or, except as sometimes happens, a rating or value is assigned based on the safety or quality of the product. Or, except as commonly happens, ranks and value are assigned to the makers, defined in this case as "workers": the technician below the professional; the breadwinner (male) over the housewife (female); the laboring person under the boss; the business person over caretakers and others who work in the "human services"; and so on, over and under, under and over.

Or, except as rank is assigned and the value of work is sifted and sorted according to gender, race, and class: Men's work valued over women's work; White people's over that of persons of color; overclasses above the poor. That kind of sifting and sorting and assigning of monetary value to a product, or monetary value applied as the measure of the person, or groups of persons, describes the ordering of life in the United States. It is an order determined by a dominating economic context and hierarchy, reflected in the economic definitions of persons and their worth that follow from it. These definitions of persons are buttressed in turn by a rank ordering according to race, class, and gender.

To make, to be a maker: work too common or too familiar or too pointless or too endangering to the status quo to acknowledge or to value. At best, to be a maker is a recreation or a leisure time activity or personal preoccupation, unless it yields fame (money) or power (money) or privileged status (money)—whether that status is social, political, religious, scientific, or artistic. At worst, to be a maker is a serious threat to the established social order.

EFFORT REWARDED BY MONEY; WHAT WE ARE PAID TO DO

"Effort rewarded by money" (Williams, 1961, p. 112). This is the economists' definition of work I come upon as I reread *The Long Revolution*, written by the British scholar and democratic socialist, Raymond Williams, and published in 1961. I read it first, I think, in the mid-1970s. As I reread it now in 1995, alongside other, newer books, I am struck by how close that definition, and also Williams's critique of economics as an insufficient frame for governing and for social policy, are to those offered by a contemporary feminist sociologist, Marjorie DeVault. DeVault (1994) writing 3 decades later and from a quite other location than Williams, says in her closely reasoned volume, *Feeding the Family*, "the most prevalent assumption [about work] incorporates the economists' view that work is what a person is paid to do" (p. 238).

Effort rewarded by money. What a person is paid to do. Either version of work is recognizable from common usage. This is typical of the meaning assigned to work as it is positioned in the broad, societal picture—

not only in the marketplace but more widely. As I ponder this, I cannot help but recognize that much of what is happening or threatening to happen politically refers directly to these definitions of work and to the economists' framing of the purposes of society as driven by the production and exchange of goods. For example, the economic frame, and these definitions, play a determining role in who is seen as a worker and citizen in good standing in this society, and who is approved and certified to be a successful contender for employment.

The economic definitions play an equally determining role in what is thought to be possible to attain in terms of work and the workplace, and for whom. They establish the boundaries of what efforts are recognized as work, which are overlooked or disallowed, and mostly these boundaries are drawn in accordance with the dictates of a market-driven economy. Economic definitions determine in large measure what purposes and standards schools and education are expected to serve, and mainly these are dictated by the requirement to supply the work force to fuel the economic machine.

This economic conceptualization of reality and the definitions of work and worker that follow from it set the direction and limits for public policy. These conceptualizations and definitions figure majorly in currently proposed, debated, and enacted legislation, including Proposition 187, capping welfare, ending affirmative action—to name only a few. These conceptualizations and definitions, and the received economic order that ratifies them, color every dimension of the social and political and educational landscape in which we find ourselves, here, in the United States at the tag end of the twentieth century.

My thoughts stray in another direction. If this is so, then we are all influenced subtly or not so subtly, collectively and individually, by the narrow vision of a society whose primary purpose is to promote economic activity. I ask myself, how do I and others experience ourselves and our work in a society in which making and the process of making is not regarded as serious work, unless it is for pay? I wonder to myself, how does the failure of making as a context for valuing work, as a definition of work, translate in individual lives, in job choices and in the understanding and expectations of workplaces? Especially, I wonder, how do I and other people evaluate work that isn't only for pay?

I begin my response to these questions at a personal level. Recently a family reunion brought me back to my homeplace in rural Minnesota. For me, it was the first time in more than 40 years to be together at the same time with the cousins who were my companions growing up. As adults, some stayed; some of us scattered. Usually on my return visits I would coincide with some but not others. Among those who stayed is a cousin I have seen regularly over the years. I had not crossed paths with another cousin very dear to me since he was about 22 and I, 25. Both cousins are now retired.

The cousin who stayed is a dedicated quilter—which she refers to as a hobby although she regularly contributes work to a charitable cause and for which she sometimes receives a small commission. Catching up with the cousin I hadn't seen in so long, we reminisced about his eagle eye and passion as a child for finding and collecting fossils and arrowheads; an ability I both admired and envied. He said that his childhood dream was to be an archaeologist. He told me he didn't follow through on that dream, deciding on economics instead. He realized, he said, as he grew older and had to concern himself with employment and job security that, judged by those standards, archaeology seemed, as I recall his words, "a sort of fringey profession." He retired early, ready to liberate himself from the confines of an office job. He talked about the gardening and restoration of old furniture that added dimension to his work during the office and breadwinning years. Just recently he had taken over a lawn service business. Outdoor work. No longer tied to a desk or an office. Yet, he recognizes, as he says to me, that this will be true only if he can control the growth, else he will be back doing paperwork.

I think about the obituaries I read regularly in the local paper and first wrote about in "Poets of Our Lives" (see Chapter 1). As I observed there, these are glances into lives, offering merely a glimpse, but a glimpse that is nevertheless evocative. Looked at from this new angle, I recognize how very carefully in these life commentaries a person's employment is distinguished from what our local paper refers to as "avid pursuits." These pursuits include such activities as growing gardens, volunteering at the hospital, doing fine handwork, traveling, reading. Although every one of these involves effort, and appears to reflect exceedingly strong, sustained commitment, none of them counts as work. Effort rewarded by money. What a person is paid to do.

SICKNESS/HEALTH/WORK

When I first read Adrienne Rich's book, *What Is Found There: Notebooks on Poetry and Politics* (1993), I came across a poem quoted by Rich that leapt out at me then and, thinking now about work, returns to mind with doubled force:

> *it's like being sick all the time*, I think, coming home from work,
> *sick in that low-grade continuous way that makes you forget*
> *what it's like to feel well, we have never in our lives known*

what it is to be well. what if I were coming home, I think,
from doing work that I loved and that was for us all, what
if I looked at the houses and the air and the streets, knowing
they were in accord, not set against us, what if we knew the powers
of this country moved to provide for us and for all people—
how would that be—how would we feel and think
and what would we create? (Brodine, 1980, p. 58)

When I first encountered the poem, I learned from Rich's references that it is a stanza from a longer poem by Karen Brodine titled, "June, 78," published in her book *Illegal Assembly* (1980). Rereading the poem, and this stanza in particular, and struck afresh by the pairing of the dual imagery of sickness and health with the act of creating, I have adopted the concluding line as title for this talk.

Low-grade sickness and vague fever, a persisting physical low ebb, a condition of being that undermines vital energy, any delight in life and even the memory of health. I think to myself when I read Brodine's words, "How true. That is just how it is." I think of my eldest sister who suffered from rheumatic fever during her adolescence and how it became not possible to think of her not sleeping for extended periods of time, occasionally around the clock. I think of children I knew years later at Prospect School who, denied even minimal dental care, ran those kinds of near continuous fevers, dropping off to sleep in the book corner. Undermining fevers punctuated by periodic acute pain from rotting teeth—pain that wiped out energy to think of anything except that they wished heartily for the day when their teeth would fall out and they could get false ones.

And I think to myself that this is just how it seems to be, and has seemed to be for some time now, around work and employment and the workplace. A malaise, a low-grade illness, a downheartedness that haunts the work premises. Too many people are either underemployed or forced to work two jobs to make ends meet. Too many have employment that denies them the barest minimum of security or none at all in case of illness or hard times in the family. Too many are living too close to the margin of what will sustain life. Too many who once had job security are living in weekly anticipation of "pink slips," in dread of finding themselves discards on the economic rubbish heaps in the name of "corporate efficiency." At the same time this ruthless downsizing is happening, the higher-ranking CEOs are making 140 times more than the average worker earns—gaining the United States the dubious distinction of having the widest discrepancy in income between those at the top and those at the bottom of any industrialized nation in the world.

I think how in this society those who are poor, who don't have money, are devalued and degraded as persons. Where I grew up, "they don't have nothin'," scornfully (if ungrammatically) ranked a family categorically as "shiftless" and dismissed them from further consideration. Shiftless in a "pull yourself up by your bootstraps" brand of hubris, equaled then as it still equals, worthless. I remember a gentle, well-liked boy in high school who after a party or school event always asked to be let off not at his door but a good quarter of a mile away. I never saw his house although he came to mine often. I remember an angry, proud poor boy in high school. Smart, unbending, he was the target of every small-minded, authority-conscious adult in the high school, and conveniently dismissed as "a bad apple." The stigma of poverty. A moral flaw. "Poverty here [in Europe] is decent and honourable. In America it lays one open to continuous insult on all sides" (in Hyde, 1983, p. 277). The words are Ezra Pound's from a letter to a friend in which he is explaining the advantages of Europe for artists living hand to mouth, struggling to put bread on the table.

Whole groups of persons stigmatized in this society by the white supremacist hold on the "goods" of the society are kept at the bottom of the ladder by the prevailing economic order. For them, poverty has sharper cutting edges than for a white poet. "To be a poor man is hard, but to be a poor race in a land of dollars is the very bottom of hardships" (p. 6). The voice is, of course, that of W. E. B. Du Bois (1989/1903) speaking to America in 1903, at the turn of the twentieth century—speaking as truly to America now at its close.

Everyone in this society, but especially youth, are targeted and blitzed by images of the wealth and fame and glamour of the very few. Most of the targeted are without prospect of jobs or anything more than a gambler's longest odds of tasting the opulent fruits of this capitalist society. Too many people, but again, especially youth, are without access to ways of changing anything, of having their own lives mean something or, to quote Cornel West (1993), "a chance to believe that there is . . . a meaning to struggle" (p. 18).

Existing in this sort of life prison, numbness and destruction may seem all there is to wish for—as those children at Prospect, denied dental care, wished to rid themselves of their own teeth. Numbing "nothingness" with drugs. Numbing "no way out" with reckless, life-threatening wildness, or by falling back from life, dropping out in despair. Numbing destruction with destructiveness itself, for the rage of being locked out, hammering back with intensified rage aimed at self or others or both.

Poverty, the absence of money. Poverty, the absence of status and voice. When economics rules the purposes of society, this is an ultimate invisibility.

"WHAT WOULD WE CREATE?"

Holding these thoughts in mind, I return to the poem. I read on. In the middle the tone alters. The reflective, "I think," is joined with another inflection: That of someone, a woman, wondering aloud to herself, "what if . . . ?" and with that wondering, the "what might be" challenges the hard-edged definitions of "what is." Imagination stirs. Hope whispers. "What if," Brodine asks herself and us, "What if I were coming home . . . from doing work that I loved and was for us all?" And "what if," she continues, "I looked at the houses and the air and the streets, knowing they were in accord, not set against us . . . ?" Loved work: for me, for you, for all of us; accord, nothing set hard against us—not houses nor streets nor the air. With those words she opens up a space—a space with room for all to breath, to live, to hope. And imaginatively widening the margins of possibility still further, she dares to think, "what if we knew the powers / of this country moved to provide for us and for all people?" (p. 58).

Daring to picture to herself a healthy society, a society that moves *for*, not *against* the people, the poet asks herself, "How would that be—how would we feel and think / and what would we create?" (p. 58). As I read these wonderings and the daring dream of health, I feel with a jolt the potency of that final phrase, "what would we create?"

I play with these thoughts: What would we create if we all had *some* work that we love? I reread the poet's phrase about loved work, and write it out in my own hand, so I can trace the thought: "What if I were coming home, I think, / from doing work that I loved and that was for us all . . ." (p. 58). Tracing the words, I hear them now in a slightly other way. I hear them with the emphasis on *all*—as in *all* of us, *all* the people: "work that I loved and that was for us *all*." In this reading, I hear an undersong: Not only to have work I love and others to have work they love but to have all our work—yours, mine—contribute to and benefit all people. The ambiguity magnifies the thought, complicates it. What the poet invites us to aspire to, to wonder about, and to visualize has, as I am hearing it now, three folds, each enfolding the next: *To have work that I love; for all of us to have work we love; for all of us to have loved work that contributes to and benefits all.*

This loved work Brodine speaks of I recognize as related to a strong recurring thread in conversations with friends and colleagues, quite a few of whom have of late found their jobs unsettled and unsettling. For several, their livelihood has been, or is right now, threatened, and for others it has been necessary to lower their standards of living to match pay cuts. Striving to make jobs more than *just* employment has been a preoccupation for some.

This is what Brodine is talking about. Reflecting back on these conversations, I hear us struggling for words, searching for a vocabulary to talk about work of a kind that is loved. Work that calls and has an answering power. Work that has the power to delight, to satisfy, to lead on, to lend meaning to life and being, for us—and for all.

For many in this room teaching is that work, the medium that satisfies and frees and contributes. Just recently I have become acquainted with a new teacher in one of the schools I work in. One morning I was there quite early. So was she. I observed the hour and she replied, "I love teaching. I can't wait to get here every morning." With those words, she gave my own work a great lift. I went on to an intense, demanding meeting, buoyed by them.

The teacher's loved work and the work Brodine is speaking to are efforts for which Lewis Hyde in his intriguing book, *The Gift: Imagination and the Erotic Life of Property* (1983), reserves the word "labor" (p. 50). It is a word Hyde uses to designate work "that sets its own pace," offering as examples, "writing a poem, raising a child, developing a new calculus . . ." (p. 50). These labors are efforts Hyde says "cannot by their nature, be undertaken in the willed, time-conscious, quantitative style of the market" (p. 106). Reading Hyde's words, I hear a resonance with what anthropologist Clifford Geertz (1973) calls "deep play" (pp. 432–433). Deep play . . . loved work . . . labor, which like serious play absorbs the worker, the player into its time frame. Work in which effort and productivity can't be measured by the hour. Work that like deep play, and I would say all imaginative acts, defies quantification and calculation.

I wonder to myself: How within the prevailing economic frame, in which effort is measured by the hour or the piece, or by accrued power, perks, and privilege, do you describe that work? What is its status? What is its worth—and to whom? Within what societal contexts does this work achieve significance and importance? And: *What would happen to us all, if no one did that work?*

Making, to be a maker; indisputably, a human destiny. A destiny that does not discriminate by age or gender or race or class. A destiny that equalizes and joins us. Children make things. So do adolescents and adults of all ages, and from all ranks and walks of life. Girls and boys; men and women. Africans and Europeans and Maoris and Eskimos and Native Americans. Tools made by the worker to do work come down to us carried in glaciers from what we in the Common Era call "the Ice Age." The paintings glow fresh from the making in dark caves in southern France, works created by the hands of people dead now time out of mind. As is visible from the cave walls, from older makings, newer ones evolved.

THE WORK OF CARING FOR; WOMEN'S WORK

As the work of making fades from consciousness, I realize to myself loved work must inevitably fade with it. Without reverence for making, without caring attention to the strong desire to make, "loved work" is effectively relegated to the status of "pastime," "private preoccupation," "leisure activity," "hobby," or "recreation." From the angle of economic activity, it occupies a status below that of entertainment—which is after all in a "nonmaking" society, a society dominated by business concerns, a stellar money-maker. I am alerted by the void left by making to other absences— to other efforts not rewarded by money that are hard to see and hard to talk about and hard to justify in the prevailing economic order.

I think of women's work, sometimes referred to as "gendered work." Certainly that work is close kin to the work of making and "loved work"— but politically, socially, and educationally it also seems to me distinguishable. Marjorie DeVault, in *Feeding the Family* (1994), speaks of this work as "activity that produces the sociability and connection of group life . . . essential to . . . central cultural rituals of everyday life" (p. 228). And expressing reservation about the phrase, she also speaks of these daily life activities as "caring work" (p. 239), or as I understand it, the work of caring *for*.

Necessary work. Work that weaves together the complex fabric of family and group life. A friend told me many years ago now of a correspondence between two nineteenth-century New England women. As I recall the story, it was a correspondence conducted only during the harsh winter months. In fairer weather the women walked between their houses some many miles to visit. Except for the summer hiatus, the letters between these New England women went back and forth quite regularly. But there were occasional gaps. Following one quite extended lapse, the partner who had not responded wrote with an apology to her friend for the long silence. The reason stated with out explication was this: I have been so busy these past months keeping things from happening.

I have never *so far* repeated this story to a woman who did not immediately intuit the nature, if not the content, of the work that had been so preoccupying: working with great care and effort to keep the fabric of intimate, familial relationships from ripping apart in unmendable ways. Gendered work. Women's work. Keeping the circle from breaking. Attending to intimacy and to companionship, attending to the tastes and the aspirations of individuals, attending to the small and large comforts of life. As DeVault (1994) describes it, "the active, artful competence of women building social ties, constructing groups and maintaining and connecting them, in households, workplaces, and communities" (p. 242). In a wage-based definition of work, this is work, relational work, that mostly doesn't count.

Women's work. I recall thinking, when I first heard the story of the interrupted correspondence, of the time "stolen" to maintain these two women's relationship. I thought of my own grandmother walking not so many miles, but a fair distance, to spend time with her sister. My mother told me that my grandmother made that walk, with a ball of thread or yarn in her apron pocket so that she could tat or crochet or knit. Not to waste the time. I don't recall witnessing this "working while walking" since the grandaunt in question died when I was very young. But I have a vivid mental image of my grandmother's hands doing what I so often did see them doing: making something—a braided rug, a scarf, a throw for the back of a chair.

A third sister completed this nineteenth-century trio of immigrant women. She was the eldest, Clara, who came to America first, and then brought the others, including her mother. "Let's pick the berries while we rest," is a phrase my mother attributed to her, which might fairly be claimed as a family motto. I know I heard it from my infancy—often with a wry, disparaging laugh, yet clearly the phrase captured for the women of my family an image that resonated: the image of work without ceasing.

Gendered work. Work that needs doing. Work for which time is stolen. Work to do while we rest. Necessary work. DeVault (1994) in her book talks about human service work, in general, as falling outside the wage-based definition of work. She tells, for example, of a study of the work of nurse's aides—not nineteenth-century women, women now—who are kept so busy doing charts and graphs that they speak of having to "steal the time" to be with their patients. DeVault reports that these aides "act on a logic of 'caring for,' as well as 'tending' their patients, but they operate within an organizational scheme that recognizes only physical care" (p. 240).

Charts filled in, statistics calculated. What counts is what can be measured. The relational, the personal, to sit and talk with a sick person, to invite their ideas and concerns, fall through the net of that definition of work. Yet any of us who have been ill ourselves, or who have had the care of an ill family member, knows the incalculable value of friendly interest, of conversation. And perhaps most of all, we know the value to the patient, even if irrecoverably impaired by illness or age, of being recognized and treated as still a person—a person with wants, desires, hopes and fears, joys and sorrows. Women's work. The recognition and valuing of persons. The recognition and valuing of the very young, the aged, the impaired.

I think of teaching. The image of stolen time resonates. Time stolen from a prescribed curriculum to make room for a child's interests. Time stolen from direct instruction to make space for children's choices and for the teacher to be, as educator Lillian Weber (1991/1997c) says, "joined with them" (pp. 64–65), attentive to, and interested in what they are making and what they are learning. And I think about the time and money and effort given by teachers to make the classroom rich in media and opportunities for children.

I think about the male teachers I have known, especially at the elementary level, called on by family and others to justify their choice of a profession that pays so little, that commands so little power and recognition—that is, after all, "women's work." I think about the administrators I have known who understood their work, and especially the work of leadership, to pivot on *caring for* the social and intellectual life of the school. Administrators, that is, who steal time from the paperwork and other bureaucratic tasks they are paid to do in order to frame issues so they are talkable, in order to make collaborative work and study opportunities for teachers, in order to bring parents and others in the community into the school, in order to create *public spaces* for shared perspectives.

This is all-important work. But it would be a sad mistake, as DeVault (1994) says, not to recognize, "the pitfalls built into any too easy association of 'woman' with 'care'" (p. 243). If the work of caring for and of sociability is important work, work that has *significant social benefit*, then, as she observes, "mystifying and romanticizing [it] . . . will no longer do" (p. 242). DeVault points out that this "necessary work might be shared more widely, and better supported in our institutional lives, so that women are not expected to produce sociability at the expense of equity" (p. 241). But, as she also says, "the practical policy problems of adequately recognizing and supporting this work remain to be solved" (p. 242).

Explicating the consequences of this void, she says that if "women's contributions to social life" are to receive due recognition and status, it will be necessary to "mov[e] beyond [a] wage-based mode of thought and [to rethink] definitions of work" (p. 238). The term "work," DeVault (1994) observes, "is a label, a part of the language we use for defining reality" (p. 238). Given its definitional status for determining what is real and what is significant and valued, she says, "What is most important . . . is to see that *the concept of work itself is a powerful political tool in the construction of knowledge, both everyday and scientific*" (p. 239, italics added).

This linking of the definition of work with the definition of reality and identifying the idea of what work is (and might be) broadens the base. Speaking from that widened context, DeVault (1994) says that the questions we ask about work must change. As she phrases it, "Instead of 'What is work?' we might ask: What are the consequences of calling this activity work and not that one? Who benefits from such a definition? What kinds of questions and issues does it obscure?" (p. 239).

THE NARROWING OF SOCIAL THINKING AND POLICY

With DeVault's questions as context, and the boundaries of work expanded to include the work of making and of caring for, I find my attention turning again to the broader societal picture. How, I wonder to myself, does the narrow definition of a work as "effort for wages" figure in the welfare debate? By this definition, women on welfare, poor women, tend to be characterized as a group as "not working," as "not in the labor market or pool" and so as "noncontributing members of society," by which is really meant, the economy. In a society driven by economic pursuits, the definition of nonworker effectively renders them nonpersons, socially and politically. The vocabulary that creeps in around the edges of this debate reflects this relegation to a less than human status. That vocabulary is often righteous and scapegoating, and sometimes hate-filled and venomous. As a group, I have heard women on welfare referred to as "cheaters," "welfare queens," "freeloaders," "drains on the system," "parasites feeding on 'our' tax dollars."

Yet, these are women, as DeVault (1994) points out, who care for and raise children, keep households together, participate in neighborhood life, and involve themselves in other kinds of activities that contribute to the social quality of life. DeVault quotes a woman who holds a low-paying telephone job, which the woman herself describes as "a bitch" as preferring to do that rather than "sitting at home" (p. 188). DeVault describes another as caring for six children and working in a community group. The activities of a third woman she summarizes this way: "She keeps track of all the kids on the street in her area, serves as secretary for a neighborhood organization, and helps Spanish-speaking mothers deal with their children's problems at school" (p. 188).

DeVault is reporting from extended interviews with a small number of women. I, and many in this room, are also aware of echoing stories heard from women who are parents in the schools.

These women DeVault talked with emblemize *effort* put into all sorts of things, but mainly it is effort that falls outside the definition of "work for wages." So it doesn't "count." This is, of course, not to say that poor women should not also have access to paid employment—and access not merely to jobs that are "a bitch." But for that access to happen there would, of course, have to be parallel access to education (not merely job training) and reliable child care. And something else, too: *respect* for women, especially poor women, and *trust* in their desire to work for their own benefit and that of their children; that is, trust in their human desire to make lives. But by pointing in this direction, I do not wish to drop a veil over the work poor women do, and do, as DeVault (1994) says, with artfulness and ingenuity—and *are doing right now.* This is work from which, as DeVault points out, all of us can learn. She cites, for example, bell hooks's 1984 essay in which hooks advises middle-class women like me "to rethink" work and the hierarchical nature of the labor market, "tak[ing] as a model working-class women's diverse and creative strategies for supporting themselves and others" (quoted in DeVault, 1994, pp. 238–239n).

Reading hooks's words, I think to myself: In another sort of society, guided by other images and visions, with a multiform or broader view of its purposes, this invisible work of "diverse and creative strategies for supporting [self] and others" would have value and status and worth.

EXTENDING THE WELFARE EXAMPLE

The welfare example coincides with other examples and applies in several other directions. California's Proposition 187 also rests on premises about work and who works and who is qualified to receive the benefits associated with contributing to the economy. As noted in *The Nation* (Scheer, 1995), Governor Pete Wilson has on other occasions admitted that California has "a near permanent shortage" of workers in certain categories. Yet, the illegal immigrants who do these needed and miserably recompensed jobs are now cynically defined by him as depriving others of work and of benefiting from the economy without returning value to the society.

I think about the shrinkage of manual work in general. Sebastiao Salgado in his book *Workers* (1993) both honors manual labor and foretells the worldwide trend away from labor-intensive work in compelling photographic images. In a dedication at the beginning of the book, he writes, "This book is an homage to workers, a farewell to a world of manual labor that is slowly disappearing and a tribute to those men and women who still work as they have for centuries" (n.p.). The subtitle of Salgado's book is *An Archaeology of the Industrial Age.*

With a sharp pang of regret, I remember how I tried to "make nice" in the face of my watchmaker father's hurt, bitter feelings when, with the advent of the throwaway watch, he accurately prophesied the rapid demise of his trade.

On television, I watch South African workers protesting the opening of a Pepsi Cola bottling plant. South Africa is struggling with high unemployment. What prompts the protest of what is featured in the news clip as Pepsi's investment in the South African economy? The bottling plant is a state-of-the-art factory, requiring few workers and only those with highly specialized skills. The investment is in consumers but not in workers, not in makers.

The forced labor of a current generation of sweatshop workers in the garment industry offers still another example of the cruel twists given to the prevailing economic definition of work. This is work performed for minimal pay, under conditions of virtual slavery, that profits powerful and wealthy manufacturers and retailers—and allows the rest of us to benefit from cheaper clothing prices at the expense of their slave labor.

Slave labor. Forced toil. Backbreaking. Soul crushing. Images of whips and chain gangs and shackles. Slave labor equals work without recompense, work extorted from the worker. Slavery—the ultimate manipulation of what constitutes a self, a person: to be deprived of the power to work and to benefit, however minimally, from your labors; to be deprived of the power to act freely on your own behalf and the behalf of those you love; to be brutalized by work and kept ignorant in order to maintain the myth of subhumanness required to justify these acts of inhumanity.

"I will never do any work in this prison system as long as I am not allowed to get my G.E.D." (p. 8). These are once again the words of Jimmy Santiago Baca (1992). Strong words. Dangerous words. A gauntlet thrown down to the captain in charge of the prison reclassification panel. A refusal by Baca to cooperate in his own brutalization. The captain's response? "You'll never walk outta here alive. Oh, you'll work, put a copper penny on that, you'll work" (p. 8). Baca tells us the classification the captain handed down: He was to be sent forthwith to "deadlock maximum security in a subterranean dungeon" (p. 8).

A narrowed definition of work; a narrowed definition of education. An economic definition of reality. A political and social order that pivots on economic activity and business concerns. Where does that leave institutionalized education and the schools? I think almost precisely where Raymond Williams (1961) prophesied when he pointed out that if economics is the determining activity of a society then, "All forms of human organization . . . must be reshaped in light [of it]" (p. 105). And specifying the consequences, says that in such a society, "we speak of work as the 'labour market' and argue about education primarily in terms of the needs of 'the economy'" (p. 106).

It is a matter of observable fact that in the United States, to the degree that education is locked into an economic definition of reality, it also is locked into the rank ordering and the narrow standards associated with work defined as "effort rewarded by money." Once imprisoned by this view of "reality," it is exceedingly hard to escape the parallel standard for the school and the student of "effort rewarded by grades"—a standard that carries in its train, a host of other economically driven preoccupations: testing, tracking, gatekeeping.

All of these are practices that I further recognize to function to sustain the received economic order and hierarchy of a privileged few at the top, with denial of access to achievement the fate of hosts of others; others who are then blamed for their failure and for not fulfilling the school agenda. Blamed as they will later be blamed and held accountable for not filling a slot in the economic system and, by not being employable, not contributing as citizens.

It is equally hard so long as the economic definition of reality maintains its largely uncontested hold on what is recognized as effort and valued as work, to escape the view of children, and especially adolescent children, as commodities to be exchanged on the market. And it is also hard to think of their educations in terms other than what makes them optimally marketable, either for jobs or for further training to fit them to the economic system, even when there is serious question that the economic system can provide those jobs.

Raymond Williams (1961) says, and I see it as having special significance for the exploitation of youth:

> In the twentieth century, as perhaps never before in history, people could without loss of respect talk of "selling" themselves (an operation with archaic connections with the devil), . . . and "being in demand," even when the processes they were engaged in were not commercial in any ordinary sense. (p. 105)

Williams from his vantage point is reminded of selling one's soul to the devil. For me, what leaps to mind are the connections with being sold, as children and women sometimes are, by those who exercise power over them (usually males), into slavery or prostitution or servitude.

It is also a matter of observable fact that since the 1980s, and continuing into the 1990s, schools have been increasingly cast in a business mold, with the vocabulary of business dominating the discourse. Efficiency, cost effectiveness, downsizing, accountability, measurable outcomes are much more frequently heard in the upper reaches of the school hierarchy than talk of children or learning or teaching, except as these also are framed by the terms and assumptions of an economic order.

Right now there are severe cutbacks in funding for education. There is every reason to be believe there will be more. In many locations, class size is increasing. Societal attitudes toward children, and especially adolescents, are increasingly punitive. Cuts are most slashing and punishing attitudes most extreme in urban areas where the educational need is greatest. Especially the basic need for opportunity and the basic need for real work—not easy work, but sustaining, absorbing, *effortful work*. This is the work Brodine calls "loved work" and Hyde names "labor" or "labor of gratitude" (1983, p. 50). This is the work Baca (1990) describes in his poem "A Song of Survival" that would "define my heart with the world into one" (p. 66), that would be the long-sought opportunity to "expend my full worth" (p. 65).

We might ask: How will we sustain a wider view of work and opportunities when the work we are doing becomes so cramped by difficulty? And we might ask, how can we afford not to? And we might ask, how are we going to sustain our vision?

SUSTAINING A VISION: A COLLECTIVE WORK

Adrienne Rich (1993) asks us to "imagine a society in which strong arts programs were integral elements of a free public education" (p. 231). She asks us to "imagine a society in which, upon leaving school, any worker was eligible as part of her or his worker's benefits, to attend free arts workshops, classes, retreats, both near the workplace and at weekend or summer camps" (p. 231). Imagining with her, I reimagine great social and educational ventures in our past and some that are current, and what they have kept alive for us in vision and possibility. I recall the WPA Arts Projects . . . the English Workingmen's Colleges . . . the Freedmen's Bureau . . . Hull House . . . the Highlander Folk School . . . the Emancipation Schools . . .

Recalling these large works, I find myself reminded of words written in the first quarter of the twentieth century by the German philosopher Max Scheler in his book *The Nature of Sympathy* (1913/1973). "The moral value of a community," Scheler writes, "varies in proportion to the total resources of love at its disposal" (p. 163). Reading the book in the early 1970s, I had to read these words and the surrounding text many times to fully comprehend Scheler's meaning. What I came to understand is that in speaking of love, and love as a moral resource, Scheler is not resorting to sentiment, or mouthing romantic rhetoric. *He is speaking of love as action.* Reminded of his words now in the context of other reading and thought, I understand Scheler is speaking of love in ways similar to Lewis Hyde when he speaks of "labor of gratitude." He is speaking of love as Brodine uses it in "loved work" or as Rich and Baca use it in relation to the loved medium. He is speaking of caring for.

Speaking this language of action, labor, and caring, Scheler is speaking in language close to the phrase another writer, Elizabeth Newson

(1978), uses in relation to children's need for "unreasonable care" (quoted in Weber, 1990/1997a). He is speaking of what my husband, Lou Carini, calls "disinterested interest." That is, interest in something or someone not for one's own gain or aggrandizement but instead an interest that makes room for some other—a painting, a person, an idea—to *be* in its own right. To appreciate and even cherish that person. To recognize and even cherish the painting. To honor and even cherish the idea. But not to own it or market it or appropriate it in any way as merely a commodity or object of use (Carini, 1995). Scheler is speaking of what Lillian Weber (1990–1993/1997b) in her "call to action" paper, "Black or Multicultural Curriculum—Of Course, But What More?" describes as "work that [has] value and *is* a real contribution" (p. 135).

Scheler's conceptualization of love, Newson's of "unreasonable care," Lou Carini's of "disinterested interest," and Weber's of work that contributes, like those of Baca, Hyde, Rich, Brodine, Williams, and the many others I have drawn on, offer other standards, other criteria, other contexts than money and power brokering for evaluating the worth and value of work, the value and worth of persons, and of society itself. They offer us other conceptualizations, other vocabulary, other definitions. As their words and works build on each other's, so ours can build on theirs and on each other's.

Collectively, as parents, teachers, citizens, we can speak out in the language of these definitions, conceptualizations, and visions. Collectively, we can work to create classrooms that in turn create the conditions for effortful, loved work. Collectively, we can gather the stories of these enactments and document the classrooms that create these opportunities. Collectively, we can act and speak from these powerful premises to an enlarged vision of work, the worker, and the workplace, and of schools and education in relation to them. Collectively, we can drive a wedge in the economic wall that blocks these vitalizing visions of what society and the schools can be and do.

So I wonder to myself: What if we did chart our course by these values? What if we did do the work of inventing classrooms and workplaces for the explicit purpose of creating space for making things and for loved work? What if we did that, understanding that we are by that same action creating the conditions that make it possible to recognize the maker in every child, in every person? What if we did that with the aim of carving out the space for a community of makers? What if we did all this? Then I wonder, indeed: "What would we create?" (Brodine, 1980, p. 58).

6

"To Believe Ourselves"

A teacher in Philadelphia, a teacher of 5-year-olds, told me the children have no recess or outdoor time except about 15 minutes at lunch when they are out on a bare, but littered, asphalt yard with nothing to play with or do. They come back into the classroom to start the afternoon wild and angry.

In parts of New York City and Phoenix, class sizes for the primary grades exceed 30 children.

A celebration of children . . .

In Jefferson, Colorado, Pepsi has promised 2.1 million dollars to the athletic program in exchange for advertising at games and a monopoly on the sale of soft drinks at sports events and in the school. On national broadcasting, a coach justified the trade-off, saying, "in these times everything is commercialized."

A celebration of children . . .

I read this headline in the Metro Report of the *New York Times* of October 5, 1997, "Wall Street's Frenetic? Try Eighth Grade." The opening paragraphs picture this scene: "[A parent] is in the waiting room of a tutoring center in northern Westchester County. Her 14 year old son . . . still sweaty from soccer practice and headed for a classical guitar lesson later, is struggling through a standardized test in the next room." The article itemizes the dollar cost of this rat race: $155 to be told that [her son], an A student, is a slow test taker, which she already knows; hundreds more dollars to coach him for the entrance exam for private high schools; $30,000 a year spent to send both the son and a daughter to a private middle school; thousands spent some years back on tutoring for the daughter in spelling. And so on.

A celebration of children . . .

Children, some as young as 4 or 5, are described in the media, and I am sad to say, sometimes in schools, as "violent" and "incorrigible."

The now established trend of trying youthful offenders at ever younger ages in the courts as adults was justified initially on grounds that the crimes committed were "adult," and more recently by a claim that there is a correlation between later criminality and minor offenses committed in childhood for which the miscreant received what the media like to call, "a tap on the wrist."

Nationally, and in states such as California in obscene disproportion, more money is allocated for prisons and incarceration of young men than for educating them. Black men are particularly targeted. California's prison population has risen from 19,000 in 1977 to 150,000 in 1997.

A celebration of children . . .

Lacking an adequate tax base due to the flight of industry to the suburbs, city schools with the poorest children have the least resources. With cuts in welfare, more children than ever are living in poverty. In the richest country in the world, with some states boasting overflowing coffers, we fail to provide adequate healthcare and nutrition and funds for education for ever increasing numbers of children.

A celebration of children . . .

One hundred million antipersonnel land mines—sometimes named death seeds—planted in 60 different countries daily maim and kill children worldwide. The United States has refused to join the more than 100-nation ban on these weapons. With no hint of irony, we are told the President's decision is rock solid.

A celebration of children . . .

DRIFT

It does not give me pleasure to begin a day celebrating the decade birthday of the Art of Teaching program with these bleak words. Yet, I also couldn't leave what I have said unsaid. Particularly in the past several years it has seemed to me to be majorly important not to let harsh, destructive influences on the lives of actual children pass unspoken. The urgency I feel in this respect responds not only to the brutal realness of these influences but to the *representation* of these undeniably compounding events as isolated and unconnected with each other: a sound byte here, a news item there, contextless fragments—the litter and detrita of life in the United States in 1997.

Money allocated for prisons *does* reduce the money allocated for education. A value priority *is* being established by the increases in prison building and the decline in passage of school bond issues.

The fact that government and publicly funded social programs are out of favor and that business, unregulated profit taking, and tax reduction are "in," do connect, and *do* impact the lives of families and children.

A failure to commit as a nation, both rich and powerful, to provide equal educational resources *does* condemn poor children, urban and rural, to depressed educational opportunities and *does* continue the practice of privileging the already well-heeled.

Poverty and unequalness of educational opportunity *are* related to class, ethnicity, and race and do harden and widen divisions that perpetuated make a mockery of claimed commitments to such fundamental rights as liberty, justice, and the pursuit of happiness.

Legislative attempts to dismantle public education by privatizing it— vouchers, charters, and erosion of the separation of church and state—*do* undermine democratic commitments of long standing. In many states such legislation has already been enacted.

Cuts in welfare *do* threaten the well-being of children, especially since neither child care nor adequately paid jobs for women have been taken into account. Homelessness is a fact of life in our very wealthy society.

I deliberately chose to bring these fragments from the social and educational scene in the United States in 1997 into one frame. I did that, as I said, to call attention to their compounding effects on children, on all of us. But even as I was assembling them, I had a twinge of misgiving. The thought came to me that perhaps by framing them together, it made them seem in some way coherent, as if they reflected a social or educational policy; from my point of view, a negative policy but nevertheless a consciously chosen position. I wish I could persuade myself that such a reading is credible. An articulated position can be debated: You stand for this, I for that. We differ. We can talk about that; other people can join in.

But I have to say that reading of what I assembled doesn't strike me as credible. In fact, I rather think the opposite is closer to the mark. That is, what my grab bag of examples reflects is the *absence* of any thought out, coherent social or educational policy. According to my reading of what is happening in the society in 1997, the examples are merely the fallout from a quite other and, in this society, dominant sphere—the economic. As I see it, what the examples I presented illustrate is the manner and degree to which economic policies majorly govern *not only the economy but all other human and societal arrangements.*

This means that business is the model for all other institutions, human relationships, and social programs: hospitals and health care, schools and universities, social agencies, the family, and so on. By translating these institutions and their purposes and concerns into economic and business terms, business language and buzzwords effectively set the boundaries and largely determine the content of the social and educational discussion.

At policy and governance levels I notice the talk about schools, hospitals, and social agencies bears this out. The discussion at these levels as in business tends to be in terms of downsizing, corporate structures, privatizing and profit, cost efficiency, and what gets results. The impersonal averaged figures and objectified generalized trends and patterns that steer the business and economic machine are, with only minor modification, replicated to steer the schools. Test scores, statistical analyses, and the trends these identify—typically summarized simplistically for public consumption as "rising" or "falling," are the standards by which the educational enterprise is judged and adjusted.

Focused on generalizable patterns and averages, the economic brokers are not much concerned with individuals. It seems to me this same impersonalness also describes quite well the education brokers. As British scholar and democratic socialist Raymond Williams (1961) says of this absence of concern for individuals and real lives, "almost one feels, in such a society, that nobody lives here" (p. 111). In much of what I read and hear I am left with much the same picture of schools: *That nobody lives there.*

TWO WORLDS AND WORLDS APART

I think this perception matches rather closely what many teachers and parents feel when they hear the schools talked about in abstractions, averages, cost factors, and so on. What is said seems to bear little or no relation to their, or the children's, actual daily lives in the classroom. What I am suggesting is that it seems that way because that is in large measure the case. It is as if there are two worlds, and those two, worlds apart. One is richly flavored, full with all the sounds, smells, textures, all the personal and individual details of children living and learning together and in the company of their teachers: exciting ideas, lively discussions, things going haywire, arguments and fights, making things, making mistakes, working out problems, things falling apart, puzzlement, frustration, things reworked and put back together again, wonder and sudden leaps in understanding—"oh, I get it, I can do it—let me."

This is a highly colored world, messy and uneven, situated and influenced by everything local and circumstantial. Nothing lacks human context. Everything and everyone has a history. Nothing is transparent. Each moment is continuous with all the others. Things tend to be uncertain as to specific outcome and not, except in broad terms, altogether predictable.

In this world what matters is timing, experience, improvisation and invention, a honed sense of possibility, the teacher's confidence in her- or himself and the children, and perhaps most of all, a sense of humor. Close to the bone working knowledge has immeasurably more weight and sustaining power in this world than any amount of specialized know-how or expert knowledge.

When Anne Sullivan (quoted in Keller, 1954) writes about her decision to change her approach to teaching Helen Keller, she speaks from this stance and this kind of knowledge:

> *I have decided not to try to have regular lessons for the present. I am going to treat Helen exactly like a two year old child. It occurred to me the other day that it is absurd to require a child to come to a certain place at a certain time and recite certain lessons.* . . . The child comes into the world with the ability to learn, and he learns of himself, provided he is supplied with sufficient outward stimulus. He sees people do things, and he tries to do them. He hears people speak, and he tries to speak. *But long before he utters his first word, he understands what is said to him.* (pp. 257–258)

Sullivan says that her decision and these insights came from observing a 15-month baby in the household and that it was these observations that led her to a method for teaching Helen:

> These observations have given me a clue to the method to be followed in teaching Helen language. *I shall talk into her hand as we talk into the baby's ears.* I shall assume that she has the normal child's capacity for assimilation and imitation. *I shall use complete sentences in talking to her,* and fill out the meaning with gestures and her descriptive signs when necessity requires it; but I shall not try to keep her mind fixed on any one thing. I shall do all I can to interest and stimulate it, and wait for results. (quoted in Keller, 1954, p. 258)

In making that decision, Sullivan was going against the expert knowledge and learning theories of her day. What is illustrated in that story is what I am talking about: reliance on local circumstances and context, reliance on her own observations as grounds to rework and adjust her practice, and most of all reliance on her confidence in the ordinary capacity and desire of children (and people) to make sense of the world. Sullivan did not doubt that Helen, even though blind, deaf, and mute, had these capacities and this strong desire.

Many in this room know all about this kind of confidence in children and all about this classroom world. Many also know that it finds its most adequate representation not in reports and charts and profiles but in the form of story and in the language of the arts. Story, and art more generally, has in common with this world a reliance on specificness and vividness of detail. A story can't be told in general or in outline. Story depends on evoking the complexity of human feelings, human connections, and human variety that are the very stuff of this world. Stories spiral and loop, escaping at every turn straight lines and geometric conformations, as children and people more generally tend also to do. For example, the child surges forward in her understandings. There is a pause. A stepping back. A time of settle and sedimentation. A time when at a superficial glance nothing much seems to be happening—except that when the next arcing ahead happens, it begins from a different place, gathering up and building from the preceding surges, recombining, and sometimes transforming, the whole.

In this world, the teacher's attitude is, *and must be,* one of attending and inquiry. Attending to the child's surges of interest and understanding. Noticing the reflective pauses. Noticing puzzlement or bewilderment or frustration or doubt. Thinking to her- or himself: "Well, I have been doing it this way—is it working for the children? Who is thriving, and for whom is this not accessible? What can I learn by noticing this child or that one more particularly? What in how I have been going about things is getting in the way of the children learning? How can I make some change?" And so on.

This is an important point. I feel I can't stress it enough. *In this world, there is always room for improvement.* There is always the necessity to rethink. There is always the necessity to revisit, and from that revisiting to envision other possibilities. As with the child learning, there is a spiraling effect: an arcing toward, a touching back, a regathering, a surging ahead. This attitude of inquiry and attending with care—both carefully and caringly—is different in essence from adopting this model or that, this definition of literacy or that.

This world of daily life in classrooms and schools, with its density of detail and variety, with its necessity to constantly evaluate and adjust, slips through the net of abstractions, averages, and general trends. I want to emphasize this. Averages and patterns can't encompass this world or provide compass for mapping and negotiating it.

This is my broad-stroke sketch of the one world. What of the other? It is different as can be from what I have described. Different in its accoutrements. Different in distance from the lives of children and teachers and families. Different in its responsibilities. I will start with responsibilities. A board or a superintendent or even a principal doesn't spend the kind of time with children that parents and teachers do. That isn't wrong and it doesn't make those jobs unimportant. It does mean that those more remote from the classroom necessarily have more limited knowledge of children and the classroom, and that these limitations are worth thinking about.

About 8 or 9 years ago now I read a letter to the editor written by an experienced school board member from a town near where I live that made this point about boundaries and distinctions of responsibility well. The gist of what she said, and the occasion for her letter, was disapproval of what she saw as interference in the school program and day-to-day life of the school on the part of some of her board counterparts. Directing the school program, she said, was not part of the board's function. The main function of boards, she said, was broad oversight of the schools, fiduciary stewardship, the maintenance of the physical plant, and, with input from others, making the final decisions on hiring. She said she thought fulfilling these responsibilities was a very big and important job. These sentiments were not common then. I haven't heard anything comparable since.

Board buildings, administrative offices and suites are like banks and corporations, a world children rarely enter, although quite often board buildings and offices, and banks too, are decorated with children's artworks or photographs of children and classrooms. When children are present and featured in the board and governance world, it is usually ceremonial: graduation, awards won by individuals or teams, performances to celebrate a ground breaking or some other occasion.

These buildings aren't meant for children. This is where the *business* of the schools gets done. Their furniture is for adults. Their calendar hinges on months, quarters, and years. The pace and rhythm are cyclical and mostly predictable. There is a formality and routine. It isn't that people aren't busy but the busyness is different from the kind of busy where every minute is packed with 25 or 30 children. There are many meetings. There are reports to compile, figures to be averaged, projections to be made, and so on. Children are sometimes the subject of these reports but as aggregates or in composite profiles, not typically as individuals with names. Prescribed sequences, goals, objectives, and excellence in all things are easy to schematize from this distance—and to mandate.

Mostly it is an ahistorical world. Things come and go. Thematic curriculum or guided reading is "in"—and then, "out." Some other is substituted. In time, themes and guided reading (bearing other names, perhaps) will be "in" again. What is missing is the understanding that curriculum or how to teach reading or math or science or geography has do with *continuous* grappling, *continuous* thinking and rethinking, *continuous* evaluating and re-evaluating. What is missing is the understanding that teaching, like learning, like living, is always carrying its history with it—not in order to replicate it, but in order to reflect, look again, amend, and propel forward as much as possible what is positive and energizing.

This isn't a world like the classroom which lends itself to story. Mostly this is a world where what is *countable* is what counts. Graphs are favored. This is a world where accountability is at the center and is the priority— not people, not individual children; not the actualities of learning and teaching. Objectivity and statistical analyses tend to overweigh particularity, context, and circumstance. Trends and patterns and summarized reports with bulleted points tend to smooth out or erase this kind of individual variation. It doesn't count. It is merely anomaly, an epiphenomenon, not real in the real world of policy projection and decision making.

Of course there are also classrooms that mirror these same priorities, and sometimes in the most hierarchized, top-down districts there is extraordinary pressure on teachers to make efficiency and outcomes their only priorities. There are also classrooms that except for minor details replicate boot camps. There are boards and districts and governance officers who do choose other values and set other priorities, but it seems to me it is harder all the time for those choices to be made and sustained.

There aren't a lot of superintendents (or chancellors or state commissioners) who stand out for their breadth of social and educational vision or for far-reaching ideas of what is possible educationally or for their philosophical or intellectual leadership. It isn't that there aren't women and men who have the capacity to articulate that kind of vision or sense of possibility or coherent philosophy. It seems that just isn't what the job is *about*. Even so, there are always some. Just as there are always some board members, like the one I mentioned, who understand that there is *both reason and obligation to establish limits* on their activities and power. But once positioned at the top, at the governance level as either superintendent or board member, it is very difficult to withstand the pressures to speak in the language of that world and to think in its terms.

I suspect these pressures contribute to the rapid turnover in superintendencies. I suspect they contribute to the decline in quality and supply of candidates. As superintendents come and go quickly there is a point of view that sees some positive advantage for children, teachers, and principals. The idea is that with such rapid turnover, those on the ground floor of schools can go about their work with only minor disruption as one regime succeeds another. Yet, twice now at fairly close range, I have watched a zealous new superintendent dismantle a district. In both cases, what was so noticeable by its absence was recognition or regard for a history in the schools that was local and contextual, and any desire or perhaps developed capacity to think in those historical and human terms.

SPLIT WORLDS AND THE CONSEQUENCES OF SPLIT VISION

Once the economic order defines the society and the habit is formed of thinking only in the terms of that order, one consequence is that other and wider values of human worth and dignity and children's rights to well-being, safety, and education are overruled, and ruled out, are cast adrift. As these wider values and larger purposes drift, neglected and untended, debate tends to be not about ends but means. What education is *for* and its aims in terms of quality of life and the right of persons to some choice and some degree of freedom in exercising those choices are irrelevant to a discussion constructed in terms of efficiencies and outcomes.

If the real-world, bottom-line aim and justification of education are already established and effectively restricted to equipping and supplying well-trained soldiers to man the economic machinery, marching under the banner, "School to Work," then all that remains to be discussed is the "how": the means, the technicalities, and the technologies necessary to accomplish the task. Getting the job done, getting those scores up, whipping that school into shape, achieving those outcomes, that's what is worth talking about and what counts. In this rendering of education, grades and scores are the equivalent of money: They have purchasing power. The higher the grades and scores, the greater their exchange value in the college and job marketplace. It is this restricted context that frames the push for national standards.

This fallout, this drift has enormous human consequence and enormous educational and social consequence. To adopt a phrase of Muriel Rukeyser's (1949/1996), as "we exalt the means" (p. 43) and leave purposes and aims unattended, memory for them dims. Memory of our human possibilities. Memory of what we are and might be. Memory of ideas of ourselves that were forged only with great effort and often at the cost of terrible human struggle. Memory for the words that animate those visions. When memory dims, as Rukeyser says it:

> Less and less do we imagine ourselves and believe ourselves. We make a criterion of adjustment, which glorifies the status quo, and denies the dynamic character of our lives, denies time, possibility, and the human spirit. This impoverishment of imagination affects our society, our culture deeply. (p. 43)

I have adapted Rukeyser's phrase about belief in ourselves as title for this talk which I have named, "To Believe Ourselves."

As Rukeyser (1949/1996) suggests, the consequences of this lapse of belief in ourselves are far-reaching and complexly interrelated. For example, if the idea of the person and of the person's right to a status of worth, dignity, and freedom is eroded, so are the ideas of liberty, equality, and justice for all. This is language deeply rooted in our culture, words whose animating power is so closely braided together with conceptualizations of the person as to be inseparable. It is just this definitive point, which is so admirably made by philosopher and historian of ideas Isaiah Berlin (1969/

1988) when he derives conceptions of freedom from "views of what constitutes a self, a person" (p. 134), and advises us that when views of the person are manipulated, then "freedom can be made to mean whatever the manipulator wishes" (p. 134).

What I hear in Berlin's words and in Rukeyser's is that it is the images, the ideas, the views of the person shaping a societal or educational vision that are the only reliable starting place, compass, and anchor for shaping a societal or educational vision. If those images, and the ideas and words that give them agency, are manipulated to conform with other ends and other values, the direction and shapes of institutions central to our kind of society and the direction and shapes of the lives of very actual people are drastically altered by that manipulation. Words that once had the power to move, are no longer hearable; ideas that once deeply influenced human conduct and aspirations lose what Muriel Rukeyser (1949/ 1996) so aptly names their "obligating power" (p. 43).

Weightless, these once animating words, these once vital ideas are elevated to ceremonial status or serve a merely decorative function—in much the way that "child centered" decorates so many school mission statements across the country. They are words with a noble and pleasing ring to mouth on state occasions, and ideas to varnish the pocked surface of a vacated premise, an empty house. But, with a wink, we are told that, of course, they don't fit into the "real" world of bottom lines and growing the economy. In the "real," real world the only stars by which the nation's course can be successfully charted are the values real in that real world, and those values are primarily economic.

Berlin's essay "Two Concepts of Liberty" was published in 1969. Rukeyser's lines appeared even earlier—in the middle of this bloody century of war and economic expansionism. The evidence is compelling that time has not reversed this drift toward economics as the shaper of all our human arrangements, or restored memory of other and wider values, or remedied the absence of radical reflection.

"TO BELIEVE OURSELVES"

Why do I find it necessary to say these things, and especially to people for whom what I am saying is probably not news? Partly to gather it up in one space. Partly to force myself to face squarely the extremity of what has happened and is happening at what I perceive to be an accelerating pace. These are greatly troubled times. This is a regressive era. As I witness this falling back and speeding up, I hear some remarkable and remarkably irresponsible things being said. For example, what I think Muriel Rukeyser, that astute taker of the public pulse, would have thought not imaginable is being proclaimed without qualification, baldly, blatantly: *that the public schools and public education are failed.*

I have even heard and read this judgment couched in terms of an experiment—as if it was something we thought we would give a try, and damn, it just didn't pan out. So, consistent with the economic drift of things, the solution is to cut our losses and move on. This framing of a great and unique conceptualization and work, however imperfect and flawed in action, as a kind of technique, a piece of technological know-how, American style, is an alert not only to the assault on the schools but to a chipping away at democratic ideas and values. Aimless chipping, taps and blows struck at random, seemingly accidental and incidental, but also relentless.

But what I witness, too, is that even though besieged, those ideas, those democratic values do persist. In these pockets of energy (as I think of them), the words and the actions that give those values representation and viability remain a presence. Even now. Even with the economic order locked so firmly into place. I see that presence in grass-roots movements across the country. I see those ideas and values at work in neighborhood renewals and the creation of community garden plots. I see those ideas and values at work in social and political activist initiatives like the one that grew from the ground up in a small Vermont town with the aim of ridding the world of antipersonnel mines. I see those ideas and values at work in political activism that insists on the right of dissent. I see those ideas and values at work in the resistance to California's repeal of affirmative action. I could add to these. So could you. The list is happily a long one—just as long as the one I read when I began these remarks.

What especially fascinates and encourages me is that one place where those pockets exist, where the presence of these ideas is strong and healthy, where grass-roots energy is vibrant, is in what is proclaimed failed: public schools and public education. Fascinating and encouraging because schools harbor a long and not glorious history of conformism and buckling to authority. Schools modeled on factories. Hierarchical structures. Lockstep grading and tracking systems. It is schools that typically have provided the machinery for disenfrachisement of the oppressed, provided the definition of who is to be denied the status of being a person able to be educated, and written and enacted the exclusionary clauses to accomplish that denial. Little Rock. Separate but equal. More often than not, democratic and vitalizing ideas have come from outside the public school system or have been forced by unrelenting and massive social movements; in my lifetime, civil rights in the 1950s and 1960s.

Notwithstanding, and mostly attributable I think to just such pushes, the shaping of an education that starts from persons and is reflective of democratic values and ideas and a human order is right now in 1997 an identifiable presence in schools. Rarely the dominant presence, but present, and a much stronger presence than 30 years ago when I began to work in schools. This it seems to me is something worth exploring, worth thinking and talking about. How that presence came to be, what its roots are, and how it is describable seem important to discover. Majorly important not just in some academic sense or as an historical exercise but as a reminder of the vigilance demanded to keep these ideas and values alive in the schools—and to project forward from that history. That is surely the first priority. And from that inquiry to discover how that presence, and the ideas and values at its root, can be deepened and expanded and made both more visible and more audible. And then, how to do this when in the society and in the schools there is split vision and split allegiances: to an economic status quo and to divergent aims at equitable development of human capacity and possibility.

I have more to say about this. First, though, I find it necessary to flesh out the presence in the schools of what I named "democratic, vitalizing ideas." Here, I am adding to the picture I sketched of the classroom world. Adding to that picture, I am widening the canvas. To do this broadening out, I am drawing on my own experience in the schools now, in 1997, and in the mid-1960s when I first began in education.

The historical perspective is deliberate. I mean by asserting it to cut across the ahistorical, ever expanding present characteristic of this society in which one current event succeeds another and is interchangeable with the one preceding and the one to follow. To depend on my own experience is deliberate. It requires that I accept its limitations. Mostly, my knowledge of schools is situated in the northeast and mostly in urban schools, with some suburban districts mixed in. For the past 8 years, I also have worked quite extensively in Phoenix and its environs. In the 1960s and continuing into the 1980s I also was connected with rural schools in Vermont as well as in North Dakota.

Acknowledging these limitations, I ask as I speak from my perspective that you reflect on your own experiences. Focus especially on those times and circumstances as a student, a teacher, a parent, a citizen, a member of some local initiative that were most vital; that is, most rich with ideas and learning and possibilities, most inclusive of a spectrum of perspectives, most characterizable by doors opening—physically, mentally, and metaphorically. In other words, think of those times and circumstances when the leading, growing edge was toward inclusion, equity, and access.

1997

When I think of 1997, and look back to the mid-1960s, my immediate and most vivid impression is of the dramatically increased variety and richness of individual classrooms now compared with the 1960s. I mean this in terms of teaching practice, the way classrooms are arranged, and the kinds of materials that are available for children. It is rare these days when I am toured through a school, even one I know little about in any depth, not to spot some interesting, novel practice or a classroom that is generating its own energy in ways I would like to know more about.

Closely connected but distinguishable is the presence of teaching practice that is less isolated and significantly less rigidified by method and one-way, whole-group instruction than it was 30 or even 20 years ago. As I travel around in the northeast and in Phoenix, I see much more experimentation and greater responsiveness to individual children. If a child isn't "getting it," more teachers seem more willing, like Anne Sullivan, to set aside a method or a personal agenda and to trust themselves and the child to work out some other way for the learning to happen.

To take another example, it was startling to me to see how many schools in Phoenix were able to make multiage grouping happen once a group of teachers and parents was committed to the idea. Not all of these succeeded, some are seriously compromised, yet quite a few did flourish, and many even in the currently regressive climate are still hanging on.

From another slant there has been a virtual explosion in teacher-created collaboratives, cooperatives, and networks, and in making other kinds of connections: teachers connecting across buildings and educational levels; teachers forming alliances with parents to make something happen; teachers connecting from city to city—all of this is vastly expanded compared with the 1960s. Right here in New York City and Westchester I can think of so many that even a partial list is instructive: Hudson Valley Teachers Collaborative which has its roots in the Art of Teaching program and its meeting place here at Sarah Lawrence; the Elementary and Middle School Teachers Network; the Institute for Literacy Studies; the New York City Writing Project; the Central Park East Schools; the Lower Eastside Schools; and nearby in Mamaroneck, a parent/teacher collaborative, a practice of cross-building conferences, and by way of Mamaroneck Avenue School, connection with W. T. Machan School in Phoenix around bilingualism and the involvement of Spanish-speaking parents in the schools. What a difference from the 1960s. Teacher isolation persists but the opportunities to break that isolation are so vastly increased.

In general, there are more books in classrooms that aren't textbooks and more art and natural materials than 30 years ago. There are still workbooks and dittos but there are whole schools that rely far less, and far less heavily, on these formulaic devices than in the 1960s.

Of course, there are still rigidities and tendencies to oversystematize. There are classrooms that by implementing overzealously some idea that was in its conception liberating have ended up with a system as rigid as the one that was abandoned. The earmark of that rigidity now as then, I notice, is blame cast on children for not "doing it." The child who can't accept inventive spelling, who wants it to be right, gets read as a perfectionist or as uncooperative. The child who resists editing or strongly prefers working alone to small cooperative groups or has interests that don't fit the theme or who just "knows" the solution to the math problem and won't describe her reasoning in writing gets talked about as resistive or, worst of all, not supportive of the classroom community.

Still, broadly and positively classrooms seem to me on the whole much more open and to offer richer learning opportunities, and more access to those opportunities, than in 1965.

Taking another perspective, it is also remarkable and altogether heartening how much wider the spectrum of children included in regular classrooms is compared with 30 years ago. And again, to balance the picture, it is not so heartening to observe that more and more children tend to be referred for evaluation, with more brands of classification for labeling them—and for excluding them.

Although there are miles to go, it seems to me the dialogue among teachers and in classrooms with respect to race, ethnicity, gender, and class is somewhat stronger, somewhat more differentiated, somewhat less likely to reflect redemptionist or "doing good for" attitudes, and somewhat less likely to reduce difference or cultures to superficialities that demean or patronize. I can even name a few pioneering schools that can lay honest claim to enacting a philosophy of pluralism and committing to the vigilance and hard recursive work required to do that.

What is not being addressed, except to deplore it, is de facto racial isolation.

Just as there are some few schools enacting a pluralistic philosophy, I am aware of some examples of more democratic, less top-down schools. All of this pioneering work is tenuous and fragile but nevertheless light years it seems to me from the mid- or even late 1960s.

Along with variety and experimentation on the relatively smaller scale of schools or individual classrooms, there are some more expansive reform efforts such as the small schools movement in New York. With these, as tends to happen with reform efforts, also come new threats of division: for example, small schools split off from big schools that still serve the vast majority of children. These are splits that also may reflect a division of children: the more privileged and those not so privileged. As I know from my own personal experience, small schools or any experimental push brings its own struggles and hardships which can lead to a looking inward and some loss of sight of the larger whole. I do not say this in a spirit of critique. I say it because it is possible to learn from past mistakes and to apply that learning to decisions and choices to be made now.

There are also other seemingly more formulaic restructurings happening—sometimes, as in Philadelphia, happening when so much more is needed than the resorting of districts into clusters or forming and naming what are called "learning communities." Yet, it also is only fair to say that in two such new "clusters" of which I am aware the teacher learning communities are working and some positive, substantive change is happening from that effort.

All and all, a more complicated and vital and varied picture than in 1967. Last April, when I first did this reflecting and recollecting, I was amazed that in spite of cutbacks in funding, in spite of negative attitudes and demoralizing critique, in spite of large class sizes, teachers and parents and occasionally whole schools can sustain this kind of vitality—can, for sure, fall back, lose their bearings, seem to shut down, but also can and not expectedly resurge, pick up dropped stitches, retrieve what seemed lost, and move on to new challenges.

ROOTS

There is much here to safeguard and there is much to build upon. And there is still more. Neither the variety and richness nor the resurgences and renewals are without context and history. Teachers don't just suddenly network. That didn't just come from nowhere. The expanded teaching repertoires and opportunities for children were not dreamed up in a vacuum. The increased variety and richness I see now are the fruit of other struggles. What I am seeing in 1997 is the uneven yield born of the high aspirations and strong hope of preceding generations of teachers, of social and political activists, and of their efforts to change and to better the society and the schools.

Mostly what happened fell considerably short of these aspirations. But—and this is important—the struggles were actual, not mere utopian dreams and schemes. This means that there was difference of opinion and sometimes sharp, rending dissension. There were failures of awareness and consciousness and all manner of human blindsidedness and error. Yet these struggles also represent people working against odds to negotiate some broader vision of human capacity and possibility.

With that preamble, I am going to sketch in very broad strokes some of the major events and struggles taking shape and playing out in the decade from the mid-1960s to the mid-1970s. I do this with doubt and misgiving. Each struggle I will name, and I will name only a few, is itself a full and thorough lesson in grass-roots democracy. Each has written its own chapter (or even an entire volume) in the effort to create a human order, in the effort to make human lives the starting place, center, and anchor for the conceptualization of education and all our human arrangements. Some of these struggles were enacted in the schools; others happened in a broader social, political arena—but all of these, and many more, had strong implication for, and connection with, public education.

The most comprehensive of these struggles, the one illuminated by the broadest vision, and with the most far-reaching political, social, and educational aims, was, of course, the civil rights movement—born in the 1950s, growing in energy in the 1960s, and continuing today. Grown from the suffering and the courage of African Americans from every walk of life and precinct in the United States—ministers, sharecroppers, thinkers, domestics, teachers, laborers, jurists, scholars, factory workers, students, artists and writers, children and adults—its embrace was enormous and its energy contagious.

This is, I believe, the single most important *constructive* event of the twentieth century in the United States. This is the struggle that continues to jar and to redefine the essence and meaning of democratic ideas, values, and aims. If not for the civil rights movement, the idea of human capacity and possibility as widely distributed would be shallow in conceptualization and weak in animating power.

Another big piece of the political context was Lyndon Johnson's Great Society and the War on Poverty; as I see it, simply new growth springing from the roots of the social and arts programs of the New Deal. Opportunity Councils, Headstart, the Elementary Secondary Education Act and Title III, the Education Professions Development Act, Follow-Through—although underfunded, all these offered new options for children and adults. Prospect School and many, many others, both urban and rural, were started or reimagined as a result. To my knowledge, the Ford Foundation and Carnegie in particular, but also on a smaller scale, the Jessie Smith Noyes Foundation and the Rockefeller Brothers Fund, joined the government initiatives with grants for curriculum, for professional development for teachers, to support teacher centers, and so on. When I think of that time I feel the optimism, the sense of possibility that buoyed and inspired so many of us.

But I have to say how short a time it was before the negative influence of classist and racist attitudes and agendas, seeds sowed into these

programs from the start, were felt and felt directly. It was simply staggering to me then, and is now, how quickly the language of disadvantage,
which originally meant economic disadvantage, turned into "cultural disadvantage." A translation that persisted and re-emerged in the 1980s as
"children at risk." Along with "disadvantage" came "needy children," "children with language delay," "developmentally immature children," and so
on. All are recognizable today and all are entrenched in schools to select
out children for "special help." Most recently it is research on brain development in relation to language that fuels this discussion.

The desegregation of the schools was deeply, fatally flawed from the
start by the failure to grapple with the fact of segregated housing, white
flight, and dominating real estate interests. Busing was the weak compromise. Segregated housing and neighborhoods remain the rule. Economic
values, of course, still dominate. Equal opportunity to access and to the
goods of this society is an unfulfilled promise.

In New York City, the schools were decentralized, increasing neighborhood and local control but not without high cost. In New York City, as
in Philadelphia, teacher strikes left bitter feelings and scars that even now
simmer and throb.

At City College, Professor Lillian Weber conceptualized and enacted
Open Education and made in the process historic incursions into the way
schools are done and thought about. There was a resurgence of progressive educational philosophy. New intrepreters of that philosophy, like
Professor Weber and Dean Vito Perrone at the University of North Dakota,
struggled to create a public and inclusive base for that philosophy against
the counterpulls of elitisms engrained by its beginnings in mainly private
schools, mainly white, mainly privileged.

National Follow-Through, building from Headstart, brought in its wake
Teacher Centers. That idea spread like wildfire. Across the country, local
teacher groups came into existence. For example, in Phoenix, SMILE, created by teachers as a positive response to teacher isolation and to resist
state pressures for uniformity in teaching practice, exists today as the Center
for Establishing Dialogue.

In Philadelphia, the District 6 Advisory Center was initiated with private funding channeled through the Boston-based Education Development
Center. When that funding ceased, a group of teachers meeting during a
teacher strike made the decision to continue on a cooperative basis. That
decision evolved into the Philadelphia Teachers Learning Cooperative
which continues as a cross-school network to this day.

The Workshop Center at City College, started by Professor Weber,
opened its doors 25 years ago and continues with Hubert Dyasi as director
now. In 1972, Dean Vito Perrone convened the first meeting of the North

Dakota Study Group on Evaluation which has continued to assemble annually since that time. There are many other examples, including Prospect Center which has offered conferences and institutes since 1970, linking teachers from many parts of the country.

Headstart, National Follow-Through, and New York State's publicly funded prekindergartens opened a gate for parent involvement and in many cities created opportunities for parents to continue their own educations. For example, in Paterson, New Jersey, Director of Follow-Through at School 28, Ora Pipkin, and her associate Mary Burks made it a particular aim to enroll neighborhood parents, mostly women, in college and then to support them through to graduation so that in time they could be teachers in the local schools.

There is more, so much more. Such a full history. So many struggles. So many mistakes. So many false promises. So many tongue in cheek resolves, without the will to fulfill them. So much possibility created. So much human energy and capacity released. So much pulling back and falling short. So many contributions by so many individuals and groups to what it means to have a public education in a nation that aspires to democratic ideas and principles. So many steps taken to enact "a celebration of children."

THE WORK THAT NEEDS DOING

So much to build on and so much at stake, for the children, for all of us. This is work that is never finished, nor finishable, but it is nevertheless a work that has a foothold, an identifiable presence in the schools. A work that exists as pockets of possibility in towns and cities across the country. A work that many in this room are continuing on a daily basis in their classrooms—sometimes against all odds as the pressures of school "report cards" and other standardizing measures mount, as the discussion of national standards happens only in the terms set by these same sort of generalized trends and patterns.

A work that many in this room are continuing by *not* closing their doors or hunkering down to wait for the storm to pass but by actively seeking and connecting with every opportunity to join with others, to pool energy, to support and be supported. This takes time and it takes strong commitment especially as districts escalate committee work and make increased demand, especially on new teachers, to participate in mandated district inservice programs.

A work that many in this room are continuing by joining with colleagues to develop and articulate their knowledge of children and classrooms: by describing children and the things they make, by describing your own work as teachers, by describing classroom activities and curriculum. And by doing this careful looking and describing and evaluating, to create together the raw materials from which to tell the story of the particularized world of classrooms and children—the stories that can enact the celebration of children that is theme for this reunion.

This is a lot. The work that is always in the making, the work that needs doing, is in good hands. It is in good hands here and in many other places, some of which I have named. And yet you know and I do that more is going to be asked and required if the presence I described and the ideas and values it embodies are to be sustained and broadened. Much of what is asked, and of what I have said, can be summed up in these words: to continue to make the effort; to not give up or give in; to start with the positive history we do have and to project that history into the future with renewed commitment.

PART

Standards in the Making

There is no substitute for a sense of reality.
—Isaiah Berlin, *The Sense of Reality*

With these words, the philosopher Isaiah Berlin (1953/1997, p. 35) distinguishes a knack for seeing what *is*, a kind of sixth sense for what lies beneath the surface or is readable between the lines, from erudition in general, and scientific knowledge in particular. This sense of reality depends he says not so much on rule or method as on "powers of observation, knowledge of facts, above all experience" (p. 33). Elaborating on these capacities, Berlin adds to them the following:

> a sense of timing, sensitiveness to the needs and capacities of human beings . . . an element of improvisation, of playing by ear, of being able to size up the situation, of knowing when to leap and when to stay still. (p. 33)

And to emphasize these essential capacities, he tells us that there are "no formulae, no nostrums, no general recipes, no skill in identifying specific situations as instances of general laws [which] can be a substitute" (p. 33).

Choosing Berlin's sense of reality to introduce the two talks in this section, both of which grapple with standards, I call attention to an idea that links them. Sometimes I represent it as "what is there to work with," stressing its sufficiency for human purposes. Other times I connect a sense of reality to the requirement for close attentiveness to the particular. In the lead (and most recent) essay, "We Love the Things We Love for What They Are," I say that to achieve this level of observation, the observer has "to be in relation to" the observed as it exists in its own right. I amplify this degree and level of attachment to the observed to mean, as the title of the essay says, "to love what *is* there." In that essay in particular I devote myself to the attitudes and the kinds of idealizing standards that by elevating the gaze to abstract heights, turn me or any observer away from the patience required to see what *is*, and to see it in its full complexity. The example I offer for this order of diverting, idealized standard is the aim at perfection.

The second talk, "Valuing the Immeasurable," begins with an essay by Vaclev Havel (1992) which, like Berlin's, directs us in all human affairs to be attentive to the density, texture, and variety of events as they exist and are happening. As Havel says it, "Things must . . . be given a chance to present themselves as they are, to be perceived in their individuality" (p. A15). A main point I am making in this second essay is that to start the discussion of standards from assessment, and specifically, assessment through standardized instruments, substitutes averages and large, general trends for what is in reality immediate, compelling, and only respondable to in the particular. In connection with this, I distinguish evaluation grounded in the actualities of the child learning, which folds directly into practice, from assessment that serves only an external and regulatory function.

I argue further that the routinized, unquestioning reliance on scores to evaluate education and to set educational policy is an abdication of responsibility. I insist that this dependence on testing technology, and those expert in its applications, not only unburdens us, citizens, parents, teachers, of responsibility but relieves us as well of a voice in the making of educational policy. The result is policy set impersonally and at locations so far removed from the realities of actual children, actual classrooms, actual schools that the individuality Havel speaks for so eloquently is eclipsed.

I have so far emphasized what I am calling after Isaiah Berlin "a sense of reality." Another idea connecting these two talks, and which has equal weight, is what in the second essay I call "manyness." Here I am calling attention to the variety and diversity of humanness and to the consequent plurality of perspectives among us—culturally and also individually. In both essays, I am making the case that unless in the schools (and in the society), we learn consciously to value highly this manyness, pressures for conformity and uniformity always present, and at the moment at peak strength, cannot be resisted. Calling attention to these pressures, I also am calling attention to the chilling consequences that standardization of the schools would have for individuals, and equally for such democratic aspirations as a liberating education for all.

This part also includes besides the talks, two meditations, one on description and the other on number. In the brief meditation on description, I tell what it means to "be in relation to" and to value what is. In the longer meditation on number I explore the role it plays in a twinned human capacity for wresting from animate nature a stable world and in the same gesture conferring value on it.

The lead talk, "We Love the Things We Love for What They Are," was presented at the 1998 session of Prospect Center's Annual Fall Conference. The conference, which included a full day of reflections, recollections, and descriptive reviews, had as its overarching theme, "Discovering Human Capacity: A Place from Which to Speak; Ground on Which to Stand."

The second essay, "Valuing the Immeasurable," had its origins in a talk titled "School Change and Re-thinking the Purposes of Assessment," given in 1991 for the START program led by Marilyn Cochran-Smith and Susan Lytle at the University of Pennslyvania. Two years later when I was invited by the Philadelphia Teachers Learning Cooperative to frame a day-long conference on children's works to observe PTLC's honor of receiving the prestigious John N. Patterson Award for Excellence in Education, I took the opportunity to develop the ideas on assessment and standards introduced in the earlier talk. The talk as it appears here is the one I gave for that celebratory occasion in the spring of 1993.

The meditation "On Description" introduced seminars I held for secondary school teachers on the invitation of Professor Vito Perrone at Harvard University in the spring of 1999. The meditation "On Number" was not composed as a talk. Although never completed or circulated, I was prompted to write it in response to comments to a talk I gave at the 1987 session of the North Dakota Study Group on Evaluation. In that talk, I contested metalevel statistics and what I represented as an over-reliance on statistical analysis in general. The version presented here completes, and to an extent, updates the earlier draft.

7

"We Love the Things We Love for What They Are"

My starting place for this talk is change, and specifically the singular human capacity to change not only things but also our own *consciousness* of the world, of each other, and of ourselves. Saying this, I am saying that I and you and people everywhere can change a perspective, alter an outlook, see the circumstances in which we find ourselves from a new angle. I am saying that I, you, and humans everywhere have the capacity enacted daily to make and remake, to work and rework *whatever is there to work with.*

A day like this one devoted to describing children and their work, and the work of teaching, moves forward from this belief. Each time we join in such a description we start from the idea that something *can* change, that old habits and hindering frames of mind can be unsettled, that we can discover in ourselves the capacity to see a child or a colleague or a situation in a fresh light.

What is the extent and nature of these changes? Will they save everything, setting a life or the schools on a new and trouble-free course? Will these changes create perfect classrooms, harmonious human relationships, and smooth to silk each child's path in school and life, or our own? No. That won't happen.

Will these changes make some difference? A difference that magnifies possibility for a child and expands the boundaries of the classroom, and even the boundaries of our own perceptions in some degree? Almost certainly, yes.

Will the difference made be forever? No. That is not likely. Yet, the possibility opened up today, a change I experience in how I look at children or other adults, unlatches a door to tomorrow and the day after. What happened isn't unhappened, and can't be. There is with each liberating

145

change a new place to start from, and to touch back to. The dimensions of this kind of liberating change are not heroic or final or absolute. Yet, borrowing a phrase from my friend, Margaret (Peg) Howes, "to unfreeze what was frozen," to set something in motion, is perhaps sufficient.

Well then, if something has been set in motion, can I be assured that what is now released will move along in a fairly straight and positive direction? Can I look forward to a day when a good or successful outcome is fully achieved? No, that cannot be promised. The probability of some final outcome, of ultimate success achieved, is almost nil.

Even though the human demand for certainty as to outcomes seems not to abate, and in this era is unusually shrill and strident, it remains that the destination of things human is notoriously unpredictable. With people, as with life itself, you just never know.

RESISTANCE, ACTION, AND FALLING SHORT

Last year when I spoke in this forum, I named the talk "Regeneration," adopting that title from Pat Barker's (1991) impressive novel of what is popularly referred to as the Great War. The novel opens with a manifesto written in July 1917 by the poet Siegfried Sassoon, a much decorated hero of that war, which I read aloud, without naming at first either the war from which it originated or the author. With somewhat different purpose in mind, I am going to read it again this year. Sassoon (1930/1978) writes:

> I am making this statement as an act of wilful defiance of military authority, because I believe that the War is being deliberately prolonged by those who have the power to end it. I am a soldier, convinced that I am acting on behalf of soldiers. I believe that this War, upon which I entered as a war of defence and liberation, has now become a war of aggression and conquest. I believe that the purposes for which I and my fellow soldiers entered upon this War should have been so clearly stated as to have made it impossible to change them, and that, had this been done, the objects which actuated us would now be attainable by negotiation. I have seen and endured the suffering of the troops, and I can no longer be a party to prolong these sufferings for ends which I believe to be evil and unjust. I am not protesting against the conduct of the War, but against the political errors and insincerities for which the fighting men are being sacrificed. On behalf of those who are suffering now I make this protest against the deception which is being practised on them; also I believe that I may help to destroy the callous complacence with which the majority of those at home regard the continuance of agonies which they do not share, and which they have not sufficient imagination to realize. (p. 218)

Writing these jarring, outrageous, treasonous words, Sassoon aimed to end the war. Decorated hero or not, by writing the manifesto, Sassoon put himself at some considerable risk—certainly of imprisonment and, except for his class and connections, of execution.

Did he succeed in his aim? Did the war end? Did anything happen to dislocate the war or retard its give-no-quarter violence, or bring it to swifter conclusion? No. None of that happened. The manifesto was silenced politically almost as soon as it appeared. A fellow officer and Sassoon's friend, the poet Robert Graves, intervened and, arguing successfully that Sassoon was suffering from shell shock, had him remanded to a military psychiatric hospital. After the political storm subsided, *by his own choice*, Sassoon returned to the front, but returned unchanged in his conviction, believing as passionately as before in the truth of his declaration.

This is not a simple or transparent decision. How did Sassoon rationalize that return? On the basis of other values, values readable between the lines of his manifesto, and specifically that to return was the only protective action he could take on behalf of the men under his command, who themselves had no choice but to fight on. There is, I should add, more than a hint of suggestion that by choosing to return, Sassoon also sought death. Against all odds, Sassoon survived the war he was willing to die to stop.

What then did his manifesto accomplish? Did it matter at all or was it merely a fool's errand, an act distinguished by its utter naivete, a failed instance of a delayed adolescent rebellion? Arguably, it was all of these. As a matter of fact, the failure of Sassoon's mission is undeniable. Yet Barker (1991) writes words toward the end of her novel that cast Sassoon's action differently, more equivocally, and more thought provokingly. "It had been," she writes, "a completely honest action, and such actions are seeds carried on the wind. Nobody can tell where, or in what circumstances, they will bear fruit" (p. 249).

A war later, a young Dutch Jewish woman, a sophisticated, intellectual woman named Etty Hillesum (1983), writes in her diary, "What is at stake is our impending destruction and annihilation, we can have no more illusions about that. They are out to destroy us completely, we must accept that and go on from there" (p. 130). "Go on from there"? To where? What choices are left when barring a miracle, annihilation locks down the future, when the number of breaths left to take approaches the countable? Hillesum, like Sassoon (but oh so differently) chooses action: to speak, to witness, to be as she phrases it "the eyes and ears of a piece of Jewish history" (p. 207), and so to continue to write to the end. With that decision, with words as arrows to fate, Hillesum arcs over the collapsing boundaries of her life, and against all reason and odds dedicates her whole being to a world she will not live to see. And commits the time she has, measurable now in weeks, perhaps months, possibly as much as a year, to staring annihilation in its face, not dodging the devastation, committing it to memory (hers and ours), and to caring for those who suffer first and most when hatred and violence go unchecked, unresisted: the children, the ill, and the aged.

As Sassoon chose the front, Hillesum chooses the deportation camps. It is an act of outrageous confidence: that there will be at the end of the unspeakable horrors ears to hear those words, to join with her to value human strength and capacity in the face of human hate, in the face of nihilism and despair. By her choice Hillesum asserts that even as all that is cruel, unjust, annihilating goes unresisted, unchecked, there remains alive human kindness and caring, acts of justice and acts that are life giving, not life destroying. Rationalizing her choice, Hillesum (1983) writes in her diary: "that is why I must try to live a good and faithful life to my last breath: so that those who come after me do not have to start all over again" (p. 131).

Hillesum dies at Auschwitz November 30, 1943. Does her mission, "to go on from there," succeed? Does it fail? Can the words in any possible fashion apply? When I told her story and Sassoon's and that of a young North Vietnamese soldier, Bao Ninh (1995), last year, I said that what is at stake in each of these stories is "resistance to conclusiveness: to witness and to say, to speak to the last, to resist silencing, to understand speaking to be an action; to be memory's animater, her insistent goad: to undo the unmaking of human-ness" (Carini, 1997, p. 17). And to undo that unmaking, to *be* a maker, an enactor of that which affirms life, which insists on the possible in the face of impossibility.

It is that resistance to conclusiveness that rings in Pat Barker's (1991) words about honest actions, "[that] nobody can tell where, or in what circumstances, they will bear fruit" (p. 249). It is that resistance to conclusiveness that rings differently but as resoundingly in Hillesum's (1983) words: "so that those who come after me do not have to start all over again" (p. 131).

I add now to these stories, a story from closer to home and to school. Although I witnessed parts of this story, and some pieces of it up close, I did not live this journey. For this reason, I will merely sketch it lightly, but I do that confidently, knowing that teachers everywhere are able to tell stories of their own in fundamental ways not different from this one, and with all the rich detail of lived experience. Outlining this one story, I aim to make room for these other stories.

Mostly these stories, the one I will sketch, the one you may be holding in memory, are not on the horrific scale of cataclysm and genocide.

They have for this reason a particular merit. By their scale and their closeness to the grain of daily life, these stories affirm human capacity to do the hard, daily work of resistance, vigilance, and action on that daily scale and level. For this very reason they carry a great weight of value as testimony to the human capacity to make and remake a human world, and by doing that to resist despair and to enact hope. These are stories that generate possibility by holding ground and by enlarging it. Yet none is a "success story," in which some human struggle is resolved once and for all, putting an all-time end to injustice or other human problem. These are stories like the ones I have already told that resist conclusion.

Quite a few years ago now, at Prospect's Fall Conference, the late Bob Navarro, then a principal in Ithaca, New York, described his journey in a building, which, when he arrived, was demoralized and divided by racial strife. The history of that strife was long and bitter, the result of a district decision to merge two school communities, each of which had reasons to resent the decision, and each other. Principals came and went. Teachers transferred out. A few stayed. Starting from there, with remaining staff and bringing with him an able administrative assistant, Sandy Washington, a woman well respected in the African American community, Bob set about to remake the school, and to remake it as a school free from racism and bias in all forms. That was the vision.

Was this easy? Of course not. Was it all totally successful? Of course not. Did it change the school for the children so that their pride in going there was strong? Yes, it did. A famous story in and about the school hinges on a major breakthrough with the children. It happened through playground games initiated by Sandy Washington and her brother and classroom assistant, Todd Peterson, which brought the children from both communities together, and led in time to a championship kickball team. There is truth in that story of unifying the children through shared effort, and it took, besides terrific energy, unfaltering confidence in the kids.

Yet even so, it is the tip of the iceberg. The grueling daily story is one of unrelenting labor, of helping teachers who wanted to leave, or needed to leave, to transfer out. It is the story of reorganizing the staff and of tirelessly pushing for an equitable education for all children. It is a story of speaking out for and getting district resources, of applying for and receiving grants to establish a continuing conversation on race. It is a story of involving parents from both communities, working together to unite the school.

Did this hard work win unqualified praise? No, it didn't. Did it end racism in the city schools? Of course not. Did what happened change the conversation on race? To an extent and in some degree in locations across the district, and in the school itself, hugely. Maybe of greatest importance, it means now, and in years to come, that there is a history, that this positive thing did happen. It does mean that for a group of teachers and families and for many, many children, they were a part of making that positive thing happen. There is strength in that experience—personal strength and collective strength. There is strength in a school that has this history and holds this memory. This is not nothing. Because of this "honest action" (Barker, 1991, p. 249), there is some firm ground to stand on, so that as Hillesum (1983) says, "those who come after me do not have to start all over again" (p. 131).

REGENERATION

Telling these stories, I touch back to last year at this time and in this place and to a school story told some years ago. I touch back as well to two other stories, one enacted 80 and more years ago and the other now more than 50 years in the past, both far distant from us sitting here in both time and place. And yet, these stories different in scale, different in circumstance and time and place, touch, and touching, touch us. We know what these stories are about. We know them humanly. We can hear them—these stories of resistance, these stories taprooted to value and the crisis of values. Even the oldest of human stories of resistance, far older than any I have retold, don't lose their power to move. They live. And living they are generative. Birthing possibility, they birth the possible in us. Some people could do this. They could resist. They could hold firm. They could move forward. They could make mistakes and be mistaken; they could falter and be afraid. Just before what Hillesum (1983) calls her "acceptance," she records these words in her diary: "Mortal fear in every fibre. Complete collapse. Lack of self-confidence. Aversion. Panic" (p. 47).

Some people could do this. Yet, doing what they did, saying what they said, throwing their whole selves into their effort, didn't achieve a final solution or perfection. Things fall short. For one, desperately short; she dies, and dies with the worst of what humans have the capacity to inflict holding full reign: hate, torture, degradation, nihilism. And yet her words reach us, and as she hoped, move us. Another wishes to die—yet lives, and living does not default on his conviction. Wars continue, but the courage to resist them is helped by his rebellious words. The third commits himself to hard, recursive work and to vigilance: to doing again and yet again what has to be done, to working and reworking what is there to work with; to holding ground, to resisting the status quo, the easy out, the papering over of strife. And making that commitment, commits himself to continue when there is no end in sight, no promise of success.

No final solution. No ultimate success. Mistakes. Imperfection. Compromise. Yet these imperfect actions, these labors of love and value and conviction, are not fallen altogether away. Where then do all the flawed though honest, incomplete though hopeful acts of conscience, of resistance, of confidence in human possibility reside? These actions are, I think, the ground we stand on—the ground that grounds us. It is human ground which means ground rich in tears, in loss, in error—and in deep feeling and value.

It is the human ground that feeds our human roots, and may, if we are fortunate, in some degree safeguard us in our humanness from the temptations of god-like superiority: of loftiness; of a supreme confidence that all I and mine do is blessed and right, and all that those others do is not only wrong, but damned. It may even protect us from the false claim that I, and those I resemble, are by right of superior blood, or genes, or intellect, or morality, the rightful arbiters and judges of which ideas, which cultures, which peoples shall live, and which are dispensable. That this safeguarding is urgently and sorely needed is written in blood across human history.

Saying this, I make here a plea for the human and the human scale. Pleading for the human, I plead also for the imperfect. Faced with life, faced with circumstances not of their making, faced with bad things or that worst of evils, our own human capacity to render evil in its vilest forms, there are people who *try*. Even though unrecognized and turned aside, there are people who prove (and prove daily) to be not without resource. Time and again people discover resource in solidarity with others, and in themselves. Time and again, people are strengthened by the acts of others who in circumstances as hard or much worse, resisted and acted. Even in terrible circumstances, there are always somehow, some few among us who are not consumed by bitterness and hate, who resist becoming in one gesture the very evil they resist: the oppressed turned oppressor; the rejected turned rejecter; the persecuted turned persecutor; the terrorized turned terrorizer.

MAKING AND REMAKING WHAT IS EVER IN THE MAKING

I have been speaking to you of resistance—resistance to what I have called *the unmaking of humanness*. Speaking of resistance to the unmaking of humanness, I am speaking as well of the strong, the burning human desire to remake and regenerate that of value in humanness. Speaking of regenerative potency, I speak to humanness as plural not singular, as influenceable but not determined, as in its very nature unfinishable. I am saying that we humans, child or adult, are in motion with humanness, in motion with that which holds for us deep human value. That being in motion with value and with each other, each of us is an animater of value, and the rememberer and imaginer of humanness.

Speaking in these terms, I consciously set aside an older conceptualization of a static human nature, either good or bad, and of summable static traits or genes that define its status. I consciously set aside along with it, perfection and utopian dreams of earthly paradise. I choose another framing altogether, a framing foreshadowed in the stories I told: That humanness and human value are created and recreated in the making of them, and for that reason, are ever in the making. What is ever in the making, pluralizes. What is ever in the making, gathers energy from other lives, from other enactments of value, and energized, spirals outward from these toward new meanings and possibilities. This process of touching back and surging forward, this spiral in the making and remaking of humanness and that of value in humanness is how I understand generation and regeneration to be both continuous and novel.

Making this choice, setting aside the absolutist's frame, I make room for human choice; that is, for some degree of freedom in relation to the brute facts of existence. That people do make these choices, that in human history people quite often have resisted unchecked hatred and destructiveness, and that people do so now, seems to me infinitely provocative. Even more provocatively, each person's choices have about them that element of surprise, of novelty that in small or large degree expands what is possible for all and each of us to imagine; each enriches and alters the human repertoire. Speaking in these terms, telling the stories I have told, I am calling attention to a degree of plasticity in all human events which holds the promise of future, and not altogether foreseeable, possibility.

I am calling attention to how one act may invite and sustain the acts of others, how a social or political or educational climate can change and be changed, how a difference can be made, how a value such as respect or kindness or caring can acquire new life and animating power—and how in all these acts, small and large, humanness and human value are rebirthed. A slender opening is found in a blocked path. A closed door is set ajar. A ray of light appears. What was locked down, releases a bit. A little more breathing space is to be found. What is dormant, but alive at the root, sends out new rootlets from which spring fresh, green sprouts.

Isn't this quite close to what educating is about and for? On a daily basis, isn't it the small alterations and connections that matter? Isn't it these that stimulate the child's mind, body, and imagination, that nourish the spirit, that spark a light in a child's eyes, that affirm to that child that he or she can do it—can learn, can think, can work it out with other people, can pursue her heart's desire or his dream?

Isn't this quite close to what we were doing all day today in this conference? By giving our full attention to a child, a colleague, or a classroom, by describing and getting to know them, weren't we seeking to nurture and stimulate and affirm for each what is right now most challenging or fascinating or life promoting?

Yet, although what we did, and although what happens in classrooms between teachers and children on a daily basis is so closely matched to what we did, it isn't common for anything like this to happen in schools. It is instead altogether *uncommon* for a disciplined, regular focus on children or teaching to be a high priority in any school; although I would hasten to add, there are some. There are also teachers who meet regularly on their own time across schools to sustain this focus in their own practice. But, with these qualifications, I stay with my point: Mostly this kind of description of a child or a child's or teacher's work is resisted. And I would go further: Mostly, looking at children or teaching at all is resisted—except to diagnose, rank, score, sort, or, in some other form, assess them.

So I ask myself, with all this life, all this energy, all this growth, all this in-the-making possibility, what is it that is resisted when in schools there is resistance to looking at children or their works, or the work of teaching? What is resisted when in schools the habitual stance is to avoid looking at children and to avoid looking at teachers and teaching? What are the roots or sources of that resistance? With these questions, I turn a corner in this talk.

RESISTING CHILDREN; FEARING HUMANNESS

I start wide here—not with schools, not with children, not with teaching. I start with poetry. The poet, Muriel Rukeyser (1949/1996), in *The Life of Poetry*, writes of what she describes as resistance to poetry—to reading poetry, to making poetry a part of one's life. "What," she asks, "is the nature of this distaste?" (p. 10). She suggests that if you ask friends or perhaps yourself, you will hear these sorts of responses: One hasn't time for poetry. A second is bored by it. Another has been put off by the "dry dissection of lines" (p. 10) experienced at school. Yet another claims not to understand poetry. Poetry is "willfully obscure" (p. 10) and unnecessarily difficult, says another. Rukeyser pushes these responses further to discover a quality that links them. Using her words, "This resistance has the quality of fear, it expresses the fear of poetry" (p. 11).

Why fear? Isn't this pronouncement a shade or more melodramatic? Doesn't it claim too much for what is as easily and rightly accounted for by indifference or, as Rukeyser herself says, distaste? Aren't the reasons the fictional responders gave more to the point: boredom, lack of time or an unwillingness to *take* the time for something that is dry, difficult, and obscure? Yet Rukeyser insists on fear. She justifies her insistence on the grounds of what poetry asks of the reader, what it not only invites, but *requires*. Quoting her, "A poem invites you to feel. More than that: it invites you to respond. And better than that: *a poem invites a total response*" (p. 11, italics added).

I understand Rukeyser to mean that the fear inspired by poetry is the fear of the feelings it arouses and the root of feeling it exposes. I fear being moved—too much. I fear the totalness of the poetic requirement which can't be met by intellect alone, or by painstaking analysis. I fear being vulnerable—in that degree. I fear being wrong or foolish or overwhelmed by being *in relation to* the poem—by accepting its invitation and requirement. Perhaps behind all the other fears, I fear I may not be equal to accepting the invitation. I fear that I cannot meet the fullness of the poem adequately; that is, with an open heart, an open embrace—and make it part of my life. In short, I fear caring too much.

To paraphrase Rukeyser, the fear of caring, of strong feeling, of deep attachment—of love—is profound. By caring, by feeling deeply, by attaching, by loving, I am vulnerable. I am vulnerable through what I love. I am vulnerable to what I love. To be loved, to love is to be irrevocably and forever *in relation to*. Caring, loving make me an open door to every emotion, every feeling. Love is fearful. To resist caring, to resist love, to resist the "in relation to" fate is to wall the fortress.

So I think to myself: What is being resisted and walled out when the school resists children? Isn't it remarkably like what Rukeyser says is resisted in poetry: *the requirement of a total response? The requirement to make each child and every child a part of the school?* Isn't what is resisted a full valuing of the child not in the abstract or at arm's length, but up close? Isn't what is being resisted the requirement the child makes for a human response? Not on the condition that the child measure up to some standard or match some ideal image of excellence. Not on the condition that the child turn into someone else who fits more agreeably into the school agenda and timetable.

Isn't what is being resisted when the child is resisted, the demand the child makes for a fully human and embracing response—a response not reducible to grading the child or ranking her or assigning her to a track or some other category? Isn't what is being resisted when the child is resisted the necessity for getting to know her? To get to know her so that the school is confronted with her humanness: what she cares about, what she most desires, what gives her utmost satisfaction? To get to know her so the school is brought face to face with her actual, imperfect, and altogether remarkable capacities and possibilities, not through an abstract lens of school-approved behaviors, attitudes, and skills, but as she is?

Isn't what is being resisted by resisting the child, the child's humanizing influence on the system? Isn't what is being resisted by resisting the child the undoing of the system? So I ask: Isn't what is resisted when the system resists the child, a resistance rooted in fear?

Here is what I hear: Well, you know, there just isn't time to get to know all these children. The point is to be impersonal—strictly objective. The school's job is to get the children up to standard. The point is to raise the school's test scores. The point is to achieve the school's goals and objectives as efficiently as possible. The point is to cover the fourth- or eighth- or twelfth-grade curriculum. The point is to raise the bar. The point is getting these 5-year-olds up to speed. No more recess. No more play. The point is *not* to get to know all these children, or to care about each and every one, or to value the capacity of each, or what each has to contribute. The point is to get the job done. The point is *excellence.*

Here is what I also hear: The children are violent. The children don't care. The children are deficient. The children are language delayed. The children aren't ready for school. The parents don't take care of their children. The children are needy. The schools can't reach their goal of excellence because the children are unmotivated, rebellious, unmanageable, and the families are not supportive.

And woven in, I hear a recurring refrain in the media, from legislators, and policy makers: The children aren't achieving. The children can't read. The children can't spell. The children can't punctuate. The children can't write a complete sentence. The children don't know the multiplication tables. The children lag behind the children in other countries in math, in science. The children lack skills required by industry and business, skills needed to advance the economy.

The schools are failing. The scores are falling. The United States is losing the world cup race for top scores. Add more mandates. Add more tests. Publish the test results. Shame the schools. Shame the teachers. Shame the children. Hold the children back until they pass the tests. The teachers are failing. The teachers can't pass the teacher test; they aren't well trained. The teachers have to get better scores. Penalize the teacher education colleges if the teachers' scores don't improve. Legislate research-based methods. Legislate phonics for reading instruction. Penalize principals of schools where test scores drop.

And echoing through all I hear, I hear fear. The economic policy makers and business moguls fear loss of power and competitive edge. The moral crusaders fear the disintegration of traditional values, of falling into moral chaos. The school establishment fears public opinion, public policy makers, and public moralists. The principals and teachers and the teacher education colleges fear being "targeted" for reprisal. The parents fear that somehow their children won't measure up, won't get their share, will be denied equitable access to opportunity in school, in the society; that they will be left out or behind. The children fear failure, that they aren't good enough.

Blame abounds. There is finger pointing. Suspicion reigns. Personalized criticism and disrespect flourish. Get tough, hold their feet to the fire, push them to the wall.

Fear, unresisted, calls out the worst in all of us. Fear unresisted breeds: obsequiousness, boot-licking, groveling; contempt, meanness, rejection; covertness, cheating, diversion of blame; division, greed, narrowness; self-abasement, self-interest, self-revulsion, self-protectiveness; suspicion, hostility, hate, despair.

Fear is a hard task master. There is no ease or play, there is no openness; generosity dwindles, mutual regard declines, possibility withers, trust evaporates. *Where fear rules, freedom flies.*

Learning can be fear driven. It is possible to do that. People, including children, do learn out of fear. They learn in order to avoid punishment and pain; they learn in order to win favor or privileges or prizes. They learn in order to undercut their competitors. Too often, they learn along the way to cheat and to fawn.

Where fear rules learning, not making mistakes, not deviating from the rule, is the learner's necessary goal. The teacher's matching goal is obedience, correctness, conformity. The learner's requirement is to bow to authority; to climb the straight and narrow ladder to success. The school's aim is perfection. The unblotted copybook. The flawless performance; 1600 on the SATs and a superlative service record. Model behavior. Superexcellent. No room for also-rans.

Where fear holds the whip hand, judgment is harsh and it is swift. No second chances. No mitigating circumstances. Three strikes and you're out. No forgiveness.

Making these statements, I marry fear to perfection. It is a barren union. Fear is paralyzing to humanness; perfection narrows vision of its possibility. A perfect child? A perfect marriage? A perfect school? A perfect society? It doesn't parse.

It isn't even so much that the words are untrue as that they are so woefully inadequate: at the same time, too grand and too small; too narrow and too abstract. What is perfectible is tiny by comparison to life, to a child, to a marriage, to a school, to a society. Perfection privileges virtuosity. It privileges the solo performance. It privileges correctness. It privileges form and conformity. It privileges the stellar moment, and the brief, bright shine of success.

Privileging virtuosity, privileging correctness, privileging form, privileging the stellar moment, perfection misses humanness. It misses the effortful daily work of making and remaking. It misses the roughness of the terrain. It misses the mistakes. It misses joy and sorrow. It misses aspiration and longing. It misses desire. It misses all that is daily—the continuing on of life, of raising a family, of teaching, of educating. Missing these, it misses a lot. Perfection falls short of us humanly.

Falling short of us, the aim at perfection diverts us from humanness. It diverts us from what is there to work with—all that the child is, all that the child brings, all that the family is doing, all that the teacher is doing. It sets our sights above what *is* there, in favor of an idealized child, a model family, a star teacher, a utopian school. Perfection's loftiness makes it the easy ally of self-proclaimed superiority, of moral certitude and purity.

This is the bulwark thrown up against the child, against humanness. This is the great wall that walls the system from the child, with the child's demands for a full response, a human response. The banner it flies is excellence, its rallying cry is correctness validated by high scores, its partner is the moral crusade for purity and traditional values—which means White, Christian, absolute; which means denial of freedom; which means lockdown on diverseness and variety.

Resisting the children, resisting humanness, the system resists what might be its undoing. Resisting its undoing, the system resists also its remaking.

OTHER VALUES THAN PERFECTION; OTHER AIMS THAN PARADISE

I have taken resistance now two sides round: to resist fear, and by that resistance, to affirm human capacity and the rebirthing of human possibility; to resist humanness, and by that resistance, to open the door to fear—fear of failure, fear of inadequacy, fear of not being up to the task. Fear that masks its fear with lofty claims and aims. Aims that mask a hollowness at the center. Failed schools at one extreme, excellent schools at the other, with nothing between the depths and the pinnacle except an ever more vast and clumsy machinery of tests and "research" and mandates to hoist the unwieldy load to the heights.

This is a precarious situation. It forces people to extremes. Blanket condemnation. Personalized critique. The extreme, negative, and conclusive language leveled at schools, teachers, and children earmarks that extremeness and its lopsidedness. Precariousness requires extremes to maintain its hold, its control. Power is at stake. Careers, prestige, and money are at stake.

Precariousness, the threat of downward slide, requires ever more policy and legislative action, ever more drastic measures taken, ever more committees and commissions and task forces, ever more upending reorganizations. When the tops spin in all directions, and one reform succeeds another before the coattails of the preceding one clear the door, there is distraction. Where there is diversion, there is no time to look either closely or deeply. In a crisis of confidence, when gripped by fear, everything hinges on not looking—or you might fall.

Precariousness requires faster and faster footwork. The pressure and pace at the top are excruciating. Heads roll frequently. The tenure for superintendents, and for principals, too, shortens yearly. There are fewer and fewer candidates for these jobs.

WITH WHAT THEN DO I FACE THIS FEAR?

I face fear with the stories I have told; stories of fear resisted. Facing fear with fear resisted, I confront fear with the knowledge that resistance carries within it the seeds of rebirth. I face fear with what you and I and all of us together have been about for this day: When looking is what is most feared and most resisted, we have been about looking. We have been about looking closely, caringly, attentively at a child or a child's work or a classroom or a teacher's work. We have been about looking openly, setting aside judgment and critique. We have been about looking not to discover what is lacking or at fault or failed but all that *is* there in the child, in the child's work, in the classroom, in the teacher's work. And by opening ourselves to what *is* there, to that of value in the child, in the child's work, in the teacher's work, we give to each a full response.

Facing fear with this disciplined work of attentive, descriptive looking, I face fear with knowledge: my articulated, particularized knowlege of the child, of the work, of the teacher. Grounded in my knowledge of the child, of the work, of the teacher, the language of "failed" or "deficient" or "not up to speed" is language I can intercept and undo. This is important. I cannot intercept and undo if I doubt the ground I stand on. Fear thrives on doubt. A little niggling doubt is all that has to be there: "Well, maybe the naysayers are right. Maybe the child isn't up to speed. Maybe the work isn't up to standard." To resist fear, to interrupt fear-ridden doubt, there is no substitute for a wide-awake, attentive, examined knowledge of the child—knowledge of what is there, of where the child is heading, of the capacities the child brings with her.

Facing fear with what *is* there in the child, in the work, in the teacher's work, I face fear with the human capacity to set aside both idealization and its shadow twin, harsh critique. Exercising this capacity, I face fear with what is giving and unresistive in humanness and in myself, with what is embracing, and openhearted. I face fear with the human capacity to be fully "in relation to"—which means *to love what is there and to love it in its imperfectness, confident that although imperfect what is there is humanly sufficient.* That if I look caringly and carefully, in each child and all there is a fullness of possibility in such abundance that the only question is whether I can return a response that matches that plenitude in some adequate measure.

Facing fear with what is giving and unresistive in humanness, I am undefended. Facing fear with what is giving and unresistive to humanness, I face fear's bulwark against humanness with vulnerability—which is not to be confused with passivity or weakness of resolve.

I face fear with the confidence that with vigilance, by looking closely, attentively, lovingly, changes can be made: That fear can in some measure be tamed, that room can be made for that rebirthing which lies at the very heart of educating. Committing myself, or you committing yourself, to vigilance, committing ourselves together to attentiveness, I commit myself and you commit yourself to small things and to small changes.

Because they are small does not mean they are easy. To the contrary this path is the path of hard, recursive work, of setbacks and mistakes, and the path of courage—the courage to keep trying. And to keep trying, knowing that when all is said and done, ultimate success, a perfect resolution will almost certainly elude us.

This is not a courage born in the heat of the moment, with fire sufficient for the swift encounter. This is not a courage born of absolute certainty or shining truth. This is a courage unredeemed by promises that at the end of the struggle all that is perfect and right will triumph, and the wrong and the damned will be vanquished. This is a courage taprooted to confidence in humanness itself and in the human capacity to regenerate human possibility and hope.

It is a courage matched to its task—a courage that is and must be ever in the making; a courage that is always being learned. If I should choose to learn to resist fear, and resisting fear to place confidence in humanness, I will need you to alert me. I will need you to help me to see and to name and to do what I can in the face of fear, and most especially in the face of my own fear. I will need your confidence to sustain me, to prevent me from averting my gaze.

Perhaps you will need me because the vigil is long and lonely and you need someone to spell you, to share the load, or at least to hear the story. Perhaps your situation is one of extreme personal danger and personalized attack. Then you may need my or another's counsel to wait, to stand back, to let others more protected respond. I think here especially of teachers new to teaching, teachers untenured, young teachers fired with hope and high expectations of themselves, and the responsibility of those of us who are the elders to give this counsel.

What I and you and all of us will require of each other is practice in naming what must be resisted: seeing it for what it is, so that seeing its face, I or you or all of us together can find the courage to check its spread, to interrupt its unhindered progress. Earlier in these remarks I repeated assaultive, condemning language leveled at children, at teachers, at schools. Language that is untruthful in its extremeness and conclusiveness. Doing so, repeating these words, I run the risk of privileging them. That I did so knowing the risk is a measure of the urgency I feel that this is language I have to learn so that I can learn to intercept it. For example, I have to learn to say, and am learning to say, "I don't participate in that language—the language of failed schools, failed children, failed families, failed teachers."

I have equally to learn to name and to say unhesitatingly, and am learning to say, where I see capacity and possibility, to name what I know is working for children, for teachers, for schools, and to be alert to every opening to insert this other, and positive, language. Will my refusal to participate in assaultive language matter? Will other more qualified, life-fostering language I insert prevail? I don't think that is likely; but to some degree, by my refusal, by my insertions, the climate is changed. Faced down, extreme statements do tend to be modified. Some thawing or warming of the atmosphere does happen. The conversation does take a somewhat other course. There is more room to speak.

I can learn from you. We together can learn from others. I know how much I have learned and how much I am strengthened by Toni Morrison's (1994) assertion that "we *do* language" (p. 22), her insistence that language *is* action, and not merely a representation of action. I know how much I have been alerted by her to language that is, as she names it, "faux," "malign," "mindless," "calcified," "commodity driven" (p. 16); language that obscures, language that, as she phrases it, "is language designed for the estrangement of minorities, hiding its racist plunder in its literary cheek" (p. 16). Learning from her, I learn, too, the lesson she teaches, *that this is the language of systems, that this is language gutted of humanness, that this is language, as Morrison says, that must be "rejected, altered and exposed"* (p. 16, italics added). I take courage from her.

I gain courage and strength from friends and colleagues, who are practiced in maintaining what the naturalist Barry Lopez (1992) calls "a hard and focused anger" (p. 42). "A hard and focused anger" which, foregoing personalized critique of persons, has as its aim to impede and disrupt the unchecked, mindless churnings of the system. I have a good friend, Jane Andrias, Director of Central Park East I, who uses language I love to name these acts of resistance that insert humanness into official, impersonal routines. Jane says that when the system threatens to overshadow a child or to harm the child, she "brings the child with her" to whatever committee or official body is passing judgment and making decisions.

She brings the child by bringing the child's works and by bringing letters about the child from the child's teachers. She brings the child by bringing the child's parents with her and by strengthening the parents' advocacy for the child. By bringing the child (and the child's parents) she makes a space for humanness. By bringing the child, by bringing the child's parents, the child and the family in some degree acquire faces in the midst of facelessness, a personal and particular existence in the midst of featureless forms and generalized judgments.

Will this kind of practice, this seeking out of opportunity to insert or juxtapose humanness to the routinized churnings of the system, this vigilance in affirmation of human capacity, make any real difference? Does it really change anything? I have heard Jane say that the impact she has won't change the system. I think I know what she means when she says that. I think she means she won't stop the system's wheels from grinding, and that is likely true. I think she may mean that she won't be able to affect more than the few children in the huge New York City system for whom she has direct responsibility. That probably is also true, although since lives are lived on the scale of one, the influence she does have isn't measurable by the same yardstick as "system changing"—if it is measurable at all.

Yet undeniably she is changing something. And so are any of us anytime I or you or all of us together do this speaking out for children, for families, for humanness. I am interested in what this change is, this less-than-system-changing change.

What I think is that the child's particularized presence, the school director's particularized presence, the parent's particularized presence, your particularized presence or mine do important work: the work of troubling the bureaucratic waters, of helpfully disrupting the official agenda. Your presence, mine, the child's, the parent's puts a spanner in the well-oiled works. Our human presences and resistiveness hinder to some degree the smooth turning of the system's wheels. This is beneficial to the child and to the parent: to be visible, to be insisted upon, to be there.

This insistence on humanness that brings the child and the family into view is beneficial to a system that needs reminding that systems, all systems, cause harm to individuals, and more generally to humanness. And that unresisted and unchecked, that harm will with a certain inevitability be grievous.

This insistence on humanness is useful to all of us. Like the stories I sketched earlier, these honest, positive actions that "travel on the wind," these stories that hinge on the human capacity to try, to make small changes, establish a referent point for us all. Told and reflected on, these stories begin to compose a history. A history lives if it is heard and told. A history lives if it is told in the voices of those who are making it. A history in the making flourishes when taprooted to other histories reflective of its own values: of confidence in resistance, of confidence in humanness, of confidence in the human capacity for regeneration.

This is a century and a nation forged in war and genocide and violence. I have drawn today from that bloody history by telling stories of resistance framed by war. But there are other and more positive histories, with other and nurturing lessons to teach us. There is the history of nonviolent resistance. There is, specifically and close to home, the history of the civil rights movement. There are traditions of justice tempered by mercy, and traditions of forgiveness, which have deep roots in the African American culture. We have in these other histories and traditions, and in our own history now in the making, an enormous resource to draw upon.

As I was working on these ideas of resistance, of rebirth, of the humanly imperfect and its sufficiency, I opened my mail to discover a poem by Robert Frost (1916/1979) sent to me by my friend, Betsy Wice, dedicated teacher and member of the Philadelphia Teachers Learning Cooperative. The poem is called "Hyla Brook." It closes with a line that says with economy all that I have taken so long to say here. That line reads, "We love the things we love for what they are." I have taken the liberty to adopt that line as title for these remarks—with thanks to Frost and to Betsy. The poem in its entirety reads:

> By June our brook's run out of song and speed.
> Sought for much after that, it will be found
> Either to have gone groping underground
> (And taken with it all the Hyla breed
> That shouted in the mist a month ago,
> Like ghost of sleigh bells in a ghost of snow)—
> Or flourished and come up in jewelweed,
> Weak foliage that is blown upon and bent,
> Even against the way its water went.
> Its bed is left a faded paper sheet
> Of dead leaves stuck together by the heat—
> A brook to none but who remember long.
> This as it will be seen is other far
> Than with brooks taken otherwhere in song.
> We love the things we love for what they are.

Meditation: On Description

Describing I pause, and pausing, attend. Describing requires that I stand back and consider. Describing requires that I not rush to judgment or conclude before I have looked. Describing makes room for something to be fully present. Describing is slow, particular work. I have to set aside familiar categories for classifying or generalizing. I have to stay with the subject of my attention. I have to give it time to speak, to show itself.

I have to trust that what I am attending to makes sense; that it isn't a merely accidental or chance event. To discover the subject's coherence and how it persists in the world, I have deliberately to shift my own perspective in relation to it. I have to see and hear how it may change according to context or time. Description can't be done on a strict timetable: so much time and then the task is complete. The renowned geneticist Barbara McClintock says about observing corn plants:

> No two plants are exactly alike. They're all different, and as a consequence you have to know that difference.... I start with the seedling, and I don't want to leave it. I don't feel I really know the story if I don't watch the plant all the way along. So I know every plant in the field. I know them intimately, and I find it a great pleasure to know them. (in Keller, 1983, p. 198)

To describe teaches me that the subject of my attention always exceeds what I can see. I learn from describing a painting or a rock or a child or a river that the world is always larger than my conceptualization of it. I learn that when I see a lot, I am still seeing only a little and partially. I learn that when others join in, the description is always fuller than what I saw alone.

Describing I am *in relation to*. What I am in relation to cannot be easily or lightly dismissed. It stays. It claims me. Describing commits the described to memory. Describing is a learning by heart. When I am learning a child's artwork by heart, I pin pieces up so that my eye catches them repeatedly.

Once when I had several small paintings hanging up that way, an older boy in the school, also a painter, stopped to look at them with me. After a time, both of us looking at them, mostly in silence, he pointed out the subtle color relationships and how the layering of paint created images. He asked me who made them. I told him his sister, then only 5 or 6. He took another long, considered look, then asked, "Does she crank out many like that?"

To describe requires and instills respect. Sometimes when I am describing a drawing or a handwritten story, I trace it. Tracing it, I experience the gesture of the line and how the letters are drawn. I map in my own own hand and arm some part of the motion of the child's hand and arm. I do that when I am observing a child at work making something— a block building, a clay sculpture, a quilt. As I watch I map the child's posture onto my own body. Later, as I transcribe what I have seen, I reenact the gestures, seeking for words sufficiently apt to translate them, words that do not flatten meaning and intensity, but call them forth.

Describing describing, I am describing a creative act familiar to every artist, familiar to every child, familiar to anyone who immerses in a something which recurrently is the sole subject of attention. Describing describing, I am describing a discovering anew that refreshes and animates. I understand this enlivening of meaning to be what Ernest Schachtel (1959) means when he writes in *Metamorphosis*:

> In such perception the glance dwells on the frontiers of human experience . . . revealing hitherto unknown vistas. It has been compared with the child's glance when it is said that the artist and the wise man resemble a child. The resemblance consists in the freshness, spontaneity, interest, and openness with which the object is approached and reacted to. (p. 240)

To describe is to value.

8

Valuing the Immeasurable

I begin with a personal story, or more accurately, an image I experienced as an 11-year-old. It was a sort of waking dream but so vivid that, now, 50 years later, it remains. And remains lively. After a period of dormancy, the image, when it reappears, is immediately recognizable. Yet, with passing years and accumulated experiences, it has proved fertile with meanings, transformative of itself, changing. So I wouldn't call it engraved. A part of me, yes, but unlike an etching, still active, still ambiguous, still working on me, still surprising.

The image has a geographic landscape and a location in time: A dull end of winter day, a March Minnesota day, a bleak late afternoon sky, on the ground the last rags of dirty snow, all viewed from the second to the last seat, in the row next to the windows, in the sixth-grade classroom. Coloring the geography is a mingling of history, both world and inner: 1944, a mid-war day, an imagination filled and fired by war news, told in radio voices—Heatter, Murrow—and dramatized in newsreels and the photography of war correspondents. Sometimes in the company of my grandfather, sometimes alone, mapping that war—both theaters, as we called them—was a regular after-school occupation: the names of places and persons, the boundaries of countries, the locations of battles and bombings and raids. I was inspired by the resistance movements in France, in Greece, and especially the horseback-riding Yugoslav guerillas, among them women.

But it was children, homeless and displaced, wandering children, bombed out children, lost and fleeing children that most drew my eye and mind. I searched them out in the newsreels, the newspapers, and magazines. Absorbing myself in snatches of story, I sometimes played at being one of those children; as I recall it, usually emphasizing in that play the mythic theme of the lost child—managing on my own without adult assistance, figuring out clever escapes and hiding places, surpassing myself with ingenuity. Sometimes, my night dreams continued the drama or a child more hauntingly visited me there.

That day it was different. The children came in the daytime. From horizon to horizon they filled the Minnesota prairie: silent, row upon row, the heads of children, some with faces, some eyeless skulls, from everywhere and now, nowhere. I understood them in the instant to be all the 11-year-olds in the world. I was stunned by their sameness to me and the vastness of the difference. I lived, yet so many of them, while still children like me, had died. So many others were uprooted from their homes.

But it was their sheer numbers, their volume that awed me, rendered me speechless: *There were so many.* My own smallness, my insignificance among so many 11-year-olds was overwhelming. It was both frightening and expanding. I felt swallowed up and also liberated—torn from my cocoon. I was one among the many, a part of that multitude, joined to them whether I wanted to be or not, and also alone. In the original meaning of the word, it was awe-ful, silencing, a sudden and immediate experience of the world as big and real—not a theater or a drama, not my oyster.

Before I told this story, I said that like yeast it continues to work in me, is still potent. Rather recently, and in the context of my life in schools, the image has returned, this time with the message of what for now I will call "manyness." And I will return to that message. But first I want to connect what I have just told you from my own life with what I understand to be true for all of us people, children and adults alike.

What the waking dream emblemizes is an interior perspective, a selective, choosing eye brought to bear on life and experience. The dream arrows to a human space so ordinary, so much a part of being human as to be almost overlookable. In that space, in that inner dimension, we—you and I and all other people—are *active* as witnesses to our own actions, to the world events surrounding our lives, to the lives of others. Witnessing, we are also animaters, evaluators, and transformers of our experience. As inwardly active agents in our own lives, we are makers of meaning, reworkers of life, and interpreters of world events. As I understand it, from childhood we are inwardly full, not empty, not receptacles, but energetic acters on life.

Through the image and the surrounding times and landscape of its occurrence, if you will, the *story* of the waking dream, I have invited you into a location not your own, but unless I am much mistaken, a location knowable and understandable to you. However distant generationally that story is or quaint in its details, the feelings, the values, the experience of that dream are broadly human: to be moved by loss of home and family; to imagine oneself in those circumstances; to find excitement in dramatizing those losses and so saving oneself; to awaken abruptly to the largeness of a world one has never known; to feel oneself joined in the fate of others.

These are common and deep human experiences. My perspective, my valuing, selective eye, is, of course, very much my own. Another child of my own generation in that same midwestern family and town might have selected, animated, and transformed those same world events otherwise, or given value to, and so remembered, altogether other events. Yet that perspective so peculiarly my own has also a public dimension. As the multitude of 11-year-olds fated by World War II were imaginatively within my ken, knowable, so my 11-year-old self and my story of that experience are imaginable and knowable by others.

Through dreams, through story, through poetry, through music, through dance, through art, through cooking, through the building of houses and making of homes—in short, through our *works*—we are, as I understand it, expressively accessible to each other. Indeed, it is through each other and each other's works, that we leap beyond the confines of our own time, place, culture, self and are expanded imaginatively, spiritually—exponentially. *This is important about us: that we have selves, that we are active in the pursuit of meaning and value, that in that pursuit we are each uniquely situated, yet understandable to each other.* The recognition of that self in others is, for me, the cornerstone of educating, and is what distinguishes educating from training and schooling.

MANYNESS

In the *New York Times* for March 1, 1992, a boxed sentence on the Op-Ed page caught my eye:

We must try harder to understand than to explain. (p. A15)

It was a key sentence in an excerpt from an essay titled "The End of the Modern Era" by Vaclev Havel, who at that time was still President of Czechoslovakia. In the essay, he was talking about the complexities of a world changing and churning with ferment, uncertain as to its future shape and direction, unbalanced by the break-up of the nation states, and fragmented further by the re-emergence of ancient enmities, long suppressed. It is in that context that this time the visual image of those long ago World War II children flashed across my mind's eye, and with them, contemporary children: Bosnian children, Armenian children, Kurdish children, Somalian children. And alongside them, children here in the United States, without shelter or living in conditions of danger, who exist daily with the threat of sudden death through violent acts or tenement fires, or more slowly through starvation of the spirit.

Although on a smaller scale, the circumstances of our schools are not less complex than those surrounding the larger world. Reflecting as schools do the tension points of our societal arrangements, we discover ourselves at the turn of the century strained by divisions of class and race and overwhelmed as I was in the waking dream by our own manyness, and not only in terms of number.

Manyness. A lot. More than can be taken in. Teeming. Teeming humanity. There are too many of us. Too many to fit in. How many can we take in? Can we stretch further? Close the door. Someone has to go. There isn't enough to go around. Manyness. Scarcity. Who has to go? Those others. The strangers.

Manyness, variety, too much demand. Distress and a sense of futility mingles with fear, frustration, and anger. There is perhaps the inclination to distance ourselves, to make some space, to detach or disengage. Especially when resources of money, supplies, and that most precious of all late-twentieth-century commodities, time, are limited, we may seek efficiencies and economies. There is economy, for example, in categorizing people, in lumping them together. If each person doesn't have to be looked at, thought about, cared for, if we don't have to get to know each one, time is saved. The individuals effectively cease to exist except as "cases" or exemplars of a "class." That is, they no longer exist except as a fragment of a featureless, generalized mass.

An example: "Those children" is a phrase my ear picks up quite frequently in schools. It is a kind of working category. It points to, but does not specify, difference or variety that is not acceptable. "Those children" are the children who distance us, who stretch our boundaries, who are hard to include. "Those children" may be children who steal or hit or have tantrums; or who speak a language other than English; or who don't easily learn to read in the time frame allotted by schools or by the accustomed method; or who are black or brown or bronze; or who are 9 or 10 but as newly arrived immigrants have never been to school before. The designation casts them into a negative space: They are not us or ours. They threaten "our" standards as teachers, as parents, as a school, as a nation. By lumping them together, we are sorting them out: They don't fit into our picture of school, teaching, and learning. "Our" solidarity as a community is affirmed at the expense of their individuality.

Accordingly, the picture is simplified. The complexities of variety, individuality, similarity, and diversity carried in the train of manyness are reduced. Feelings of anger and frustration are soothed. And, with giant strides we advance toward uniformity and its near neighbors, conformity and standardization. In that neighborhood also resides the promise of certainty. It was in the name of efficiency and homogeneity that the public schools were graded, lumping together children of the same age, and by the device of grade level, of the same achievement or ability.

Yet although we yank them out by the roots, like sturdy weeds, *variety and diversity* crop up to defile the manicured lawn of the classroom. And so stiffer measures are required: tracking, ability grouping, transition grades, retention, resource rooms are instituted, all with the aim of narrowing, simplifying, homogenizing. In the aim at uniformity and certainty, children who don't learn according to plan or who don't fit the picture are given "the gift of time" or "special services" to meet their "individual needs." Elaborate measures and intricate bureaucratic machinations are required to simplify the school's delivery of its services.

And in the classroom? As it turns out, no matter how many barriers are erected, each child who comes through the door brings along his or her individuality and so inevitably makes some contribution, welcome or unwelcome, to the variety and the diversity of the class. It is common lore in schools that if a particularly unruly child, one who doesn't fit the picture or doesn't learn according to plan, leaves or is removed, another child will with promptness come forward to fill those shoes. *As variety is minimized, smaller differences stand out and assume importance.* I have been told of a high school that tracks each class 1*a* through 1*h*. I know of many public elementary schools that strongly prefer no summer-birthday 5-year-olds and resort to screening tests to ensure the right level of maturity among the entering kindergarteners. The circle grows ever tighter. Doors close. Barriers grow higher. And still there is complexity, still there is variety, still there are differences.

Many. Manyness. Variety. We are many and different. No two of us are the same. Each unique, each human. Each with a claim to life. To liberty? To justice? To happiness? Who is entitled, who is not? Who decides? Can room be made for the many? In their variety? In their diversity? In their complexity? Is the public space of the school commodious enough to embrace them all?

Can the circle be expanded? Are there enough doors in? Can the paths to learning be multiplied? Is it possible for us as educators and as citizens to rethink and reapportion our resources? Can we reorder the values that guide our educational actions? If we can't, what is stopping us?

AFFIRMING PLURALISM

In the context of the essay, Havel (1992) means that to do the work of understanding we must as people, as humans, create *radically different ways of looking at the world and ourselves.* He cautions specifically against placing trust merely in new technologies and aspiring to final, ultimate, universal solutions. He suggests instead attention to particularities, to local conditions, and most especially to the development of those dimensions of our humanness which he believes to be most worthy of our humanity—if, I might add, not always the most noticeable: among them, "an elementary sense of justice, the ability to see things as others do, a sense of transcendental responsibility, archetypal wisdom, . . . courage, [and] compassion" (p. A15). In other words, he appeals to my and your recognition of those sorts of feelings, values, and themes through which human existence may be reimaginable and transformable.

Havel says that in order to understand, "Things must be given a chance to present themselves as they are, to be perceived in their individuality" (p. A15). Specifying "things" to be people and children, I am going to repeat Havel's assertion: "[People, including children] must be given a chance to present themselves as they are, to be perceived in their individuality." And continuing:

> We must see the pluralism of the world [and of people] and not bind [them] by seeking common denominators or reducing everything to a single common equation. . . . The way forward is not in the mere construction of universal systemic solutions to be applied to reality [or to children or learning or schools] from the outside; it is also in seeking to get to the heart of reality through personal experience. (p. A15)

Or, to return to language I used earlier, to seek the heart of reality by way of each other's inner location, made enterable through story and through works—works of the hand and works of the mind. He goes on to say that such an approach promotes "an atmosphere of tolerant solidarity and unity in diversity" (p. A15), a unity based on "mutual respect, genuine pluralism and parallelism" (p. A15). He concludes these ideas by asserting that what is required of us is the rehabilitation of "human uniqueness, human action and the human spirit" (p. A15). Or, what I have been calling inner agency, a self active in the making of meaning, knowledge, and values.

So what is stopping me and you and all of us together from turning our attention fully to that refreshing and interesting task? Havel (1992) suggests that what is stopping us is not *only* scarcity and limitations of resource but a profound and far-reaching belief. It is a belief with roots stretching back in the West at least 3 centuries in a world detached from human spirit: An objective world, a technologically controllable world, a world which, like a giant puzzle, is solvable. Havel further suggests that we are hindered from the radical rethinking which is required of us for the reason that our attention is not on human agency. Instead, he says, "we treat the fatal consequences of technology as though they were a technical defect that could be remedied by technology alone. We are looking for an objective way out of the crisis of objectivism" (p. A15).

What I understand, following on these thoughts, is that what stops us as educators and as citizens in making radical changes that would allow us to educate the *many*, in all our human variety and diversity, is a view of humanness that is lacking and seriously out of balance. What is lost and found missing in the translation of humanness into object and commodity terms is the *inner dimension* which in the context of the story told earlier I called by these names: *self, witness, interior perspective, animating spirit, maker of works and meaning, transformer of experience, active agent.*

Until as educators and citizens we make room and time and educational arrangements that allow us to recognize, value, and draw forth this dimension of the children we educate, we will continue to be overwhelmed by their variety and diversity. We will continue to resort to categorizing them in order to reduce the complexity of the task. We will continue to seek technical, external solutions that will fix or alter the children so they will fit more easily into the school mold.

WHAT DRIVES EDUCATION?

Right now, *assessment drives education*. It both controls and dominates what it is possible to do in the schools. It is the strongest force against any change that goes beyond the rearrangement of received structures and inherited definitions. I distinguish here between two purposes of assessment. The first of these purposes has to do with evaluation, which has the ostensible aim of benefiting the learner. The second has to do with accountability and the regulation of schools and public education.

I understand regulatory assessment to serve the purpose of monitoring schools and of keeping track of and maintaining standards for the entire public education enterprise. As this is an exceedingly broad and ambitious purpose, it is of more than passing interest that tests, designed primarily to assess the skill-level achievements of children, should play the feature role in this arguably most important social sphere of the society.

Even when policy making addresses broad social purposes, for example, through educational programs designed to provide opportunities for children living in poverty, the *justification* for these programs is made primarily in terms of improved test scores. That is, what is valued, and deemed valuable, about these programs is not the educational opportunities and widened horizons they offer but the measurable achievement of the recipients.

There are many limitations and drawbacks to basing and justifying educational and social policy in these narrow terms, and at the expense of the children and families they presumably are designed to serve. Chief among these is the danger of defining regulation in schools or other venues as a *technological* task and abdicating responsibility for it to technical experts. I say "danger" and choose that strong word advisedly for the reason that educational policy making and the regulation of schools are not technical tasks. Properly understood both policy making and regulation have their basis in broad social and ethical principles, and are for that reason necessarily located in the political sphere of the society.

And further: In whatever venue the necessity for regulation arises (and it does in all our human and social affairs), it inevitably calls into question definitions of liberty; that is, our freedom to express and to pursue what we perceive as goods or values, and the spheres in which we may do so relatively unimpeded. It is in this respect that regulation influences, and is influenced by, our understandings and beliefs with respect to what constitutes what I have called in this essay *a self*. In other words, if I freely and energetically express my perspectives and desires and pursue what I define as happiness and worthwhile goals, I may grossly infringe on the pursuits of others.

Equally, regulation of my freedom, or of yours, whatever the justification, is fraught with perils. If, for example, I am powerful and I deny that you possess a self, or I say that you have only a poorly developed self, then I may with justification override your liberty in favor my own free reign—and exercise my self-appointed right to govern or oppress you and yours. In its nature a restraint, regulation touches on censorship, on asymmetries of power between individuals and groups, on equity, on enfranchisement, on privacy, and on the right of dissent.

In brief, regulation engages us politically and specifically in the working out of human arrangements conditioned by history and local circumstances, which by their historical nature will require revisiting, rethinking, and reworking in the light of changed circumstances. When as educators or citizens we define regulation as a technical task solvable through technological means, we place it outside human history.

It is for this reason that I understand technology to be specifically ahistorical: Each new solution supplants the previous one, rendering it obsolete, while each solution in turn draws its authority from "fact" and "law" that locate it as objectively detached from human agency. When we as citizens or educators consent to the rule of experts and place our faith in "answers" and "solutions," and, for example, reduce the basis and justification of educational policy to test scores, we abdicate our political responsibility for weighing up and balancing divergent perspectives. We rid ourselves of the social and intellectual obligation to examine the value ground of our assumptions, and to think through as well as we can, however imperfectly and with whatever inevitable human error, the implications and consequences of the actions that will follow from them.

Speaking from another location than the broadly political, testing technology also diverts us as educators. By emphasizing technological measures and solutions, testing turns our attention away from a conceptualization of educating as human work dependent on human resource. Turned aside from our own human capacities as teachers we are turned aside equally from the possibility of developing classrooms able to draw forth each and every child's capacities. When children's capacities sink from view, as teachers and parents our ability to support children's own efforts to make sense of their life experiences and the world around them is seriously impeded.

Stripped of human resource and capacity on all sides, dependency on outside expertise and technologies increases. What the tests test defines learning and achievement. It is an end-stopped assessment offering no direction other than "get those scores up" for improving the quality of children's educational experience. The idea of an evaluation that would fold directly into the lived experiences of individual learners and the wider but no less lively world of the classrooms is lost from view—and possibility.

I separate a testing technology from an evaluation able to serve these purposes on the grounds that the values invoked by testing are contradictory to those arising from the actualities of children growing and learning and from the horizons of meaning enacted in the classroom on a daily basis. A measurement-driven evaluation, which by definition refers to statistical norms and comparative ranking determined by linear standards, is not differentiated enough to accommodate this kind of complexity and particularity. The instruments are too blunt. The aims are both too narrow and too general; for example, to obtain a statistical profile of the achievement of groups on highly specific tasks and isolated skills. That is, when the focus is on measurement, we are forced to substitute small, static, additive units for events which as they are enacted in life are animated, layered, textured, complexly interlaced, and educationally potent.

THERE IS THAT IN LEARNING WHICH RESISTS MEASUREMENT

Building from this context of ideas, I am going to position two thoughts in tandem. First, there is that in learning and educating which is immeasurable. Second, at present, the measurable (the technical) is determining what is valued and recognized to be important in educating.

I am going to expand the first thought: There is that in learning and thinking, in the teaching–learning relationship, in the process of educating and being educated, which is immeasurable. Further, and here I return to the earlier story I told, there is that in us humans, a self, which is immeasurable. Immeasurable: not merely not yet measured or simply exceeding our current technological capacity.

As I understand it, the immeasurable signals what exceeds and defies object boundaries; that is, what goes beyond or below or transcends those limits. The immeasurable hints at mystery, spirit, and a largeness exceeding the agreed-upon dimensions of human perception acceptable to an objectivist rendering of the world and of humanness. The immeasurable makes me think of all those moments, when, as in my waking dream, suddenly something is understood, but both the understanding and how it occurred are not specifiable to a chain of reasoning or an aggregation of skills.

Applying the immeasurable to ordinary classroom occasions, learning to read in my experience is often like that. Although we may arrange the child's instruction according to a theory, method, and sequence of activities or exercises, it is difficult—I would say, impossible—to specify how the reading happened, or with any humility ascribe the learning to the instruction we did or the theories that dictated the practice.

The immeasurable also makes me think of those events that arouse in us awe and wonder, perhaps rendering us speechless, as I was in the wake of that image which overtook me 50 years ago. It is also what fills me when I hear a baby speak that baby's first intelligible utterance, a word. Astonished wonder: How did that happen? This is a mystery enacted anew by each baby born, repeated every day, worldwide, and ever awe-inspiring. I may be able to establish the conditions surrounding the emergence of that word or specify the neurological connections required for its occurrence, but fundamentally it's a mystery. Endlessly interesting to pursue, it inspires thought.

It seems to me in these mysteries, in these immeasurable occurrences, reside the big questions, the important questions, which impel us humans to seek and make knowledge. And unless we are afflicted with a Faustian pride, to recognize that the questions ever exceed the boundaries of the knowledge we make in their pursuit. These are the questions without solutions, amenable to no final answer. Or to return to my starting point, these are questions which are not satisfactorily addressed through technological means.

The immeasurable also returns me to Havel and the importance he attaches to the education of those dimensions of our humanness he summarizes around such immeasurables as an elementary sense of justice, openness of mind to perspectives and ideas other than our own, responsibility, courage, compassion, and wisdom. Immeasurable. Not instructable. Not testable. But actively engaged and enacted in those classrooms where teachers and children on a daily basis consent to the pursuit of unanswerable questions and to the unexpectedness of the journeys those pursuits launch.

In the negotiation of those journeys, in the give and take they require, strong bonds are formed: in the play and talk and making of works; in the ideas embraced and the choices made; in the immediacy of a here and now experience; in the exploration of worlds beyond, imagined and historical; in the energetic pursuit of interests, individually and collectively. In all of these there resides enormous educational significance, immeasurable meaning. There is that of the awe-inspiring, of wonder, in the understanding that it is here, in the schools, in classrooms that members of the rising generation, each possessed of emotional intensities and intellectual urgencies, each possessed of a self, come together, the embodiment of posterity. And come together *to work it out together*, in the particular, every day, with all that implies of without ceasing, always regathering.

I repeat: *There is that in learning and educating which is immeasurable.* When you or I or anyone else applies rulers, or their equivalent, to the immeasurable, we have to change what is immeasurable to fit the measuring stick. Specifically, we have to pare it down so that all that remains are its countable properties. Doing that we turn the immeasurable into something else (and less) than what it is. In this fashion, for purposes of measurement, thinking got defined as measurable intelligence, and then forgetting that human beings like us were the authors of the definition, we mostly understood thereafter that measured intelligence is what thinking is. Under the influence of that definition, it was easy to lose sight of, or render insignificant because immaterial and immeasurable, contemplation, imagination, meditation, insight, spiritual understanding, reflection, poetics; or what may be broadly understood as an *aesthetic*, which heretofore fell loosely within the province of thinking.

When the immeasurable isn't recognized or valued, it tends to slip from view. Out of sight, it ceases to claim our minds and attention. We forget how to see it. Left to lie fallow these kinds of experiences tend to become not talkable. The language for saying them, for exploring their meanings, grows rusty, archaic, clumsy on our tongues, and sometimes, embarrassing or forbidden. For example, it is within my own memory that in my days in college studying philosophy of science, anything smacking of the spirit was better censored than said, although interestingly, "force" was allowable. And to be dismissed as "merely subjective" was to be banished to some intellectual equivalent of Siberia.

When the immeasurable isn't *recognized* or *valued* by teachers, or by the educational community at large, the occasions when it arises in the classroom or through the expressiveness of an individual child, tend to be dismissed or noticed only as charming, or funny, or distracting, or idiosyncratic, or clever—but as incidental to the "real" work of learning and mastering skills. A lot that is educationally important in understanding the child as a learner, or the dynamic chemistry of a group of children playing together, is missed in this way. It is missed for the reason that it falls outside the accepted categories of meaning and for this reason doesn't connect for the viewer with any complexity. Or to say that another way, it lacks *allusory* power—the power to evoke other complexes of meaning.

For those familiar with Mike Rose's enlightening book, *Lives on the Boundary* (1989), it's what he *didn't* miss when he asked the student who came to the tutorial center what *she* thought was wrong with sentences red-penciled by an instructor as incomplete. In response, the student pointed *not* to the sentence fragments but to the conventionally correct declarative sentence at the beginning of the paragraph—a sentence that began with "She was." The student said she didn't want to keep repeating "she was . . . she was . . ." in the sentences following because it didn't "sound very intelligent" (p. 171) to write the same words over and over and that wasn't the kind of writing she wanted to do.

Rose grasped in the student's critique of her composition that it was her attempt to vary sentence structure—to surpass herself as a writer—that led to the faulty sentences. Or, to say that another way, Rose understood from her aesthetic (immeasurable) and her aims (immeasurable) that the student was striving to be writerly. That is, she was aiming not for correctness but to expand her writing repertoire and her stylistic fluency.

There is a world of difference between those two aims and a world of difference in the teaching response they call forth. Or there is if I or you hear it—which is to say if you or I possess the wealth of understandings of writing and of learning and of humanness which permit us to perceive the significance of her emphasis, and appreciate the strength of her desire. And, I would add, if as teachers we are not blocked from those perceptions by a mind-set that would dictate that her aims, while perhaps admirable and even moving, are, of course, misplaced and unrealizable since she doesn't have the technical "tools" or the "skills" to pursue them. If that is my mindset or yours, then we will see the job in quite other terms: to help the young woman to recognize these deficiencies and to set (as all of us are prone to say), more "realistic" goals.

To regather and start again: *There is that in learning and educating which is immeasurable. The measurable tends to determine what is important in educating and learning. When the immeasurable falls outside the recognized categories of meaning and contexts of value which fill the educational screen, it tends to slip from view, to be left unspoken, and to sink in value to the level of anecdotal interest.* Lacking contexts of value through which its importance is recognized, it becomes difficult to justify as having educational purpose and meaning. That is, anything happening in the classroom that can't be justified by measurement is treated with suspicion or dismissed outright as meaningless or is not noticed at all.

For example, assuming measurement as the value context for justifying educational importance, what does children's play mean? What is the importance of a child drawing or sewing or building with blocks or taping bits of cardboard scrap together? Or, for that matter, daydreaming in a sixth-grade classroom? Within this context, these are not addressable questions. Neither are these: What is the importance of an artist painting or a musician performing or composing or a scientist inventing a theory? Or for that matter, what is the importance of a life lived or the enacting of a life?

With respect to schools, it is teachers called upon to justify a classroom world rich in activity and play who experience the stress of these questions most severely and with the greatest immediacy. More than once I have heard teachers who have accomplished these kinds of classrooms, or are developing them, characterize their lives as deeply and uncomfortably divided between the immeasurable actualities of children learning and growing and the demands to justify that learning and growing in terms contradictory to those immeasurable actualities—that is, in terms that deny their importance.

They and, as I will come to, many of the rest of us are caught in the kind of double-talking, double-thinking of those forced to shift back and forth between two worlds. In this instance, I understand those worlds as the daily, lively world of personal, firsthand experience, and the superimposed world of secondary interpretations. I am going to liken that daily, lively personal world of the classroom to the home life of any immigrant or member of a disenfranchised population: a place of intimacy and relaxation, where the speech is vernacular, the rituals and gestures understood, where you are valued for yourself.

The superimposed world I will liken to the alien tongue and manners of the dominant surrounding society which must be assumed as soon as the safety of home is left behind, where little that is of importance to you is valued or recognized. In both circumstances, that of the stranger to a culture, or that of the teacher, much is lost in translation and the cost in stress is high. That double existence is emblemized whenever a kindly, well-intentioned principal says to an inspired teacher, or a superintendent says to a change-making principal, "I don't care how you do it or what means you use or anything else you do besides. I leave that to your professional judgment and expertise—as long as you achieve the outcomes." Outcomes, which it goes without saying, are tacitly understood to be measurable.

Those who straddle two worlds become adroit at translation; cunning and sly at protecting some sphere of action in which they and their students are free to be who they are. They learn the skills of rear-guard tactics calculated to unsettle the status quo, to make small openings in the confining walls. Theirs is the camaraderie and closeness of resistance movements everywhere. The energy required is enormous. The frustrations are many. A ruling preoccupation is holding ground, not allowing encroachments on the territories of freedom still intact. Occasionally there is a major crack in the prevailing structure and the opportunity to seize new ground—ground which all too often proves hard to hold since the thought and language deck is stacked in advance against the successful entry of new players, speaking with other tongues and visualizing other pictures of the world, other renditions of reality.

To say this in a slightly other way, and speaking from my own life and observation, those who resist, challenge, or stand apart from the prevailing interpretation of what constitutes "reality," or in common parlance, what is assumed as "the real world," find themselves constrained to respond to and in the terms of that inherited meaning structure. I, and many, many others, have spent long hours analyzing and critiquing standardized tests for the reason that as dissenters we won't be heard at all if we cannot speak the language of those who make and promote them, and those who accept the definitions of those experts.

Many of us have worked hard to invent better tests and alternatives to tests. We have put our energy into reducing the number of tests administered or the numbers of children to whom they are given. We have pleaded to obtain forgiveness of tests in the form of waivers for schools committed to carving out new educational space. We have angled to refer assessment to agencies external to the school system which we know to be sympathetic with our purposes and are credible in terms of expert qualifications to the district or state regulators. In every way we could think of, we have struggled to lift the pressures of accountability from the shoulders of children. These include in a few courageous instances, and with the assent and support of parents, the refusal to administer the tests at all.

These struggles have been and continue to be necessary. But they fall short, and I believe will continue to fall short, of change that is transformative. That is, change that is more than mere substitution of one model or program for another. And there are other hazards. Each time I or you translate, every time we are drawn into double-talk, we move ourselves away from the actuality of what we know to be the important and very real work of creating classrooms in which the immeasurable is valued. Removed from these actualities, we are distanced as well from the equally real work of creating and articulating the value contexts through which these settings can be understood and recognized.

I cannot stress enough how important I believe this work to be. Only rarely can any of us spare the time to plumb the meanings and consequences of such foundational ideas for educating as the conceptualization of the self or the definition of what knowledge is. I am confident that if we did take that time we would uncover important and interesting differences. I am equally confident of the variety we would discover if each of us had the opportunity to tell what we see as the grounding assumptions, the starting points from which we envision the work of educating and set educational priorities.

I emphasize variety because I believe it is from grappling with differences intensively that collectively we might arrive at a few broad, elementary principles for educating. And by that route, establish a common ground to which many could genuinely lay claim—ground wide enough to include variety without resort to the suppression of differences.

GETTING TO KNOW THE CHILDREN WE TEACH

Early in these remarks and related to the story I told from my own life, I suggested that a child's works (writings, drawings, constructions) map pathways to the child as a maker of meaning and value, to the child as self and active agent. To round out this talk, and to frame the Descriptive Reviews of Work that are the substance of this conference, I return now to that idea.

What do I mean when I say a child's works are a map or a pathway? I mean that if we as educators and parents are attentive to works, we are able to witness the child, the maker, thinking aloud, using the space of a page or a block construction or a story as territory in which to make experience, feelings, and ideas actual and renewable, while at the same time breaking boundaries into new fields of possibility.

For myself and from my own past in classrooms at Prospect School, among my most cherished observations are those of children doing just that: Drawing side by side, filling the air with commentary, carrying on a conversation with figures they are in the act of creating, or crossing the boundaries of another child's drawing to participate in the drama unfolding there. Or, to offer another example, listening to a child singing softly and happily to the fabric, needle, thread, and buttons from which she is contriving a little doll.

Later, when we, the adults, came to look at the children's works *apart* from the activity of the making of them, we brought with us this closeness to the happening, the questions arising from that closeness, and also appreciation. What we did not come with was the intention to measure or score the works or to judge them with reference to some other external standard. We did not, for example, bring to the works theoretical schemata in order to classify the makers according to developmental stage or level of intellectual functioning. We did not apply rubrics or benchmarks to the works.

We set aside these received contexts for determining the significance of the work in order to remain as much as possible with the expressiveness of the person. Within the limits of our attention and imaginative grasp, we wanted to look at the work *in its own right*. Treating the work and the maker with regard and care, we undertook to describe the work in a disciplined, serious way. We undertook to tell the work aloud among ourselves, a group of interested and concerned adults, teachers and sometimes parents, drawing on our perspectives collectively in that telling.

I want to be very clear, though, as all of us participating in this conference set forth to do this kind of describing, that the descriptions are *secondary* to the works themselves and to the maker and the contexts in which the work was created. This is the case whether the describing occurs among adults or through a parallel process among children in the classroom in response to their own and other children's works. The classroom with its activities and materials, the children, and the things they make are *primary*. I feel it is necessary and important to emphasize this because the idea of portfolio, entering as that technology did from the assessment wing, tends to make the work *secondary* to the assessment purposes it serves. And so it is not unusual to discover that works are made in schools in order to have something to put in a portfolio, which in its turn is being made in order to score or rank the contents or the student.

The distinction I am making is majorly important. I feel I can't stress it enough. Once the cart is put before the horse, the priorities are reversed: *The score or rank is valued not only over the the work itself, but over the making of it, and over all the immeasurable thought and learning which occur in that activity.* By conceiving what children make as *performances* or *products*, it seems to me portfolio assessment tends to divert attention from this active, expressive side, and from the classroom as a place that supports the child's making and doing as important in its own right.

Although not primary, the descriptions we began to do at school in response to the children's works nevertheless did prove to be important and useful. Through these exercises, we found our recognition of children, in their variety, in their complexity, enriched, sharpened, and deepened.

And further: from the descriptions, questions arose—questions that had the effect of opening our eyes wider. As I raise a selection of these, I invite you to think of the works of children you know, or works made in your own childhood play:

> What inspires this child to wonder and question?
> What does she care about deeply?
> What holds, sustains, and furthers his interests?
> What connections are being made?
> Where is this child opening up regions of thought and horizons of meaning?

And also:

> What does this child call to *my* attention?
> How are my horizons and experience being expanded?
> Where and how does this child's valuation of the world overlap with that of other children, with my own, with those of other thinkers?
> Where do this child's questions connect with those at the heart of the subject matter disciplines and with ways of making knowledge ascribable to those disciplines?

And also:

> What standards are enacted through this child's works?
> What values are embodied in those standards?
> What light is shed on external standards by this child's works and ways of knowing?

I suggest that these are educationally important questions—not answerable questions, but questions which, if entertained and pursued, can lead to the understanding needed to draw forth each child as an active thinker and learner.

Meditation: On Number

Reflecting on number, I am acutely conscious of the priority it is accorded when making large-scale decisions about educational programs and also when deciding the fates of individual children. On the large scale, in education, as in the social sciences more generally, research designs that employ sophisticated statistical methodologies proliferated as the twentieth century matured. With the advent of computer technology that proliferation shows no signs of slowing. "Research based" is now a virtual requirement for an educational program to be adopted in many states.

On the small, but inestimably important scale of individual children, although an occasional test maker or professional organization may protest, a single score on a standardized test can have a determining effect on a child's educational future. Right now, with almost exclusive reliance on standardized tests as the measure of school success, the effect of test scores on the lives of individuals can be, and often is, profound.

What is it about humans and number? So far as is knowable, number in its developed form is a human invention and talent. Number, and name, too, in certain respects, are associated with our human proclivity for pattern, for order, for connection—and for the abstract relationships that follow from these. These depend, as does number itself, on setting boundaries, on holding some "thing" constant. From this angle on the world, permanence and object properties dominate. In the West, this emphasis on consistency has yielded remarkable advances in understanding of the physical universe and in derived technologies.

Still, there are other human proclivities and other experiences, no less real, although harder to pin down. There is, for example, the human enjoyment of novelty, of mingle and flow, of tone and color, of the feel and sense of a thing, or what I will call its expressiveness. Less tangible and less amenable to number, these experiences nevertheless exercise strong influences on us. Even when dismissed as subjective, these capacities for apprehending what lies beyond or within are inseparable from imagination as they are also from wonder and awe. There is art. There is the spiritual in life.

Both perspectives are humanly indispensable: ambiguity, expressiveness, and the finite, particularized occasion have worth, and so does pattern, order, and the generalizable. I do not understand these perspectives to be oppositional but rather to describe a continuum in human perception and experience. Often both can be in play at the same time, and desirably so.

For example, I can't read a poem without apprehension and appreciation of rhythm, of the pulsing of the words, which in turn pulse indivisibly with my heart, with the flow of blood, with every breath. This experience of mingle, of participation animates meaning. Yet, as a reader, I also often stop to count out the meter of a poetic line. As a describer, when I describe writing of any kind, sooner or later I count words and syllables. I compare sentence lengths and how they vary. Inevitably, if I have many pieces of writing from the same author, through this counting, I discover patterns bridging across the collection, descriptive of this author's language sense. Or, in parallel fashion, if I am describing visual artworks, I discover repeating elements and, in the course of describing these, a kind of geometry of the composition descriptive of the artist's aesthetic.

I like to do this kind of describing. I depend on it. Counting, discovering patterns, reading or looking across pieces deepens and sharpens my understanding. When I do this kind of disciplined reading or looking, I learn the piece inside out.

But, returning to the poem as example, if my ear is deaf to beat, to the pulsations of language, no amount of counting and patterning is going to assist my understanding. Behind the counting, and the recurrence that yields pattern, there is a "rightness" of rhythm that is vaguer than number but not without relationship to it. If I fail at the level of expressiveness, if counting and pattern are my only access to the poem, I think it is safe to say, the *experience* of it is lost.

Many years ago now, I came across words from a letter written by Robert Frost (1914/1964) that say this thought with admirable humor and economy. Frost was writing about what he calls "sentence sense," of which he says, "A sentence is a sound in itself on which other sounds called words may be strung" (p. 110). And continuing, points out, "You may string words together without a sentence-sound to hang them on just as you may tie clothes together by the sleeves and stretch them without a clothesline between two trees, but—it is bad for the clothes" (pp. 110–111).

In the example I chose, the issue is one of emphasis and subordination. I may choose to emphasize order as I do when I count words or meter.

Equally, I may choose to emphasize the expressive side as I do when I trace any handwritten (or drawn) piece to join with the writer's gesture and cadence, or read aloud to restore the written to the spoken, and so to the inner location and vibrations of the voice. What seems often hard to do is to keep both perspectives, and both ends of the continuum from the animate to the ordered, in view at once—valued equally for the difference in understanding each provides. It is as if to value one, the other must be scorned. I know I sometimes catch myself doing this in reaction to what I deplore as unexamined attachment to numbers altogether detached from reality.

HOW DO I CHOOSE? WHAT IS AT STAKE?

What is at stake is that whichever end of the continuum, and whichever perspective I choose, there are consequences, and these are necessarily value-laden. That is, my choice in these matters has inevitably to do with conferring importance and worth and with setting priorities. If I opt for number, in the final analysis I opt for abstractness and what is generalizable. If I opt for expressiveness, I opt in the final analysis for the concrete particular, with its qualities of nuance, complexity, and variety.

This is what I was grappling with in 1975 when I made the case for observation and description as the appropriate methodology for the study of human phenomena. Making that choice, I was setting a value priority. The more I was in the close company of children, the more I observed, the more I was impressed that what was educationally consequential was how each of the children engaged the world, and the complexity and variety of that engagement.

Observationally, my access to that complexity and variety was through seeing the child in action—gesturally, verbally, and, most vividly, in play and in the act of making things. Watching from this angle, what was striking is the freshness and novelty and excitement that each child confers on the world—and on humanness. No matter how many drawings of houses, trees, and suns I looked at, even by the same child, I never discovered a duplication. No matter how often I observed house play or fort building, the stories enacted never grew stale by repetition. Wherever I looked variety overrode sameness. This seemed important.

Neither were the children individually explainable by reference to external constructs and categories, nor in important ways, predictable. The more I thought about this, and the more I devoted myself to staying as close to what I was seeing and hearing as I could—in which counting and patterning definitely played an important role—the more I was persuaded that where human lives and experience are concerned, the choice to move toward abstractness and generalization is fateful. More especially, I was made to think about this hard because it seemed to me that mostly when people categorized and classified and generalized about children, that happened effortlessly with no explicit decision to do so.

That is, in research circles and in educational circles, it was simply the way you did it. Even in sophisticated longitudinal studies following a child across a span of years, the categories for what to look at (and measure) and for interpreting the data gathered tended to be determined in advance. What fell outside these categories went mostly unnoticed. Speaking more broadly, in research circles and in schools, the idea of a normative child was present and widely accepted. The idea that children grow mentally (and morally) in a specifiable sequence of developmental stages was present and widely accepted. The idea that there is a normative 7-year-old brand of learning that justifies putting all 7-year-olds together in a class was present and widely accepted. The idea that you could measure a child's intelligence and rely upon that number for sorting children into categories and predicting their "success" as learners was present and widely accepted.

What seemed lost from view is that classification, generalization, and the normative, and statistical methodology more generally, cannot accommodate or illuminate individualness and particularity. And cannot do so for the good and ample reason that these methodologies are not applicable to individuals or particularized experience. Categorization is a necessary condition for statistical manipulations of data to occur. Statistics and classification apply to groups and generalized phenomena and to distinctions among such groups and classes. I draw the inference that when individuality and the concrete particular is a dominant and important feature, as I suggest it is for anything human, the function of statistical methodologies is necessarily subordinate and limited.

NAME AND NUMBER

From my own observations, the effortless decision to rely heavily, sometimes exclusively on these methodologies did a serious disservice by covering over educationally and humanly consequential complexities and particularities. Even more I was troubled by how thinking in this classificatory, normative fashion unnames the individual. If I don't have to name or look at the person I am categorizing, child or adult, on whom I also may be passing judgment, the barrier against callous treatment (or worse) is significantly lowered. Also, the classifications tend to stick. In a school district I worked in children were classified early in terms of language development. Some of these were children whose primary language was not English. The ones classified low tended to stay in that slot. As the children grew older, this was the frame through which they continued to be viewed, dramatically influencing attitudes and an important factor in how a child was tracked in classes.

On a bigger human scale, it seems to me the relationship of name and number emblemizes the tension between what is close and recognizable and valued for itself and what is removed, lacking in individual character, and devalued. For example, my name recognizes me in the flesh, in the particular, and most important, does that *through the context of my intimate relatedness to other people*. That I have a name at all means that I have some unique importance for some other persons—my parents, my family, all those who love me, and for whom my name carries me as a presence in their lives.

From this immediacy of feeling for life and its continuance, I notice that people from many cultures have some tradition of passing names from one generation to the next. Every so often studying children's writings, I have come across a story or poem about a nameless child, the point of which is that the child finds some sheltering people and through this new connectedness, a name and a life. The ritual of taking a name, or dreaming it, makes this same point about context: The name relates the person to something. Often, and especially in taking a new name, this is associated with a rebirth, a transformation of being.

Numbering people undoes the connectedness that name accomplishes. For example, substituting a number or label for my name deprives me not only of my individual identity but of the recognition that I enjoy a reckonable place, a status of worth, in the larger human scheme of things. Oppressors use numbers to place their victims outside the realm of human concern. As history tells us, and repeatedly, the nameless are easily disposed of: They are no one's grandmother, sister, friend, or lover.

THE PRIMARY VALUE OF NUMBER

The reservations I have expressed about the overweening dominance of statistical methodologies in education (and related fields) I do not extend to number in its primary functions. When I used a poem to illustrate the blending of order and pattern with vaguer experiences of rhythm and pulse, I touched on that function. As I understand it, numbers can and do have a primary place in the rendering of particularity, and the value of the finite occasion in all its variety and nuance.

Here I return to the idea that it is through number that something to which I can attach and which will hold my attachment is carved out from the mutable, shifting landscape—and held constant. From the twinned and indivisible human capacity which in one gesture confers both worth *and* constancy, I gain a world of value and, equally, a world of appreciable stability. On the side of stability, this is a world I can in some degree count upon as an arena for daily life and action. In numbers, and through numbers, I enjoy some renewable action, some element of the recurring, some clarity of outline in a world largely in flux. On the side of value, by attending with care, by selecting *this* over *that*, I equally gain a world I can count on not merely for bare physical survival, but as Whitehead (1938/1958) says it, "survival for diversified worthwhile experience" (p. 43).

This seems to me the primary function and value of number. It is at this primary level, still closely related to the event, the happening, that number is representable, I think, as descriptive. Many years ago now I saw a film on the life of the artist Edvard Munch in which percentages of the incidence of tuberculosis, prostitution, and venereal disease in Norway in the late nineteenth century were juxtaposed to the intimate, immensely complex interplay of these and other influences on the artist's life. None of these percentages explained anything or interpreted anything. Interspersed as they were throughout the film they worked as an economical device or context to connect Munch to a time and place, while Munch's highly particular life did the work of tying the numbers to the particular and excruciating experience of what it was to be in that time and place. In other words, the particular illuminated the generalized situation. For me viewing, the juxtaposition was sobering and thought provoking.

Of course, even at this close-to-the-event, descriptive level, statistics are generalizing numbers. Even at this level, number (and the boundaries number confirms) necessarily sacrifice ambiguity, expressiveness, and animation in favor of boundedness, object properties, and stability. Still, when connected to the particularities of concrete social and individual realities, it seems to me these kinds of "counts" (as I think of them) have a salutary *alerting* effect. It is highly instructive, for example, to know the numbers of Southern and Eastern Europeans who were denied entry to the United States in the 1920s and 1930s because they didn't pass IQ tests. It is also instructive to know the tiny number of Jews who survived the Warsaw Ghetto.

Right now, it is instructive to know how many children are being retained in Chicago and other urban systems intent on upholding a resolve to end what are called "social promotions," and especially the number retained for a third year in the same grade. When evaluating social and educational policy it seems to me there can be no substitute for knowing how and in what degree those policies impinge on individual lives. Counting the numbers affected may be a first and useful step in that evaluation, but standing alone and unconnected to the actual lives of actual children, the numbers are, at best, insufficient and, at worst, destructive.

DESCRIPTIVE NUMBERS AND METALEVEL STATISTICS

What seems to me important is to distinguish this alerting, juxtapositional use of statistics from the metalevels of sophisticated manipulation of data at twice and thrice remove from their point of origin and from anything in particular. I have been thinking about this because data manipulation of this kind, which has been a prevailing activity among social scientists and educational researchers for many years now, has tended to accelerate with each advance in computer technology. What I contest in this practice is the ease with which the numbers assume the character of being themselves real—and as it is usually phrased, "hard." And closely related, I challenge the typically tacit but operative assumption that numbers can themselves tell the story the way it really is; that is, that the numbers are self-evident and value-free, devoid of social and political context. *They are not.*

As in all things, there may be specific occasions that justify metalevel statistical maneuvers. My point is that it is seriously diverting to give the numbers game priority status for the reason that to do so suggests that answers to serious, complicated social and educational issues can be found by this kind of statistical analysis. This is misleading in the first place and has the added effect of calling attention away from formulating and grappling with those issues and questions too large to be easily encompassed by these technologies.

If you and I have access to the same data and numbers, and possess volumes of these, but neither of us has any immersion in the life of a classroom, or any deep observational grasp on the variety and variability of children learning, then it is altogether likely our discourse and argument are going to pivot on the abstractions close to hand. We are stuck with our abstractions for the good reason that neither of us has the experience of the actualities necessary to prompt questions that exceed the limits of the technological methodology we each embrace.

For myself, I hold that the complexities of education are immune to technological resolution or to any final solution. And further, it seems to me that these complexities necessarily fall outside any single explanatory frame. This doesn't suggest to me that there is reason to despair of inquiry. Rather, it points to a requirement to focus with maximal attention on where to start the inquiry and how to redouble efforts to promote in schools a habit of continuous questioning and examination.

When I say attention to where to start, I mean that it matters, and matters greatly, how we as educators, researchers, and above all, socially concerned citizens, *frame* issues and questions for inquiry. Here it seems to me that a first requirement is not to pare away the complexities in order to get to something manageable that can be efficiently measured—and so to put the technological cart before the horse. I suggest width of consideration has to be a first priority, and that to achieve it the great advantage is to have present many points of view. Putting the first emphasis on multiplicity of perspectives enacts a commitment to grapple with the complexities, and to do that assiduously, resisting as much as possible the easier path of paring the question immediately down to measurable size.

For example, right now, national standards in education are proposed as a response to test results that by some interpretations indicate decline, with testing the technology of choice to measure the impact of imposing such standards. To impose and enforce national standards is a major *political* decision. In response, an inquiry is asked for that breaks into the technological circle in which what defines the problem is proposed as its solution.

Breaking in, I want to start wide. That is, I want to identify and flesh out as much as possible the social, educational, and political contexts for understanding the issue. For example, I want to hear from policy makers how nationalizing standards is projected to positively affect resources for schools. I want to hear from teachers how they perceive its influence on their opportunities for growth. I want to hear from teachers, schools, children, and parents across a wide spectrum how individual children's learning opportunities are likely to be affected. I especially want to hear about this from the communities that tests have historically discriminated against and I want to be certain those communities have access to that history. And that is just the beginning.

I want to explore across a spectrum of perspectives the question of how we *can* know what children know, and the related question of who *needs* to know what children know, and *for what purposes*. I want to start rolling alongside any cross-sectionally designed statistical design, inquiries into individual children's learning spanning time and ultimately carried across every level of schooling. This it seems to me is the necessary particularized piece to chasten and weight to the level of reality what mass-scale statistical comparisons tend to mask.

What I am saying is that these proposals about standards and achievement are not abstract issues, of research interest only, or issues that can be addressed merely by reference to rising and falling scores. These are complex social and educational issues that have wide and often specific, extreme, and long lasting repercussions in individual lives and in the society as a whole. These are issues that require a posture of broad, continuous inquiry, engaged in not only by professional researchers, but by those closest to the realities of schools and educating. Education is simply too important to the health of a society to be left strictly to the rule of experts.

A NUMBER STORY

To conclude this meditation, I wish to acknowledge its source in a story Alfred North Whitehead tells in *Modes of Thought* (1938/1958). It says so well, and delightfully, what number accomplishes in individuating experience, and in the valuing of the individual, that I repeat it here almost in its entirety:

> We were in a charming camp situated amidst woodland bordering a Vermont lake. A squirrel had made its nest in our main sitting-room, placing it in a hole in brickwork around the fireplace. She came in and out to her young ones, ignoring the presence of the human family. One day she decided that her family had grown up beyond the nursery stage. So, one by one, she carried them out to the edge of the woodland. As I remember across the years, there were three children. But when the mother had placed them on a rock outside, the family group looked to her very different from its grouping within the nest. She was vaguely disturbed and ran backwards and forwards two or three times to make quite sure that no young squirrel had been left behind. She was unable to count. . . . All that she knew was that the vague multitude on the rock seemed very unlike the vague multitude in the nest. Her family experiences lacked the perception of the exact limitation imposed by number. As a result she was mildly and vaguely disturbed. (pp. 106–107)

This little tale has given me much food for thought.

PART **IV**

Generation/Regeneration

A society that devours its own young deserves no automatic
or unquestioning allegiance.

—Pat Barker, *Regeneration*

Across the talks I chose for this book, I speak of the generative and regenerative in connection with growth and change which, surpassing the additive and substitutional, is organic and transformative. In this concluding part of the book, composed of a single talk, called "To Help Us Start Strong," after words of Toni Morrison from her Nobel Lecture (1994, p. 27), I turn to the root of that word: to birth. Calling attention to this root meaning, I signal the responsibility of all of us, the elders, to act in the midwifery role that Morrison specifically ascribes to language and which I apply to assisting at the birth of the succeeding generation. What I cast as the elders' responsibility, I cast also as "our other chance": to affirm human continuance and its transformative potentialities.

What I do not spell out in this talk, although it is implied, is a truth about human growth and learning so self-evident it hardly requires saying: that human growth and human learning are from the start and inevitably intergenerational. For this reason there is a certain roughness of experience inherent in the process. I have my experience and my generation, you have yours, we touch and sometimes connect but as often, miss. Yet, I am on your horizon and you are on mine. If I am the older, I have grappled with experiences you who are younger are just now encountering for the first time. Yet, equally, if I am the older, you are confronted with circumstances and contingencies of living which I can glimpse only through you. What I do at my peril is to turn my face away from yours or to hide mine from you. This is the unrelenting and fruitful tension that binds us, even as we may reject each other. Even so, even rejecting, we are caught in this inescapable embrace.

In many of the talks preceding this last one, and especially perhaps in "We Love the Things We Love for What They Are," I am striving for what it is to enact the generational responsibility, and how it is that we, the elders, so often fail and miss our chance—from impatience, from cynicism, and, driving these, from fear. It seems that on all sides now we, the elders, rush to pronounce that the children are just like us, adults, and to be treated and judged accordingly. There is a leveling of generational difference. There seems little right now that hinders the strong denial that there even is a distinguishable time of childhood or a time of youth or, for that matter, a time of adulthood or of age. The harm in this rendering of life as same and uniform is great, perhaps incalculable. It is this harm I point to with the epigram taken from Pat Barker's novel, *Regeneration* (1991), which frames this last part of the book.

In step with Barker's words, at the start of this concluding talk I play off our human animating powers against all that imperils humanness through the forgetting of those powers. Yet, by the end of the talk it is not so much the perils or the generational miss I emphasize as the generational connection, and the power that connecting can confer on us—both elders and youth. I do that primarily through the story of a child, scheduled by school standards to fail, who teaches us her elders lessons in humanness and generosity, and what it is to teach and what it is to learn, that are unforgettable.

Ending as I do with a child and with a child's lessons in courage, the talk at its conclusion opens up and outward, affirming hope. Confirming openness and a main theme of this book, that there can be no final solutions to humanness and human activities (for which education is emblem), the talk ends with a question—a question, as I say in the last line, left hanging.

This talk is a revised version of a keynote address for a regional meeting of the National Council of Teachers of English held in Montreal in June 1997. In keeping with the theme of that conference, I titled the address "Reflection Refracted." I chose to rename this version to match revisions I made to focus more sharply on generational responsibility.

9

"To Help Us Start Strong"

Babies start strong with the world, hungry for it as they are for the nurturing breast. This hunger shows itself in ways anyone who cares to look can notice. For example, babies everywhere gaze around at things. Gaze is I think the right word for that looking about, not aimed at anything in particular, that little babies do. An open-ended looking, a willingness to take it all in. And then, of course, just by the act of gazing, the baby gets caught up in the world, in things. A bird in flight. A cat or a puppy. A merry-go-round. Voices. A firetruck. A ring of keys. Music. Gazing, the baby notices; noticing, the baby attends; attending, the baby discovers—what she fancies, what strikes terror, and where she and the world meet and part. A memory: I am holding my tiny 4-week-old son. He rears back suddenly and stares at me, frowning, as if to say, "Who are you?" or "How did I land here?" My husband catches the moment with the camera. It is my favorite.

The baby starts strong in relation to the world, and with particular intensity, to people. That relatedness at first strays merely a degree or two from the reflexive. For example, somewhere, right now, someone is burping a baby, patting that baby gently on the back. Somewhere, right now, someone becomes aware of a little hand patting back. One good turn deserves another.

That's a beginning. Take it a step further. A friend of mine accompanied her daughter and son-in-law on a long drive. While my friend's daughter and her husband spelled each other as drivers, her job was to entertain the baby who was about 3 months old. She was well qualified for the job since she is an early childhood educator. All the way from North Dakota to Vermont, when the baby was wakeful, she sang songs and recited nursery rhymes. Finally arrived at their destination, exhausted and relaxing from the trip, they were amused at how focused the baby was on my friend, staring at her, unblinking. What did she want? What was going on in her mind, that she was so intent? After a time, the baby opened her mouth, and tiny as she was tried to make little laaing sounds—to start the singing again.

Babies everywhere do this reflecting back to the world. They do it by dancing, saying, singing the world back. And, dancing, saying, singing, the baby, the little child describes it. Doing that, in ways subtle and bold they announce themselves as active players in the world's making and remaking. Edith Cobb (1977), a little-known but astute commentator on childhood, remarks that other animals mostly play at being the adult version of their infant selves. So kittens mostly play at being cats and cubs at being bears or lions, depending. She calls this practice play. She observes that human babies and children are not restricted in their play to this kind of replicative practice. Instead a child plays at being anything and everything in the world that catches her fancy: a tree or a cat or a car or a skyscraper or a star in the sky. Playing at what she is *not*, possibilities expand before the child; boundaries are breached. In the child's gesturing and describing, the world receives, as Merleau-Ponty (1962) says it, "a fresh layer of meaning" (p. 407).

Thinking about how strong the baby starts with the world, I think, too, about wonder and curiosity and this getting to know by reflecting back, by describing what you see or hear or experience, and getting to know in the process what is the "not me." I think about the urgency of difference, of strangeness and the paired urgency to know: Because I am neither it nor you. Because the world exceeds me. Because there is an horizon. Because there is an opposite shore. Because even my own face reflected in the smooth surface of a stream is reversed. Because there is not only what is comfortable, familiar, and predictable but the call of the unknown; the promise of the unlooked for. Anything could happen. And might.

I think about the baby patting the patter. I think about my son rearing back, achieving the space to see, to look, to stare. I think about my friend's granddaughter calling back the song. I think about how closely these capacities, observable in the baby, the little child, for noticing and describing, for reflecting back and remembering, neighbor on the creativity we ascribe to artists.

In his memoir, *Working in the Dark*, the Chicano poet Jimmy Santiago Baca (1992) gives voice to that closeness, marrying it to a regenerative life change on the scale of the transformative, with these moving words:

> I was born a poet one noon, gazing [out a grilled cell window] at weeds and creosoted grass at the base of a telephone pole. . . . The words I wrote then sailed me out of myself, and I was transported and metamorphosed into the

images they made. From the dirty brown blades of grass came bolts of electrical light that jolted loose my old self; through the top of my head that self was released and reshaped in the clump of scrawny grass. Through language I became the grass, speaking its language and feeling its green feelings and black root sensations. (p. 11)

I think about memory and the play of memory back over a lifetime. I think about the lifework that is the recollecting, the making and remaking of a story that is part of every person's life: A life story—a life story that even as it is happening is being reworked, remade. A life story that is complicated many times over, that is never singular but mingled with and pluralized by other lives.

And is at the same time, as the novelist Eudora Welty (1984) writes, set apart from those lives. Starting with reflections on her own self and her life in her family, she writes how generational barriers dividing her from her parents, seemingly insurmountable early in life, were with later learning and reflection, leveled. As she says it:

Through learning at my later date, things I hadn't known or had escaped or possibly feared realizing, about my parents—and myself—I glimpse our whole family life as if it were freed of that clock time which spaces us apart so inhibitingly, divides young and old, keeps our living through the same experiences at separate distances. (p. 102)

And continuing, she takes the image of journey, an inward journey, to describe how such distances are bridged—not only for her, but for you or me or all of us. Making this wide, inclusive gesture, Welty affirms memory, and memory in its active mode of reflecting back, as embracing of our humanness. She says to herself, and to us:

It is our inward journey that leads us through time—forward or back, seldom in a straight line, most often spiraling. Each of us is moving, changing, with respect to others. As we discover, we remember; remembering we discover; and most intensely do we experience this when our separate journeys converge. (p. 102)

A journey—mine, yours, everyperson's—that proceeding, doubles back, interrupting and negating the smooth progressions of measured time. A circuitous journey, twining with other journeys, diverging, seldom following the straight line, rarely making the right-angle turn. A journey that as it spirals gathers up a thick and tangled skein. A journey to uncover what *is* in what was. A journey that breaking free from clock time loosens the fast hold of day and year. A journey that is all at the same time a learning, a realizing, and an imaginative discovery.

To be sailed out of time and oneself. To be transported and metamorphosed into images. To write or draw or sculpt or paint or dance or sing those images, not once but many times over, and by that making and remaking, by that doubling back and layering up, to give weight to being.

TO GIVE WEIGHT TO BEING; REFLECTING, I WITNESS

Starting with the baby starting strong with the world, with the baby's human capacities to notice, to say back, and doing that, to know and to remember, I give weight to being. Giving weight to being, I give weight to humanness. To remember, to reflect is to be doubled. To remember, to reflect is to be both agent and witness to agency. To reflect, to witness is to cast a valuing eye on life, on the world. Agent, witness, conferrer of value, evaluator—constructions of self, of person heavy with moral implication.

A reminder then: Reflecting, I look back. I look inward. I ponder. Reflecting, I weigh up. I strike balances: neither here nor there, neither this nor that, neither mine nor yours. Reflecting, blur and blend, dapple and swirl blot out boundaries previously drawn. There is no certainty as to outcomes, except the opportunity to learn, as Milan Kundera (1988) names it, "the wisdom of uncertainty" (p. 7).

A further reminder: If reflecting alone doubles, then reflecting with others quadruples and multiplies. Reflecting with others, I break the isolating grip of my own perspectives. Each of us stands at a particular and distinctive angle to what claims attention: a bird, a butterfly, a rock, a piece of writing, a painting, a garden, a quilt, a meal, a child making things—a drawing perhaps or a story or a doll contrived from a sock tied with yarn. Reflecting with others, I am expanded exponentially.

Reflecting with others, I am reminded that *sameness is antipathetic to humanness.* Except that your stance and perspective amplify and challenge mine, I freeze in place, rigidify. Reflecting with others, I am reminded that conformity, uniformity, standardization—everything that marches stiff legged in narrow lines—endangers the species.

"THINGS ARE NOT AS SIMPLE AS YOU THINK"

What is same, is flat; what is same homogenizes. What is same depletes complexity. What is same demands a constant guard against all that varies from the norm, the convention, the agreed upon. What is same rejects questions. What is same defends its sameness against all comers. War breaks out. Difference is anathema to sameness.

Reminded, I am alerted to danger. I recall with the urgency of portent, these words of Milan Kundera (1988): "in [the] race towards lightness [of being], we have crossed a fateful boundary" (p. 28). To slow that race, to pull humanness back from that boundary, Kundera inserts the novel, telling us that it is the novel's sole purpose to keep "the world of life" under a permanent light and to protect us from "the forgetting of being" (p. 17).

I am intrigued. I pay close attention when Kundera says of the novel that its spirit is double winged, and names them "the spirit of complexity" and "the spirit of continuity" (p. 18). Of complexity and the novel, Kundera tells us that the eternal truth of the novel is this: "Things are not as simple as you think" (p. 18). Of continuity, he tells us, "Each work is an answer to preceding ones, each work contains all the previous experience of the novel" (p. 18).

Simple definitions, simply rendered, yet reading this passage, I am riveted—and again, reminded. Might I not say that the joined spirit of complexity and continuity which Kundera ascribes to the novel is also the spirit of humanness, of living a human life? Might I not say that, like the novel, each life is itself a work which in the making of it is an answer to previous works, containing the experience of previous lives? Might I not, continuing the thought, say that in each life and all, yours, mine, everyperson's, "things are not as simple as you think" (p. 18)?

Large ideas: Ideas of complexity and continuity, of doubling and layering, of leading on by connecting back. Saving ideas that are, as Kundera (1988) says, increasingly hard to hear "amid the din of easy, quick answers that come faster than the question and block it off" (p. 18). Saving ideas that are increasingly slippery and hard to hold in a time that is, as he also says, "firmly focused on a present that is so expansive and profuse that it shoves the past off our horizon and reduces time to the present moment only" (p. 18). As these ideas, as true of lives as of the novel, recede in a "world grown alien" to them, what does their fading prophesy for the weight of being, for humanness?

A BIRD IN THE HAND

Kundera chooses memory and the novel to play the role of miner's canary: to signal by their peril, the peril to humanness. Another writer, Toni Morrison, alerted to that peril, chooses language and parable to tell the story of danger to the endangered species. Morrison's (1994) parable, told in her Nobel Lecture, is spun around a theme of youth at odds with age, of age unforgiving to youth. I choose to retell a condensed version of that story—partly for how it strikes chords with Kundera's, but mostly for the sake of an unexpected moral twist.

Briefly, the story pivots on a challenge by some young people to an old, blind, Black, wise woman to prove her clairvoyance. Laughing, the young people approach her carrying a bird in their hands, a bird Morrison (1994) chooses "to read . . . as language" (p. 12). Eager to unmask her as a fraud, the young people ask the old woman, "Is the bird . . . living or dead?" (p. 11). Her response, slow in coming, is stern and ambiguous: "I don't know . . . whether the bird you are holding is dead or alive, but what I do know is that it is in your hands. It is in your hands" (p. 11). Meaning, as Morrison spells it out, that the life or death of language is in the hands of those who hold it. If it is in your hands, it is your responsibility.

For the old, Black, blind, wise woman, whom Morrison fashions as a writer, language is, as the novel is for Kundera, a work—a work in the making, a work closely woven with being. As she phrases it, the writer woman thinks of language "partly as a system, partly as a living thing over which one has control, but mostly as *agency*—as an act with consequences" (p. 13, italics added). Constructing language as agency, Morrison confers on it a power of consequential action so potent that, as she says, even "moribund, it is not without effect" (p. 14). Robbed of its animating powers, Morrison tells us that the *active effectiveness* of language exists only in its negative and "policing duties" (p. 13) or, as she also says, as it "thwarts the intellect, stalls conscience, suppresses human potential" (p. 14). Its *deathliness* is recognizable in intolerance for new ideas, an inability to imagine or shape novel thoughts, and, using Morrison's words, by "the tendency of its users to forgo its nuanced, complex mid-wifery properties, replacing them with menace and subjugation" (pp. 15–16).

So it matters, and matters greatly, whether this bird is alive or dead. There is implication that the young people may have killed it or that it is, in their hands, dying. Still, the old, blind, wise, Black writer woman has, it would seem, performed her duty by informing them of that responsibility. Her hands it would appear are clean. At this point of seeming moral resolution comes the twist in the tale, heralded by the entry of third parties, unnamed visitors, whose role is that of questioners. The questions Morrison (1994) requires the visitors to ask are these: "Who are they, these children? What did they make of that encounter [with you]? What did they hear in those final words: "The bird is in your hands" (p. 22)?

Posing these questions, Morrison turns the tables on the old woman and on herself. She revisits the encounter with the children but this time from their perspective: the perspective of those who are young; the perspective of those who are inheriting a language, and indeed the perspective of those who are inheriting a world pillaged by those who traveled it ahead of them: the elders—whose numbers include the old, blind, Black, wise writer woman herself.

Specifically, Morrison suggests in response to the visitors that perhaps the children didn't have *anything* in their hands. Perhaps the question, "Is the bird we hold living or dead?" (p. 23) was asked merely to get the old woman's attention, to get her to take them seriously. Perhaps the question asked meant something different and bigger. Perhaps, as Morrison phrases it, the question meant: "Could someone tell us what is life? What is death?" (p. 23).

THE GIFT OF YOUTH TO AGE: OUR OTHER CHANCE

Or, perhaps, as I hear it in my own mind in response to Morrison's words, the young people, the children were by asking the question, offering the old woman an unspoken but huge opportunity—a gift. Perhaps just by seeking her, by asking *anything*, they were saying: "*Here is your other chance.* After the pillage, the rape, the devastation, the immeasurable acts of violence inflicted on humanness, the body counts that exceed the imaginable, here is your chance, your only chance to rebirth possibility—world possibility, human possibility." And I hear them saying, "To get this other chance, you need us. Please talk to us. Please tell us. Please don't leave us here, alone—stranded."

This is what I hear the children asking, and, by asking, breaking the seal on the generational casements, flinging them wide so that air and light can enter the stale, shamed house of the elders. What I hear is that by coming to the house and banging on the door with questions, with their bodies, the children are brave and the children are generous. What I also hear is that the children are forgiving. Forgiving even when the shamed and shameful elders, oblivious to their crimes, name them, the children, the violent ones, the incorrigible ones, and legislate and finance, not schools and the children's education, but jails and their imprisonment.

What I hear is that the children inherit the wind—a wind sown with the destroying seed of values degraded by the elders to be only and merely economic. If wealth and gain are the only values, then what about children? What is their worth? When values are downgraded to material gain, how can the elders value children except in economic terms: that is, as commodities for exchange on the economic market? In this construction of "worth" and "value" and "real world," what is to hinder the elders from ridding themselves of those who don't "measure up" in these narrow terms?

What I also hear in Morrison's parable is that the children, those children who once started strong with the world, are afraid. I recognize this.

This is the fear I sometimes see and feel among children when I am in the schools. The children's lives are short, untried. The children's lives are unsafe. Some will die tragically of want and destructiveness. Many will experience the random and untimely deaths of friends and relatives. They will learn early in their short, untried, unsafe lives that the elders don't always count these deaths, these tragedies, these losses—because those killed, those maimed and foreshortened by loss and too early sorrow don't really count. They are the children prophesied to be failures. They are the children foreordained to be dropouts. They are the children cast for the role of losers in the competitive, dog eat dog economy that rules their lives. They are the children at the very bottom of a ladder on which the rungs for climbing upward are positioned ever higher, ever further out of reach.

The children further up, the children with a foot on a higher rung, are afraid, too. They might slip. They might fall. Hanging tight, they ask, in paraphrase of Morrison's words, "Is this all there is? Is this what life is? *If there isn't anything more, what is death?*" The elders are silent. The elders pretend not to hear the children, blocking their ears with the dead, annihilating words of judgment, swiftly rendered: "The children are arrogant. The children can't learn. The children have no language. The children aren't interested in knowledge. The children are irresponsible. The children are spoiled. The children are violent and destructive. The children don't care." I have heard all these words in the media—and shamefully, even in schools.

The most damning of these judgments is the last named: The children don't care. This judgment strikes to the core of humanness. Passing that judgment condemns the children to some isolating Siberian outpost of humanness—an outpost reserved for those who have no hope of their lives, for those who are lost to the deep human desire for their lives to hold some meaning. And who, not caring and lost to desire, are also and necessarily lost to human warmth, who are invulnerable alike to loss and sorrow and love.

The great point and virtue of Morrison's parable is to oppose this devastating judgment and to oppose it unconditionally: The children *do* care— they care terribly, hopefully, and with all their hearts. Caring, the children are vulnerable; caring, the children are naked in their strong desire for life. Even as the elders rush to reseal the casements of the house, the children, caring so passionately, strive to push them open again, reaching for a hand to hold, straining their ears to catch some healing word. They do this, even as they see so glaringly with their sharp, probing, youthful eyes that the elders are marred by falseness, that the elders blame as they also deny their own role in the devastation; that the elders are more eager to reap profits and to maintain appearances than to stand for and with the children.

Even so the children's generosity is unbounded—unbounded by their very desperation, unbounded by their very desire. The children need the elders. The children need the healing words, the honest words. As Morrison's parable spells out, the children need the elders to tell truly *their* desires, what *they* most wanted of *their* lives, what they meant to do when *they* were young, what they did do that *matters* to them. The children need the elders to tell them where in their living they found joy and worth and meaning, where they went astray, and perhaps especially, to tell the values that name their generational and personal struggles.

The children want to hear it all. Truly. The children's humanness is fragile. Without this telling, how can they weave together the sparseness of their own experience? How can they forge a language for naming themselves and their struggles? How can they find their own way in those struggles or continue the story if the elders mock, reject, and condemn with swift, merciless judgment? The children in Morrison's (1994) parable ask the old, blind, wise, Black writer woman, "Is there no context for our lives? No song, no literature, no poem full of vitamins, no history connected to experience that you can pass along *to help us start strong*?" (p. 27, italics added). They say to her: "You are an adult. The old one, the wise one. Stop thinking about saving your face. Think of our lives and tell us your particularized world" (p. 27).

The politics of reflection is announced by reflection's absence, with a moral consequence caught with uncanny precision in the closing lines of a poem written by William Carlos Williams (1938/1986–88) in the first quarter of this century of catastrophic destruction—and forgetting: "No one / to witness / and adjust, no one to drive the car."

JENNY'S STORY

Morrison's parable is spacious, porous, encompassing. Within that roomy scaffolding, I now insert another story. A particularized story. A story of a particular child. I do this to animate story and memory, to give weight to being. I tell this one story to call into your minds, your particularized world, your particularized stories. I do this purposefully to spill the vivid colors of the particular life, the particular world over the deathly grays of generalization and classification, those neutralized hues that paint humanness impersonally, and the human world flat. It is a virtue of story that it cannot be told in general or categorically or impersonally. It is a virtue of story that its weight, like the weight of a lived life, resides in the density of the specifics.

I also tell this story from an urgent sense of the responsibility of the elders to remember and, remembering, to bring the children into the story:

One by one, in pairs and trios, called by their names, not numbers or la-
bels or ranks, so that the children will not be hidden from us, and we from
them. I tell this story knowing that the story of this child, and the remembered children she calls to your minds, confers on us, their elders, the re-
viving, invigorating gift of each child's uniqueness—and of the particularized variety among them, those miraculous differences that are the
crown of our humanness.

Here is the story, woven together at points with the story of how it
got made and told, and occasionally offering glimpses of other stories, also
bearing on reflection and reflective practice, but that in this talk go mainly
untold.

The Prospect Center in Vermont where I am based holds an annual
summer institute attended by teachers from around the country, including teachers from New York, Philadelphia, Phoenix, Chicago, and other,
smaller cities and towns. In the summer of 1996, a group of us were involved for an intensive 3 days of reflection and description centered on a
little girl who happened to be from Phoenix; a little girl named Jenny.

Jenny's teacher, Cecilia Espinosa, prepared for the child study while
still in Phoenix by involving both Jenny and her mother, since neither of
them would be with us in Vermont. Jenny, for example, helped to choose
the drawings, writings, and constructions that we would describe and, on
her own, added to these some photographs and a few treasured objects
from home. The seriousness with which she made her selections, and her
trust that these would be respected, is emblemized for me in one of those
objects. It was a little box packed full with small folded papers. Attached
was a note from Jenny inviting us to look at the box but to please not read
the papers as they were her prayers and private. I watched many adults
in the larger institute stop by during those 3 days to look at Jenny's collection. Every one of them picked up the box. No one touched the prayers.

To accompany the collection, and so those of us doing the study could
hear Jenny's voice, her teacher and mother made a tape of Jenny talking
about some of her drawings and writings. Jenny's mother, Tisa Williams,
added in her picture of Jenny by taping a portrayal that included stories
of Jenny from her earliest years and from her daily life within the family.

To carry out our study, we used a disciplined method of inquiry called
the reflective, descriptive processes—originated at Prospect and developed
in practice by several generations of teachers from a variety of locations.
From among these we especially made use of the processes called the
Descriptive Review of Children's Works and the Descriptive Review of the
Child. Before we dived into these descriptions, Jenny's teacher sketched
for us the school context: W. T. Machan—a big school, overcrowded, with
class sizes pushing upward of 30, classes mostly bilingual and mostly

multiage. We learned that because of that arrangement for grouping children she had taught Jenny for the past 3 years.

It was in listening to Cecilia talk about the school and her classroom, that we caught glimpses of those other stories—the stories that wouldn't get told fully that summer; stories still waiting to be told. A teacher's story of how she went about creating a multiage classroom for both English and Spanish speakers. A teacher's reflection on that experience and how a class continuing together for 3 years helped relieve the strain of big classes and the fragmentation of transiency. A teacher's story of how continuities and human bonds were further strengthened by welcoming and supporting children (and parents) in their own first language; by providing lots of materials for writing, drawing, and constructing; and by giving children freedom to make the kinds of choices reflected in Jenny's big collection of work. An important story to tell, and especially so at a time when teaching and the schools are devalued.

And, around the edges of this story and Jenny's story, we could discern the outlines of still another story: A story of how a large public school staff, under the leadership of principal Dr. Lynn Davey, had worked together as a whole for nearly a decade to figure out how to use what resources they had, and especially their human resources, to support continuity and opportunity for the children. Another important story to tell, and majorly important at a time when media and legislatures rush to proclaim the failure of the public schools.

With these partially glimpsed outlines of bigger stories as context, we turned to Jenny's story, starting with description of her drawings and writings. Making that study of Jenny's works, we overviewed the entire collection to discover the large prevailing themes and recurrent motifs. At intervals, we paused to reflect on what seemed important words called to our minds by what we were seeing and reading, words like "round" that captured for us both the circularity and the fullness of forms that appear in her drawings. We took note as well of how often, especially in our descriptions of the writing, we found the words "brave" and "honest" on our lips.

We were moved to those words again as we listened, crowded around the tape recorder, to Jenny's mother's description of her daughter—a portrayal to which Jenny's teacher added the dimension of Jenny in school. Their descriptions, each from her own perspective and in the context of a variety of circumstances, allowed us, the group assembled in Vermont, to visualize Jenny's presence. We heard them talk about how she moves, including characteristic gestures, and her pace and rhythm. We learned about what interests her deeply and her preferences. From these and our firsthand knowledge of her work, gained through close, collaborative description, we gained a sense of her aesthetic. We heard stories of her relationships at home and in school, and her friendships. We heard about ways she typically sets out to learn something and her ways of thinking through an idea or problem.

The combined description of Jenny's works with the descriptive review of her as a person and learner yielded rich insights and prompted deep thought. It was a moving experience. I know each of us came to the close of those 3 days spent in Jenny's company with particular moments engrained in memory—moments that sparked our imaginations, that renewed our commitment to a humanly centered education. What electrified me happened when I was listening along with everyone else to Jenny herself speaking on tape as she talked about the drawings she had made and pieces she wrote from kindergarten through grade 2.

The writings in particular, and Jenny's retelling of those writings on tape, are shot through with big human stories, and especially stories of the struggle for human rights and identity by those denied both. Among these were the stories of Cesar Chavez, Martin Luther King, Rosa Parks, Harriet Tubman, and Helen Keller. To give a little of the flavor of Jenny's retelling of these stories that moved me so, I offer the following excerpt from the transcribed tape:

> There was this boy in my class that I liked . . . and at the time . . . we were learning about Martin Luther King and Cecilia was reading lots of books about Martin Luther King. So [my friend and I] decided that we want to make a book about Martin Luther King. So it was both by us and illustrated by us, and it was in English and Spanish . . . and it told about his life and then it told that he, that he liked to play stuff and . . . one day his friends they didn't come to play with him but they came and they told him that they can't play with him anymore and he was really sad and he went home and asked his mom and dad why . . . can't they play with me . . . and then his mom told him about it . . . that when she was a little girl . . . White people didn't want them [Black people] so the White people made them to be slaves . . .

Hearing Jenny herself speak for the first time, I listened to how serious she was and how deliberate. I was struck that she included in her retelling the full picture of how the book came to be, including how she and her writing partner worked together coequally on it—drawing all the illustrations and writing the book in two languages. I smiled when later in the tape she mixed into the twentieth century's civil rights story, Harriet Tubman as the woman who didn't move to the back of the bus, and then corrected herself when an adult (her mother or teacher) whispered in the background, "Rosa Parks."

But even as we listened to Jenny's confusion, Barbara Batton, a teacher from New York who was a participant in this child study, pointed out that Jenny had got the names *wrong* but the idea *right*, and by doing that, she had made a larger connection. Rosa Parks and Harriet Tubman, separated by a century, are nevertheless equivalent figures, players active in the same struggle, inspired by the same strong desire for freedom. They have the same value-weight, if I may put it that way. So: A mistake of fact, but a powerful memory at work, able to make the connections of value unerringly. "That's Jenny," we said to each other.

By the time we listened to Jenny speaking on tape, telling with such thoroughness how her book on Martin Luther King came to be, we had already described and reflected on some of these retold stories. We understood as we listened to Jenny describe how she went about the writing that, for her, revisiting and reworking ideas is a dominant mode of learning. You might say Jenny learns what is important to her reflectively; that is, by heart. Or, you might say she learns by weaving what she judges to have value into her own thought and being. In our inquiry group, we called it, "making the idea or story her own."

Later we learned through her mother's and teacher's portrayals in the Descriptive Review of the Child that the value connections extended to herself, and specifically and directly to her actions in the classroom. This is an example given by her teacher: A new child entered the class, a boy who fought and teased quite relentlessly. One child, a girl, became a particular target of that teasing. The children tended to shy away from or exclude him. The more he was on the outside, the worse he acted. Jenny did something that is very hard to do. She befriended both the boy and his chief victim. She invited the boy to be her partner for projects. That is, she joined him, and persisted in that even when some adults in the school advised her that she shouldn't as he would be a bad influence.

Collapsing a much longer story, when she had the privilege of asking someone to join her for a lunch date with the teacher, Jenny asked both the boy and the girl he tended to victimize to be her specially invited guests. Through Jenny's generous reaching out to both, they began to get to know each other as Jenny had got to know each of them. By making herself the bridge, Jenny softened the aggressor, reassured the victim, and opened the circle to include both. As we came to the close of this 3-day reflective inquiry, the word "brave," engraved in our minds and present on our lips, was emblem, too, of a continuing human story:

Brave Harriet. Brave Rosa. Brave Jenny.

LESSONS FROM JENNY

Why choose this particular story to tell? Why pair Jenny with Morrison's (1994) parable and Kundera's (1988) "spirit of the novel" (p. 18)? For so many reasons. I choose her first for all Jenny teaches about slowness, and how slowness is not merely the opposite of quickness. I choose her for how, by teaching that, she jars the simplistic, binary school thinking about children in which quick equals bright equals smart and slow equals dull equals stupid. I choose her because with that sharp jarring, space is made for learning and thinking that do not conform with quickness, and for ideas and knowledge that are precluded by standards of economic utility and efficiency. I choose Jenny because the basic truth about people (and novels) that "things are not," as Kundera (1988) points out, "as simple as you think," shines through what she teaches (p. 18).

I choose Jenny because she is the child who typically is devalued and downgraded in the school market exchange. She is the child who tends to be classified early as not up to standard. She is the child slated not for "poems full of vitamins" or a "history connected to experience" (Morrison, 1994, p. 27), but the thin fare of skill drills and learning fragmented into tiny pieces, devoid of idea or meaning. Choosing Jenny particularizes what tends to be missed when differences in thinking and learning are proclaimed to be disabling, and variety is treated as an affront to the school agenda.

Viewed from another perspective, choosing Jenny illuminates the educative potency of story—the literature, the stories the children in Morrison's parable are pleading for. Through her hunger for story, for a history connected to human values and human struggle, she bears witness to that deep desire observable from infancy in her and Everychild to join with life, to join with learning. Through giving the stories her close, loving attention, by copying them over, by retelling them, by caring intensely enough to do that, Jenny recreated the stories, the lives and the saving ideas and values embedded in those stories. It is unlikely that a teacher would set the standard of copying over stories for a 7-year-old. Yet Jenny set that hard, laborious standard for herself. If there is nationally a serious concern and interest in standards, Jenny by her actions illuminates the very heart of the matter.

Through her courage to enact the ideas and values emblemized by those stories in her daily life in the classroom, she gives specific detail and vibrant meaning to what the children in Morrison's (1994) parable are asking for when they plead with the old, wise, Black, blind writer woman "to help us start strong" (p. 27). To start strong, as Jenny specifies it, means to know that your story catches up the threads of previous stories. To start strong means to know that your life builds on other lives. To start strong means to know that you are necessary, a contributor to the bigger human story, both valued and valuable. To start strong means to know that you are not alone.

I choose Jenny because she is a bearer of that great gift, the generational gift of the children, of youth to age: *our other chance.* The other chance, which as Morrison (1994) says in relation to language, but I apply more broadly, to exercise our "mid-wifery properties" (p. 15) to assist in the rebirthing of human possibility. For me, to be assisting agent in that rebirthing says adequately what it is to be a teacher, a parent, an elder. For me, the rebirthing of possibility, the passing on of "mid-wifery properties" from one generation to the next exposes the taproot value of educating and its highest standard.

Finally, I choose Jenny for her reminder to me *that there is no virtue in reflection* except that reflection is rooted in valuing; except that reflection retrieves and memory reanimates large and saving ideas; except that together these human gifts increase awareness of difference, leading to some coherent action. And even perhaps, as remembering did for Jenny, makes imaginable, and so doable, acts of courage on the daily and human scale that expand human possibility, and give weight to being.

Having said this, and having chosen Jenny, I am going to turn the tables on *my*self. *Any* child, and most certainly including the particularized child each of you is remembering, can teach lessons of this order: different lessons, and differently enacted, but of equal value—if each is treated seriously, if none is trivialized, if none is prophesied into failure. These are all stories waiting to be told; all lessons waiting to be learned.

STORIES NOT TOLD; QUESTIONS LEFT HANGING

And what of those other stories—the teacher's story, the school's story? What of those big stories in the wings of Jenny's story—big stories only waiting for a cue to enter? What about all the other like, but oh so tastily different stories, tellable by teachers and schools across the country, except that these voices, the voices of particularity and complexity are blocked—blocked as Kundera (1988) says, by the "din of easy, quick answers" (p. 18). Vouchers. Charters. Tax deductions for contributions to private schools. National standards.

These are the easy answers in response to the proclaimed failure of the schools. These are the convenient if transparent solutions that pave the road to the privatization and standardization of the public schools. The question is: How in the rush to the judgment and execution of the public schools can these stories be made hearable—these particularized stories, not of total failure, not of stunning success, but the stories of schools in the making? How can the case for variety and particularity and complexity be heard over the "johnny one note" song of national standards and standardization more generally?

These are hard questions. Reflecting on those questions, I or you might ask another, even more urgent. This time reading the bird in the parable as commitment to a public education for the public good, I might ask, or you might, "Is it living . . . or is it dead?" I leave the question hanging.

APPENDIX

The Reference Edition
of the Prospect Archive

The *Reference Edition of the Prospect Archive* was published in 1985 through the sponsorship of the North Dakota Study Group on Evaluation and funding from the Jessie Smith Noyes and Bush Foundations. The reference edition reproduces the collections of 36 children (artworks, writings of all kinds, and 3-D constructions) in microfiche and colored slides, spanning 5 through 9 years of a child's school life. Besides the reproduced works, the published collections include a catalogue of the child's works by year according to motifs, media, and themes; a bound typescript of teachers' weekly narrative records and twice-yearly narrative reports to parents; and typescripts of selections from the child's written production.

Conventions adopted for reproducing the children's works and related materials include the following:

1. To protect the privacy of the children and their families, each child was assigned a pseudonym; placing parentheses around the child's name on slides, narrative reports, and typescripts of written work is the convention adopted to indicate that practice. (Please note that for this book, the first time a pseudonym appears, quotation marks are substituted for parentheses.)
2. Each item in a child's collection was numbered. The first number refers to the child's age; the numbers following the decimal indicate the place of the item within the year's production; for example, (Sean) 4.1 is the first item in the file for the academic year in which he was age 4. A second decimal—for example, 4.1.2—is the device for revision when an item surfaced after numbering of the collection had been completed for that year. It is to be kept in mind that many pieces of work went home; the numbering system does not take that additional production into account.

On undated work, the letters "nd" (no date) are substituted for the age of the child. The letters "HC" before the number indicate that the item came from a "Home Collection" placed in Prospect's keeping; the letter "B" before the number indicates a work larger than 12"x17" and possibly as large as 3'x 4'. Another indicator of an item's dimension is the apparent size of the label relative to the size of the image: for example, when the label appears very small, the work is of a very large dimension; when it is large, the work is small.
3. "Patches" that appear on some items mask the child's actual name or other biographical data.

One copy of the reference edition is housed at Prospect Center; the other at the University of North Dakota, Grand Forks (Special Collections, Chester Fritz Library). Rental of slides and other materials can be arranged by writing to Prospect Center, P.O. Box 328, North Bennington, VT 05257; 802-442-8333.

Acknowledgments. Vito Perrone, formerly Dean of the Center for Teaching and Learning at the University of North Dakota, and subsequently Director of Teacher Education at Harvard Graduate School of Education, was instrumental in proposing the project to publish the reference edition and obtaining the funding to make that possible. Dirck Roosevelt, Director of Prospect Center during the years that included the publication of the reference edition, facilitated the project in many ways.

The following persons—Prospect staff, Board members, former Prospect students, Friends of the Archive, and Noyes Scholarship recipients—assisted in planning, preparing, and producing the reference edition, many on a voluntary basis, under the leadership of Patricia Carini: Beth Alberty, Mary Anderson, Jon Barber, Corinne Biggs, Jodi Blake, Peter Carini, David Carroll, Vincent Corcoran, Jon Crispin, Susan Donnelly, Tom Fels, Robin Goodman, Sheela Harden, Darlene Headwell, Peg Howes, Barbara Karmiller, Jane Katz, Margie Larner, Jeanne McWaters, Ruth Medeiros, Rebecca Morton, Cinda Morse, Diane Mullins, Alice Seletsky, Ferrilyn Sourdiffe, Frances Stillman, Steel Stillman, Cecelia Traugh.

(Portions of the text for this Appendix were excerpted from the Prospect Center newsletter of November 1993, Eds., Margaret Himley and Lynne Strieb, and from the "Introduction to the Reference Edition of the Prospect Archive," 1985, © Prospect Archive and Center for Education and Research.

References

American Psychiatric Association. (1994*). Diagnostic and statistical manual of mental disorders* (4th ed.). Washington, DC: Author.

Baca, J. S. (1990). A song of survival. In *Immigrants in our own land and selected early poems*. New York: New Directions Books. (Original work published 1979)

Baca, J. S. (1992). *Working in the dark: Reflections of a poet of the barrio*. Santa Fe, NM: Red Crane Books.

Bao Ninh (1995). *The sorrow of war: A novel of North Vietnam*. New York: Pantheon Books.

Barfield, O. (1963). *Worlds apart*. Middlctown, CT: Wesleyan University Press.

Barker, P. (1991). *Regeneration*. London: Plume.

Berlin, I. (1988). Two concepts of liberty. In *Four essays on liberty*. New York: Oxford University Press. (Original work published 1969)

Berlin, I. (1997). *The sense of reality: Studies in ideas and their history*. New York: Farrar, Straus & Giroux. (Original work under title "Realism in History," October 9, 1953, the Elizabeth Cutter Morrow address, Smith College, Northampton, MA)

Bishop, E. (1994). Chemin de fer. In *The complete poems: 1927–1979*. New York: Noonday Press, Farrar, Straus & Giroux. (Original work published in 1946)

Brodine, K. (1980). June, 78. In *Illegal assembly*. New York: Hanging Loose Press.

Bussis, A. M., Chittenden, E. A., Amarel, M., & Klausner, E. (1985). *Inquiry into meaning: An investigation of learning to read*. Hillsdale, NJ: Erlbaum.

Carini, L. (1995). *Ethics and aesthetics: An essay in spiritual humanism*. Unpublished manuscript.

Carini, P. F. (1975). *Observation and description: An alternative methodology for the investigation of human phenomena*. Grand Forks: University of North Dakota Press.

Carini, P. F. (1979). *The art of seeing and the visibility of the person*. Grand Forks: University of North Dakota Press.

Carini, P. F. (1982). *The school lives of seven children*. Grand Forks: University of North Dakota Press.

Carini, P. F. (1997). *Regeneration*. Unpublished manuscript.

Cather, W. (1941). *O pioneers*. Boston: Houghton Mifflin.

Cobb, E. (1977). *The ecology of imagination in childhood*. New York: Columbia University Press.

DeVault, M. (1994). *Feeding the family: The social organization of caring as gendered work.* Chicago: Chicago University Press.

Dewey, J. (1963). *Experience and education.* New York: Collier Books. (Original work published 1938)

Dewey, J. (1980). *Democracy and education.* In J. A. Boydston, P. R. Baysinger, & B. Levine (Eds.), *John Dewey: The middle works, 1899–1924: Vol. 9. 1916.* Carbondale and Edwardsville: Southern Illinois University Press. (Original work published 1916)

Dickinson, E. (1951). I felt my life with both my hands. In T. H. Johnson (Ed.), *The poems of Emily Dickinson.* Cambridge, MA: Belknap Press of Harvard University Press. (Original work composed 1862)

Dinnage, R. (1996, February 15). Death's gray land. *The New York Review of Books, 43*(3), 19–21.

Dorris, M. (1993). *Working men.* New York: Henry Holt.

Du Bois, W. E. B. (1989). *The souls of black folk.* New York: Bantam Books. (Original work published 1903)

Frost, R. (1964). *Selected letters of Robert Frost* (L. Thompson, Ed.). New York: Holt, Rinehart & Winston. (Original letter written 1914)

Frost, R. (1979). Hyla brook. In E. C. Lathem (Ed.), *The poetry of Robert Frost: The collected poems, complete and unabridged.* New York: Henry Holt. (Original work published 1916)

Fussell, P. (1977). *The great war and modern memory.* New York: Oxford University Press.

Geertz, C. (1973). *The interpretation of cultures.* New York: Basic Books.

Gleik, J. (1987). *Chaos: Making a new science.* New York. Penguin Books.

Graham, M. (1935, April 28). *Frontier.* Guild Theater, New York City.

Havel, V. (1992, March 1). Address to the world economic forum, Davos, Switzerland. *New York Times, 141*(48892), A15.

Heller, E. (1975). *The disinherited mind: Essays in modern German literature and thought.* New York: Harcourt Brace Jovanovich.

Hillesum, E. (1983). *An interrupted life: The diaries of Etty Hillesum* (A. Pomerans, Trans.). New York: Pantheon Books.

Himley, M. R. (with Carini, P. F.). (2000). *From another angle: Children's strengths and school standards.* New York: Teachers College Press.

hooks, bell. (1994). *Teaching to transgress: Education as the practice of freedom.* New York: Routledge.

Hyde, L. (1983). *The gift: Imagination and the erotic life of property.* New York: Vintage Books.

Joyce, J. (1948). *The portrait of the artist as a young man.* New York: New American Library, Penguin Signet.

Keller, E. F. (1983). *A feeling for the organism: The life and work of Barbara McClintock.* New York: W. H. Freeman.

Keller, H. (1954). *The story of my life.* Garden City, NY: Doubleday.

Kundera, M. (1988). *The art of the novel* (L. Asher, Trans.). New York: Grove Press.

Lessing, D. (1994). *Under my skin: Volume one of my autobiography, to 1949.* New York: HarperCollins.

Lopez, B. (1992). *The rediscovery of North America*. New York: Vintage Books.

Lorde, A. (1984). Poetry is not a luxury. In *Sister outsider: Essays and speeches*. Freedom, CA: Crossing Press.

Magnus, R. (1961). *Goethe as a scientist* (H. Norden, Trans.). New York: Collier Books, Men of Science Library. (Original work published 1906)

Matthaie, R. (1971). *Goethe's color theory* (H. Aach, Trans.). New York: Van Nostrand Reinhold.

Merleau-Ponty, M. (1962). *The phenomenology of perception* (C. Smith, Trans.). London: Routledge & Kegan Paul.

Mintz, N. L. (1959, May). Concerning Goethe's approach to the theory of color. *Journal of Individual Psychology, 15*, 33–49.

Morrison, T. (1970). *The bluest eye*. New York: Washington Square Press.

Morrison, T. (Ed.). (1992). *Race-ing justice, en-gendering power*. New York: Pantheon Books.

Morrison, T. (1994). *Lecture and speech of acceptance upon the award of the Nobel Prize for literature*. New York: Alfred A. Knopf. (1993 Nobel Lecture in Literature)

Newson, E. (1978). Unreasonable care: The establishment of selfhood. In G. N. A. Vesey (Ed.), *Human values* (pp. 1–26). Atlantic Highlands, NJ: Humanities Press.

Quindlen, A. (1992, March 1). To defray expenses. *New York Times, 141*(48892), A15.

Rich, A. (1993). *What is found there: Notebooks on poetry and politics*. New York: W. W. Norton.

Rodriguez, L. J. (1993). *Always running, la vida loca: Gang days in L.A*. New York: Simon & Schuster.

Rose, M. (1989). *Lives on the boundary: The struggles and achievements of America's underprepared*. New York: Free Press.

Rukeyser, M. (1996). *The life of poetry*. Ashfield, MA: Paris Press. (Original work published 1949)

Salgado, S. (1993). *Workers: An archaeology of the industrial age*. New York: Aperture Books.

Sassoon, S. (1978). *Memoirs of an infantry officer*. London: Faber & Faber. (Original work published 1930)

Schachtel, E. (1959). *Metamorphosis: New light on the conflict of human development and the psychology of creativity*. New York: Basic Books.

Scheer, C. (1995, September 11). L.A.'s immigration woe: "Illegals" made slaves to fashion. *The Nation, 261*(7), 237–238.

Scheler, M. (1973). *The nature of sympathy* (P. Heath, Trans.). Hamden, CT: Shoestring Press. (Original work published 1913)

Scott, O. (1976). Pre- and post-emancipation schools. In R. Dropkin & A. Tobier (Eds.), *Roots of open education in America* (pp. 13–20). New York: City College Workshop Center for Open Education.

Shakur, S. (1994). *The autobiography of an L.A. gang member*. New York: Penguin Books.

Weber, L. (1994). *Reflections*. New York: The City College Workshop Center. (Original work composed 1986)

Weber, L. (1997a). The authority of the teacher. In B. Alberty (Ed.), *Looking back and thinking forward: Reexaminations of teaching and schooling* (pp. 90–95). New York: Teachers College Press. (Original work composed 1990)

Weber, L. (1997b). Black or multicultural curriculum—of course, but what more? In B. Alberty (Ed.), *Looking back and thinking forward: Reexaminations of teaching and schooling* (pp. 128–140). New York: Teachers College Press. (Original work composed 1990–1993)

Weber, L. (1997c). Inquiry, noticing, joining with, and following after. In B. Alberty (Ed.), *Looking back and thinking forward: Reexaminations of teaching and schooling* (pp. 48–67). New York: Teachers College Press. (Original work published 1991)

Welty, E. (1984). *One writer's beginnings*. Cambridge, MA: Harvard University Press.

West, C. (1993). *Race matters*. Boston: Beacon Press.

Whitehead, A. N. (1958). *Modes of thought*. New York: Capricorn Books. (Original work published 1938)

Whitman, W. (1986). *Leaves of grass: The first (1855) edition* (M. Cowley, Ed.). New York: Penguin Classics.

Whitman, W. (1992). I hear America singing. *In selected poems of Walt Whitman*. New York: Gramercy Books. (Original work published 1860)

Whitman, W. (1992). Song of the broad-axe. In *Selected poems of Walt Whitman*. New York: Gramercy Books. (Original work published 1856)

Whitman, W. (1992). There was a child went forth. In *Selected poems of Walt Whitman*. New York: Gramercy Books. (Original work published 1855)

Williams, R. (1961). *The long revolution*. New York: Columbia University Press.

Williams, W. C. (1986–88). To Elsie. In A. W. Litz & C. J. MacGowan (Eds.), *The collected poems of William Carlos Williams* (Vol. 1). New York: New Directions Books. (Original work published 1938)

Williams, W. C. (1986–88). Asphodel, that greeny flower. In A. W. Litz & C. J. Mac-Gowan (Eds.), *The collected poems of William Carlos Williams* (Vol. 2). New York: New Directions Books. (Original work published 1944)

Index

Andrias, Jane, 161
Assessment, 5, 48, 95, 142, 143, 153, 171–73, 180. *See also* Measurement; Standardization

Baca, J. S., 46, 48, 49–50, 51, 52, 53, 102, 104, 117, 119, 194–95
Bao Ninh, 148
Barfield, Owen, 76
Barker, Pat, 53, 67–68, 146, 147, 148, 150, 191, 192
Batton, Barbara, 205
Berlin, Isaiah, 19–20, 50, 51, 129–30, 141, 142
"A Bird in the Hand" (Morrison), 197–99, 200, 201, 206, 208
Bishop, Elizabeth, 21
Blake, Joan, 2
Brodine, Karen, 108, 110–11, 119, 120
Burks, Mary, 138

Caring, 90, 112–16, 154, 200, 206
Carini, Louis, 2, 6, 120, 148
Cather, Willa, 21
Change/reform: and civil rights, 131; continuous, 138–39; and generational responsibility, 191; and human capacity, 145; incremental, 90; less-than-system, 161; as making difference, 145–46; and perfection, 94–95, 145; radical, 171; regenerative, 8–9, 90; and schools as collective work, 98; and schools in the making, 89–90, 94–95; and standards in the making, 152–53, 159; as struggle, 135–38; and "to believe ourselves," 131; as transformative, 85, 90, 191, 194; and unfinished work in education, 138–39; as unpre-

dictable, 146; and valuing the immeasurable, 171, 178–79
Chiang, Fay, 46
Children: "bringing" the, 161; capacities of, 196; "celebration" of, 121, 122, 138; at center, 9, 95, 98, 130; confidence in, 125–26; destructive influences on, 122; getting to know, 179–81; gifts of, 199–201, 207; inclusion of wider spectrum of, 134; as makers of knowledge, 79–83; and making, 20; media images of, 121–22; as open to world, 193–194; pathologizing, 69–71, 121–22, 155; resisting, 153–57; rights of, 128–29; social attitudes toward, 118–19; "special help," 137
Clark, Pam, 93
Classrooms: comparison of 1960s and 1997, 133–35; efficiency of, 128, 129; manyness in, 169; as two worlds, 177–79
Cobb, Edith, 83, 194
Cochran-Smith, Marilyn, 143
Conformity/sameness, 70, 95, 97, 131, 156, 196–97
Connections, making: and generational responsibility, 192, 205, 206; and knowledge making, 80, 82–83, 85–87; and learning, 85–87; and number, 186; and standards in the making, 152–53; and stories, 2, 11–15, 16, 85–87; among teachers, 133, 137; and works, 15, 112–13

Davey, Lynn, 93, 203
"Deep play," 45–46, 111
Democracy, 2, 15, 16, 48, 97, 131, 132, 133–35, 136, 142
Description: as basis of work at Prospect, 3–7, 10–11, 90–91; and generational

215

About the Author

Patricia F. Carini is a co-founder of Prospect School (1965–1991) and the Prospect Archive and Center for Education and Research (1979–present) in North Bennington, Vermont. At Prospect, she began the Collections of Children's Works; directed the Archive Scholars and Fellows program, which culminated in publication of the *Reference Edition of the Prospect Archive*; and developed observational, descriptive methods for study of children and their works and the documentation of schools. She has introduced these methods of study in public schools across the country, including Boston; Grand Forks, North Dakota; Ithaca, New York; Mamaroneck, New York; New York City; Paterson, New Jersey; Philadelphia, and Phoenix. Her previous publications include *Observation and Description: An Alternative Methodology for the investigation of Human Phenomena* (1979); *The Art of Seeing and the Visibility of the Person* (1979); and *The School Lives of Seven Children* (1982). Patricia F. Carini is an honorary member of the Prospect Center Board and a charter member of the North Dakota Study Group on Evaluation. In 1998, she was awarded a Doctor of Humane Letters degree by Bank Street College.